'It is a voice of a true original and a voice of America'
Katharine Sale, *Financial Times* Books of the Year

'The book no one thought he could write'
Hanif Kureishi, *Guardian* Books of the Year

'Brilliant, fascinating and gobbled up in one sitting'
Griff Rhys Jones, *Observer* Books of the Year

'Vivid, romantic and far more revealing than anyone dared hope'
John Preston, *Sunday Telegraph* Books of the Year

'Lucid and engaging, rendered in gorgeous prose, his first volume of reminiscences was full of glimpses into its author's humanity . . . *Volume Two* cannot come soon enough'
*Mojo* Book of the Year

'A startling insight into one of the most important artists of the twentieth century'
*Independent* Books of the Year

'Every line of *Chronicles* reverberates with the marrow-shaking snarl of the mesmerizing American voice that first signed up with Columbia records in New York City in 1961 . . . You realise why Dylan will always be part of the unofficial soundtrack of our lives. *Chronicles* takes its place next to *On the Road* and Guthrie's *Bound for Glory* as an essential record of an American artist's manifest destiny'
Robert McCrum, *Observer*

'A delight . . . lucid, engaging and incredibly direct. Dylan has taken back his own story from his biographers . . . He has more real literature in him than a thousand professors'
David Sexton, *Evening Standard*

'A startling event . . . [*Chronicles*] shows Dylan's extraordinary command of language, married in the book to an uncanny recall of events and a masterly narrative sensibility'
*Observer*

'If you want a magisterial portrait of the invention of a great artist, you will be mesmerized . . . a gorgeous, lyrical account of his arrival in snowbound New York. This memoir, like his songs, is an indispensable map to the light and darkness of our age'
Liam Carson, *Irish Independent*

'Dylan's writing never loses its richness, its sense of crystalline observation . . . Readers hoping to gain admittance to Dylan's inner sanctum may be surprised by how far in they are allowed to venture'
John Preston, *Sunday Telegraph*

'A book which measures up to – and in many respects surpasses – the highest hopes anyone could have had of it. The narrator of *Chronicles* turns out to be a superbly candid and engaging character, with a sharp descriptive eye . . . If you've always wondered how this man transformed the supposedly antique certainties of folk music into the soundtrack to the most self-consciously forward-looking of decades, this book has the answer'
Ben Thompson, *Independent on Sunday*

'An extremely good book indeed, actually, a great one. If you are not weeping with gratitude by the end, then frankly, the age has passed you by . . . I cannot remember a book that has made me happier than this one'
Bryan Appleyard, *Sunday Times*

'With this rich, intermittently preposterous, often tender work, Bob Dylan has delivered more than many of us dared hope for'
Mike Marqusee, *Guardian*

'Charming . . . Enthralling . . . One hears a lovely shyness in Dylan's acknowledging the unlikely distance he has travelled . . . It's the kind of moment that renders this a wholly engrossing and unaccountably touching memoir'
Anthony Quinn, *Daily Telegraph*

'A double delight: besides being a treasure trove for Dylan fans, it is also sparklingly well-written . . . Slowly and deftly, *Chronicles* peels away some of the enigma that still swirls around Bob Dylan, and leaves you hungrier than ever for *Volume Two*'
Patrick Humphries, *Sunday Express*

'Dylan might turn out to be his own most illuminating critic and biographer . . . taut, atmospheric prose encompassing six decades of life and work and demonstrating a sure grasp of what he did, why he did it and how he felt while it was being done . . . *Chronicles* is good enough to bring even the most disillusioned stray back into the fold'
Richard Williams, *TLS*

'[Dylan] has decided to tell his story, and it is as riveting, poetic, poignant and funny as some of his best songs . . . It sizzles with biting one-liners and radiates honesty'
Shusha Guppy, *Daily Mail*

'Brilliant . . . arresting . . . fascinating . . . Some phrases in *Chronicles* are as good as his best songs. Many anecdotes are mesmerizing. The style is staccato, spare, poetic . . . Dylan can tell a bloody good story'
Edward Smith, *Spectator*

'A delightfully happy riposte to the library of books that ponder his status as poet, rock god and cultural icon . . . priceless'
*Sunday Times*

'*Chronicles* is a singular book. Never has a rock star put pen to paper with such skill'
Christopher Bray, *New Statesman*

# BOB DYLAN

# Chronicles

## Volume One

POCKET
BOOKS

LONDON • SYDNEY • NEW YORK • TORONTO

First published in Great Britain by Simon & Schuster UK Ltd, 2004
This edition published by Pocket Books, 2005
An imprint of Simon & Schuster UK Ltd
A Viacom company

1 3 5 7 9 10 8 6 4 2

Simon & Schuster UK Ltd
Africa House
64-78 Kingsway
London WC2B 6AH

www.simonsays.co.uk

Simon & Schuster Australia
Sydney

A CIP catalogue record for this book is available from the British Library

Designed by C. Linda Dingler

ISBN 0743478649
EAN 9780743478649

Printed and bound in Great Britain by
Cox & Wyman Ltd, Reading, Berkshire

# CONTENTS

# 1

# Markin' Up the Score

LOU LEVY, top man of Leeds Music Publishing company, took me up in a taxi to the Pythian Temple on West 70th Street to show me the pocket sized recording studio where Bill Haley and His Comets had recorded "Rock Around the Clock"—then down to Jack Dempsey's restaurant on 58th and Broadway, where we sat down in a red leather upholstered booth facing the front window.

Lou introduced me to Jack Dempsey, the great boxer. Jack shook his fist at me.

"You look too light for a heavyweight kid, you'll have to put on a few pounds. You're gonna have to dress a little finer, look a little sharper—not that you'll need much in the way of clothes when you're in the ring—don't be afraid of hitting somebody too hard."

"He's not a boxer, Jack, he's a songwriter and we'll be publishing his songs."

"Oh, yeah, well I hope to hear 'em some of these days. Good luck to you, kid."

Outside the wind was blowing, straggling cloud wisps, snow whirling in the red lanterned streets, city types scuffling around, bundled up—salesmen in rabbit fur earmuffs hawking gimmicks, chestnut vendors, steam rising out of manholes.

None of it seemed important. I had just signed a contract with Leeds Music giving it the right to publish my songs, not that there was any great deal to hammer out. I hadn't written much yet. Lou had advanced me a hundred dollars against future royalties to sign the paper and that was fine with me.

John Hammond, who had brought me to Columbia Records, had taken me over to see Lou, asked him to look after me. Hammond had only heard two of my original compositions, but he had a premonition that there would be more.

Back at Lou's office, I opened my guitar case, took the guitar out and began fingering the strings. The room was cluttered—boxes of sheet music stacked up, recording dates of artists posted on bulletin boards, black lacquered discs, acetates with white labels scrambled around, signed photos of entertainers, glossy portraits—Jerry Vale, Al Martino, The Andrews Sisters (Lou was married to one of them), Nat King Cole, Patti Page, The Crew Cuts—a couple of console reel-to-reel tape recorders, big dark brown wooden desk full of hodgepodge. Lou had put a microphone on the desk in front of me and plugged the cord into one of the tape recorders, all the while chomping on a big exotic stogie.

"John's got high hopes for you," Lou said.

John was John Hammond, the great talent scout and discoverer of monumental artists, imposing figures in the history of recorded music—Billie Holiday, Teddy Wilson,

Charlie Christian, Cab Calloway, Benny Goodman, Count Basie, Lionel Hampton. Artists who had created music that resonated through American life. He had brought it all to the public eye. Hammond had even conducted the last recording sessions of Bessie Smith. He was legendary, pure American aristocracy. His mother was an original Vanderbilt, and John had been raised in the upper world, in comfort and ease—but he wasn't satisfied and had followed his own heart's love, music, preferably the ringing rhythm of hot jazz, spirituals and blues—which he endorsed and defended with his life. No one could block his way, and he didn't have time to waste. I could hardly believe myself awake when sitting in his office, him signing me to Columbia Records was so unbelievable. It would have sounded like a made-up thing.

Columbia was one of the first and foremost labels in the country and for me to even get my foot in the door was serious. For starters, folk music was considered junky, second rate and only released on small labels. Big-time record companies were strictly for the elite, for music that was sanitized and pasteurized. Someone like myself would never be allowed in except under extraordinary circumstances. But John was an extraordinary man. He didn't make schoolboy records or record schoolboy artists. He had vision and foresight, had seen and heard me, felt my thoughts and had faith in the things to come. He explained that he saw me as someone in the long line of a tradition, the tradition of blues, jazz and folk and not as some newfangled wunderkind on the cutting edge. Not that there was any cutting edge. Things were pretty sleepy on the Americana music scene in the late '50s and early '60s. Popular radio was sort of at a standstill and filled with empty pleasantries. It was years before The Beatles, The Who or The Rolling Stones would breathe new life and excitement into it. What I was playing at the time were hard-lipped folk songs with fire and brimstone servings, and you didn't need to take polls to know that they didn't match up with anything on the radio, didn't lend themselves to commercialism, but John told me that these things weren't high on his list and he understood all the implications of what I did.

"I understand sincerity," is what he said. John spoke with a rough, coarse attitude, yet had an appreciative twinkle in his eye.

Recently he had brought Pete Seeger to the label. He didn't discover Pete, though. Pete had been around for years. He'd been in the popular folk group The Weavers, but had been blacklisted during the McCarthy era and had a hard time, but he never stopped working. Hammond was defiant when he spoke about Seeger, that Pete's ancestors had come over on the *Mayflower*, that his relatives had fought the Battle of Bunker Hill, for Christsake. "Can you imagine those sons of bitches blacklisting him? They should be tarred and feathered."

"I'm gonna give you all the facts," he said to me. "You're a talented young man. If you can focus and control that talent, you'll be fine. I'm gonna bring you in and I'm gonna record you. We'll see what happens."

And that was good enough for me. He put a contract in front of me, the standard one, and I signed it right then and there, didn't get absorbed into details—didn't need a lawyer, advisor or anybody looking over my shoulder. I would have gladly signed whatever form he put in front of me.

He looked at the calendar, picked out a date for me to

start recording, pointed to it and circled it, told me what time to come in and to think about what I wanted to play. Then he called in Billy James, the head of publicity at the label, told Billy to write some promo stuff on me, personal stuff for a press release.

Billy dressed Ivy League like he could have come out of Yale—medium height, crisp black hair. He looked like he'd never been stoned a day in his life, never been in any kind of trouble. I strolled into his office, sat down opposite his desk, and he tried to get me to cough up some facts, like I was supposed to give them to him straight and square. He took out a notepad and pencil and asked me where I was from. I told him I was from Illinois and he wrote it down. He asked me if I ever did any other work and I told him that I had a dozen jobs, drove a bakery truck once. He wrote that down and asked me if there was anything else. I said I'd worked construction and he asked me where.

"Detroit."

"You traveled around?"

"Yep."

He asked me about my family, where they were. I told him I had no idea, that they were long gone.

"What was your home life like?"

I told him I'd been kicked out.

"What did your father do?"

" 'lectrician."

"And your mother, what about her?"

"Housewife."

"What kind of music do you play?"

"Folk music."

"What kind of music is folk music?"

I told him it was handed down songs. I hated these kind of questions. Felt I could ignore them. Billy seemed unsure of me and that was just fine. I didn't feel like answering his questions anyway, didn't feel the need to explain anything to anybody.

"How did you get here?" he asked me.

"I rode a freight train."

"You mean a passenger train?"

"No, a freight train."

"You mean, like a boxcar?"

"Yeah, like a boxcar. Like a freight train."

"Okay, a freight train."

I gazed past Billy, past his chair through his window across the street to an office building where I could see a blazing secretary soaked up in the spirit of something—she was scribbling busy, occupied at a desk in a meditative manner. There was nothing funny about her. I wished I had a telescope. Billy asked me who I saw myself like in today's music scene. I told him, nobody. That part of things was true, I really didn't see myself like anybody. The rest of it, though, was pure hokum—hophead talk.

I hadn't come in on a freight train at all. What I did was come across the country from the Midwest in a four-door sedan, '57 Impala—straight out of Chicago, clearing the hell out of there—racing all the way through the smoky towns, winding roads, green fields covered with snow, onward, eastbound through the state lines, Ohio, Indiana, Pennsylvania, a twenty-four-hour ride, dozing most of the way in the backseat, making small talk. My mind fixed on hidden interests . . . eventually riding over the George Washington Bridge.

The big car came to a full stop on the other side and let me out. I slammed the door shut behind me, waved good-bye, stepped out onto the hard snow. The biting wind hit me in the face. At last I was here, in New York City, a city like a web too intricate to understand and I wasn't going to try.

I was there to find singers, the ones I'd heard on record—Dave Van Ronk, Peggy Seeger, Ed McCurdy, Brownie McGhee and Sonny Terry, Josh White, The New Lost City Ramblers, Reverend Gary Davis and a bunch of others—most of all to find Woody Guthrie. New York City, the city that would come to shape my destiny. Modern Gomorrah. I was at the initiation point of square one but in no sense a neophyte.

When I arrived, it was dead-on winter. The cold was brutal and every artery of the city was snowpacked, but I'd started out from the frostbitten North Country, a little corner of the earth where the dark frozen woods and icy roads didn't faze me. I could transcend the limitations. It wasn't money or love that I was looking for. I had a heightened sense of awareness, was set in my ways, impractical and a visionary to boot. My mind was strong like a trap and I didn't need any guarantee of validity. I didn't know a single soul in this dark freezing metropolis but that was all about to change—and quick.

The Café Wha? was a club on MacDougal Street in the heart of Greenwich Village. The place was a subterranean cavern, liquorless, ill lit, low ceiling, like a wide dining hall with chairs and tables—opened at noon, closed at four in the morning. Somebody had told me to go there and ask for a singer named Freddy Neil who ran the daytime show at the Wha?

I found the place and was told that Freddy was downstairs in the basement where the coats and hats were checked and that's where I met him. Neil was the MC of the room and the maestro in charge of all the entertainers. He couldn't have been nicer. He asked me what I did and I told him I sang, played guitar and harmonica. He asked me to play something. After about a minute, he said I could play harmonica with him during his sets. I was ecstatic. At least it was a place to stay out of the cold. This was good.

Fred played for about twenty minutes and then introduced all the rest of the acts, then came back up to play whenever he felt like it, whenever the joint was packed. The acts were disjointed, awkward and seemed to have come from the Ted Mack *Amateur Hour*, a popular TV show. The audience was mostly collegiate types, suburbanites, lunch-hour secretaries, sailors and tourists. Everybody performed from ten to fifteen minutes. Fred would play for however long he felt, however long the inspiration would last. Freddy had the flow, dressed conservatively, sullen and brooding, with an enigmatical gaze, peachlike complexion, hair splashed with curls and an angry and powerful baritone voice that struck blue notes and blasted them to the rafters with or without a mike. He was the emperor of the place, even had his own harem, his devotees. You couldn't touch him. Everything revolved around him. Years later, Freddy would write the hit song "Everybody's Talkin'." I never played any of my own sets. I just accompanied Neil on all of his and that's where I began playing regular in New York.

The daytime show at the Café Wha?, an extravaganza of patchwork, featured anybody and anything—a comedian, a ventriloquist, a steel drum group, a poet, a female impersonator, a duo who sang Broadway stuff, a rabbit-in-the-hat magician, a guy wearing a turban who hypnotized people in the audience, somebody whose entire act was facial acrobatics—just anybody who wanted to break into show business. Nothing that would change your view of the world. I wouldn't have wanted Fred's gig for anything.

At about eight o'clock, the whole daytime menagerie would come to a halt and then the professional show would begin. Comedians like Richard Pryor, Woody Allen, Joan Rivers, Lenny Bruce and commercial folksinging groups like The Journeymen would command the stage. Everyone who had been there during the day would pack up. One of the guys who played in the afternoons was the falsetto-speaking Tiny Tim. He played ukulele and sang like a girl—old standard songs from the '20s. I got to talking to him a few times and asked him what other kinds of places there were to work around here and he told me that sometimes he played at a place in Times Square called Hubert's Flea Circus Museum. I'd find out about that place later.

Fred was constantly being pestered and pressured by moocher types who wanted to play or perform one thing or another. The saddest character of all was a guy named Billy the Butcher. He looked like he came out of nightmare alley. He only played one song—"High-Heel Sneakers" and he was addicted to it like a drug. Fred would usually let him play it sometime during the day, mostly when the place was empty. Billy would always preface his song by saying "This is for all you chicks." The Butcher wore an overcoat that was too small for him, buttoned tight across the chest. He was jittery and sometime in the past he'd been in a straitjacket in Bellevue, also had burned a mattress in a jail cell. All kinds of bad things had happened to Billy. There was a fire between

11

him and everybody else. He sang that one song pretty good, though.

Another popular guy wore a priest's outfit and red-topped boots with little bells and did warped takes on stories from the Bible. Moondog also performed down here. Moondog was a blind poet who lived mostly on the streets. He wore a Viking helmet and a blanket with high fur boots. Moondog did monologues, played bamboo pipes and whistles. Most of the time he performed on 42nd Street.

My favorite singer in the place was Karen Dalton. She was a tall white blues singer and guitar player, funky, lanky and sultry. I'd actually met her before, run across her the previous summer outside of Denver in a mountain pass town in a folk club. Karen had a voice like Billie Holiday's and played the guitar like Jimmy Reed and went all the way with it. I sang with her a couple of times.

Fred always tried to make a place for most performers and was as diplomatic as possible. Sometimes the room would be inexplicably empty, sometimes half-empty and then suddenly for no apparent reason it would be flushed with people with lines outside. Fred was the man down here, the main attraction and his name was on the marquee, so maybe a lot of these people came to see him. I don't know. He played a big dreadnought guitar, lot of percussion in his playing, piercing driving rhythm—a one-man band, a kick in the head singing voice. He did fierce versions of hybrid chain gang songs and whomped the audience into a frenzy. I'd heard stuff about him, that he was an errant sailor, harbored a skiff in Florida, was an underground cop, had hooker friends and a shadowy past. He'd come up to Nashville, drop off songs that he wrote and then head for

New York where he'd lay low, wait for something to blow over and fill up his pockets with wampum. Whatever it was, it wasn't a huge story. He seemed to have no aspirations. We were very compatible, didn't talk personal at all. He was very much like me, polite but not overly friendly, gave me pocket change at the end of the day, said "Here . . . so you'll keep out of trouble."

The best part of working with him, though, was strictly gastronomical—all the French fries and hamburgers I could eat. At some point during the day, Tiny Tim and I would go in the kitchen and hang around. Norbert the cook would usually have a greasy burger waiting. Either that, or he'd let us empty a can of pork and beans or spaghetti into a frying pan. Norbert was a trip. He wore a tomato-stained apron, had a fleshy, hard-bitten face, bulging cheeks, scars on his face like the marks of claws—thought of himself as a lady's man—saving his money so he could go to Verona in Italy and visit the tomb of Romeo and Juliet. The kitchen was like a cave bored into the side of a cliff.

One afternoon I was in there pouring Coke into a glass from a milk pitcher when I heard a voice coming cool through the screen of the radio speaker. Ricky Nelson was singing his new song, "Travelin' Man." Ricky had a smooth touch, the way he crooned in fast rhythm, the tonation of his voice. He was different than the rest of the teen idols, had a great guitarist who played like a cross between a honky-tonk hero and a barn-dance fiddler. Nelson had never been a bold innovator like the early singers who sang like they were navigating burning ships. He didn't sing desperately, do a lot of damage, and you'd never mistake him for a shaman. It didn't feel like his endurance was ever being tested to the utmost, but it didn't matter. He sang his songs calm and steady like he was in the middle of a storm, men hurling past him. His voice was sort of mysterious and made you fall into a certain mood.

I had been a big fan of Ricky's and still liked him, but that type of music was on its way out. It had no chance of meaning anything. There'd be no future for that stuff in the future. It was all a mistake. What was not a mistake was the ghost of Billy Lyons, rootin' the mountain down, standing 'round in East Cairo, Black Betty bam be lam. That was no mistake. That's the stuff that was happening. That's the stuff that could make you question what you'd always accepted, could litter the landscape with broken hearts, had power of spirit. Ricky, as usual, was singing bleached out lyrics. Lyrics probably written just for him. I'd always felt kin to him, though. We were about the same age, probably liked the same things, from the same generation although our life experience had been so dissimilar, him being brought up out West on a family TV show. It was like he'd been born and raised on Walden Pond where everything was hunky-dory, and I'd come out of the dark demonic woods, same forest, just a different way of looking at things. Ricky's talent was very accessible to me. I felt we had a lot in common. In a few years' time he'd record some of my songs, make them sound like they were his own, like he had written them himself. He eventually did write one himself and mentioned my name in it. Ricky, in about ten years' time, would even get booed while onstage for changing what was perceived as his musical direction. It turned out we did have a lot in common.

There was no way to know that standing in the kitchen of

the Café Wha? listening to that smooth, monotone drawl.
The thing was that Ricky was still making records and that's
what I wanted to do, too. I envisioned myself recording for
Folkways Records. That was the label I wanted to be on.
That was the label that put out all the great records.

Ricky's song ended and I gave the rest of my French fries
to Tiny Tim, went back into the outer room to see what Fred
was up to. I had asked Fred once if he had any records out
and he said, "That's not my game." Fred used darkness as a
musically potent weapon, but as skilled and powerful as he
was, there was something that he lacked as a performer. I
couldn't figure out what it was. When I saw Dave Van Ronk I
knew.

Van Ronk worked at the Gaslight, a cryptic club—had a
dominant presence on the street, more prestige than anyplace else. It had mystique, a big colorful banner out front
and paid a weekly wage. Down a flight of stairs next to a bar
called the Kettle of Fish, the Gaslight was non-booze but you
could bring a bottle in a paper bag. It was shut down in the
day and opened early in the evening with about six performers that rotated throughout the night, a closed drawn circle
that an unknown couldn't break into. There weren't any au-
ditions. It was a club I wanted to play, needed to.

Van Ronk played there. I'd heard Van Ronk back in the
Midwest on records and thought he was pretty great, copied
some of his recordings phrase for phrase. He was passionate
and stinging, sang like a soldier of fortune and sounded like
he paid the price. Van Ronk could howl and whisper, turn
blues into ballads and ballads into blues. I loved his style. He

was what the city was all about. In Greenwich Village, Van Ronk was king of the street, he reigned supreme.

Once on a cold winter day near Thompson and 3rd, in a flurry of light snow when the feeble sun was filtering through the haze, I saw him walking towards me in a frosty silence. It was like the wind was blowing him my way. I wanted to talk to him, but something was off. I watched him go by, saw the flash in his eye. It was a fleeting moment and I let it go. I wanted to play for him, though. Actually, I wanted to play for anybody. I could never sit in a room and just play all by myself. I needed to play for people and all the time. You can say I practiced in public and my whole life was becoming what I practiced. I kept my sights on the Gaslight. How could I not? Compared to it, the rest of the places on the street were nameless and miserable, low-level basket houses or small coffeehouses where the performer passed the hat. But I began to play as many as I could. I had no choice. The narrow streets were infused with them. They were small and ranged in shape, loud and noisy and catered to the confection of tourists who swarmed through the streets at night. Anything could pass for one—double door parlor rooms, storefronts, second story walk-ups, basements below street level, all holes in the wall.

There was an unusual beer and wine place on 3rd Street in what used to be Aaron Burr's livery stable, now called Café Bizarre. The patrons were mostly workingmen who sat around laughing, cussing, eating red meat, talking pussy. There was a small stage in the back and I played there once or twice. I probably played all the places at one time or another. Most of them stayed open 'til the break of day, kerosene lamps and sawdust on the floor, some with wooden benches, a strong-armed guy at the door—no cover charge and the owners tried to offload as much coffee as they could. Performers either sat or stood in the window, visible to the street, or were positioned at the opposite end of the room facing the door, singing at the top of their voices. No microphones or anything.

Talent scouts didn't come to these dens. They were dark and dingy and the atmosphere was chaotic. Performers sang and passed the hat or played while watching tourists file past, hoping some of them would toss coins into a breadbasket or guitar case. On weekends, if you played all the joints from dusk 'til dawn, you could make maybe twenty dollars. Weeknights it was hard to tell. Sometimes not much because it was so competitive. You had to know a trick or two to survive.

One singer I crossed paths with a lot, Richie Havens, always had a nice-looking girl with him who passed the hat and I noticed that he always did well. Sometimes she passed two hats. If you didn't have some kind of trick, you'd come off with an invisible presence, which wasn't good. A couple of times, I hooked up with a girl I knew from the Café Wha?, a waitress who was good to the eye. We'd go from place to place, I'd play and she'd take up collection, wear a funny little bonnet, heavy black mascara, low laced blouse—looked almost naked from the waist up under a capelike coat. I'd split the money with her later, but it was too much of a hassle to do it all the time. I still made more when she was with me than when I was working on my own.

What really set me apart in these days was my repertoire. It was more formidable than the rest of the coffeehouse players, my template being hard-core folk songs backed by incessantly loud strumming. I'd either drive people away or they'd come in closer to see what it was all about. There was no in-between. There were a lot of better singers and better musicians around these places but there wasn't anybody close in nature to what I was doing. Folk songs were the way I explored the universe, they were pictures and the pictures were worth more than anything I could say. I knew the inner substance of the thing. I could easily connect the pieces. It meant nothing for me to rattle off things like "Columbus Stockade," "Pastures of Plenty," "Brother in Korea" and "If I Lose, Let Me Lose" all back-to-back just like it was one long song. Most of the other performers tried to put themselves across, rather than the song, but I didn't care about doing that. With me, it was about putting the song across.

I had stopped going down to the Café Wha? in the afternoons. Never stepped foot in there again. Lost touch with Freddy Neil, too. Instead of going over there, I began hanging out at the Folklore Center, the citadel of Americana folk music. That was also on MacDougal Street, between Bleecker and 3rd. The small store was up a flight of stairs and the place had an antique grace. It was like an ancient chapel, like a shoebox sized institute. The Folklore Center sold and reported on everything that had to do with folk music. It had a wide plate-glass window where records and instruments were displayed.

One afternoon I went up the flight of stairs and wandered in there. I browsed around and met Izzy Young, the proprietor. Young was an old-line folk enthusiast, very sardonic and wore heavy horn-rimmed glasses, spoke in a thick Brooklyn dialect, wore wool slacks, skinny belt and work boots, tie at a careless slant. His voice was like a bulldozer and always seemed too loud for the little room. Izzy was always a little rattled over something or other. He was sloppily good natured. In reality, a romantic. To him, folk music glittered like a mound of gold. It did for me, too. The place was a crossroads junction for all the folk activity you could name and you might at any time see real hard-line folksingers in there. Some people picked up their mail there.

Young occasionally produced folk concerts by the unmistakably authentic folk and blues artists. He'd bring them in from out of town to play at Town Hall or at some university. At one time or another I saw Clarence Ashley, Gus Cannon, Mance Lipscomb, Tom Paley, Erik Darling hanging around in the place. There were a lot of esoteric folk records, too, all records I wanted to listen to. Extinct song folios of every type—sea shanties, Civil War songs, cowboy songs, songs of lament, church house songs, anti–Jim Crow songs, union songs—archaic books of folk tales, Wobbly journals, propaganda pamphlets about everything from women's rights to the dangers of boozing, one by Daniel De Foe, the English author of *Moll Flanders*. A few instruments for sale, dulcimers, five-string banjos, kazoos, pennywhistles, acoustic guitars, mandolins. If you were wondering what folk music was all about, this was the place where you could get more than a vague glimmer.

Izzy had a back room with a potbellied wood-burning stove, crooked pictures and rickety chairs—old patriots and heroes on the wall, pottery with crossed-stitch design, lacquered black candlesticks . . . lots of things having to do with craft. The little room was filled with American records and a phonograph. Izzy would let me stay back there and listen to them. I listened to as many as I could, even thumbed through a lot of his antediluvian folk scrolls. The madly complicated modern world was something I took little interest in. It had no relevancy, no weight. I wasn't seduced by it. What was swinging, topical and up to date for me was stuff like the *Titanic* sinking, the Galveston flood, John Henry driving steel, John Hardy shooting a man on the West Virginia line. All this was current, played out and in the open. This was the news that I considered, followed and kept tabs on.

As far as keeping tabs on things, Izzy kept a diary, too. It was some sort of ledger that he kept open on his desk. He'd ask me questions about myself like, where it was that I grew up and how did I get interested in folk music, where I discovered it, stuff like that. He'd then write about me in his diary. I couldn't imagine why. His questions were annoying, but I liked him because he was gracious to me and I tried to be considerate and forthcoming. I was very careful when talking to outsiders, but Izzy was okay and I answered him in plain talk.

He asked me about my family. I told him about my grandma on my mom's side who lived with us. She was filled with nobility and goodness, told me once that happiness isn't on the road to anything. That happiness is the road. Had also instructed me to be kind because everyone you'll ever meet is fighting a hard battle.

I couldn't imagine what Izzy's battles were. Internal, external, who knows? Young was a man that concerned himself with social injustice, hunger and homelessness and he didn't mind telling you so. His heroes were Abraham Lincoln and Frederick Douglass. *Moby-Dick*, the ultimate fish story, was his favorite tall tale. Young was besieged with bill collectors and dictates from the landlord. People were always chasing him down for money, but it didn't seem to faze him. He had a lot of resilience, had even fought city hall into allowing folk music to be played in Washington Square Park. Everybody was for him.

He'd pull out records for me. He'd given me a Country Gentlemen record and said I should listen to "Girl Behind the Bar." He played me "White House Blues" by Charlie Poole and said that this would be perfect for me and pointed out that this was the exact version that The Ramblers did. He played me the Big Bill Broonzy song "Somebody's Got to Go," and that was right up my alley, too. I liked hanging around at Izzy's. The fire was always crackling.

One winter day a big burly guy stepped in off the street. He looked like he'd come from the Russian embassy, shook the snow off his coat sleeves, took off his gloves and put them on the counter, asked to see a Gibson guitar that was hanging up on the brick wall. It was Dave Van Ronk. He was gruff, a mass of bristling hair, don't give a damn attitude, a confident hunter. My mind went into a rush. There was nothing between the man and me. Izzy took the guitar down and gave it to him. Dave fingered the strings and played some kind of jazzy waltz, put the guitar back on the counter. As he put the guitar down, I stepped over and put my hands on it and asked him at the same time how does someone get to work down at the Gaslight, who do you have to know? It's not like I was trying to get buddy-buddy with him, I just wanted to know.

Van Ronk looked at me curiously, was snippy and surly, asked if I did janitor work.

I told him, no, I didn't and he could perish the thought, but could I play something for him? He said, "Sure."

I played him "Nobody Knows You When You're Down and Out." Dave liked what he heard and asked me who I was and how long I'd been in town, then said I could come down about eight or nine in the evening and play a couple of songs in his set. That was how I met Dave Van Ronk.

I left the Folklore Center and went back into the ice-chopping weather. Towards evening, I was over at the Mills Tavern on Bleecker Street where the basket-house singers would bunch up, chitchat and make the scene. My flamenco guitar–playing friend, Juan Moreno, told me about a new coffeehouse that had just opened on 3rd Street, called the Outré, but I was barely listening. Juan's lips were moving, but they were moving almost without sound. I'd never play in the Outré, didn't have to. I'd soon be hired to play at the Gaslight and never see the basket houses again. Outside of Mills Tavern the thermometer was creeping up to about ten below. My breath froze in the air, but I didn't feel the cold. I was heading for the fantastic lights. No doubt about it. Could it be that I was being deceived? Not likely. I don't think I had enough imagination to be deceived; had no false hope, either. I'd come from a long ways off and had started from a long ways down. But now destiny was about to manifest itself. I felt like it was looking right at me and nobody else.

# 2

# The Lost Land

I SAT UP in bed and looked around. The bed was a sofa in the living room and steam heat was rising out of the iron radiator. Above the fireplace, a framed portrait of a wigged colonial was staring back at me—near the sofa, a wooden cabinet supported by fluted columns, near that, an oval table with rounded drawers, a chair like a wheelbarrow, small desk of violet wood veneer with flip-down drawers—a couch that was a padded back car seat with spring upholstery, a low chair with rounded back and scroll armrests—a thick French rug on the floor, silver light gleaming through the blinds, painted planks accenting the rooflines.

The room smelled of gin and tonic, wood alcohol and flowers. The place was a top floor walk-up in a Federal style building near Vestry Street below Canal and near the Hudson River. On the same block was the Bull's Head, a cellar tavern where John Wilkes Booth, the American Brutus, used to drink. I'd been in there once and saw his ghost in the mirror—an ill spirit. Paul Clayton, a folksinger friend of Van

Ronk, good-natured, forlorn and melancholic, who must have had at least thirty records out but was unknown to the American public—an intellectual, a scholar and a romantic with an encyclopedic knowledge of balladry—had introduced me to Ray Gooch and Chloe Kiel, the occupants of the place. I walked over to the window and looked out into the white, gray streets and over towards the river. The air was bitter cold, always below zero, but the fire in my mind was never out, like a wind vane that was constantly spinning. It was midafternoon and both Ray and Chloe were gone.

Ray was maybe ten years older than me—from Virginia— he was like an old wolf, gaunt and battle-scarred—came from a long line of ancestry made up of bishops, generals, even a colonial governor. He was a nonconformist, a noninte- grator and a Southern nationalist. He and Chloe lived in the place like they were hiding out. Ray was like a character from out of some of the songs I'd been singing, someone who had seen life, done deeds and lived romances—had traipsed around, had a broad grasp of the country, its conditions. Though there was an undercurrent of upheaval reverberat- ing, and in a few years the American cities would tremble, Ray took little interest, said the real action was "in the Congo."

Chloe had red-gold hair, hazel eyes, an illegible smile, face like a doll and an even better figure, fingernails painted black. She worked as a hatcheck girl at the Egypt- ian Gardens, a belly-dancing dinner place on 8th Avenue— also posed as a model for *Cavalier* magazine. "I've always worked," she said. They lived as husband and wife, or brother and sister, or cousins, it was hard to tell, they just lived here, that's all. Chloe had her own primitive way of looking at things, always would say mad stuff that clicked in a cryptic way, told me once that I should wear eyeshadow because it keeps away the evil eye. I asked her whose evil eye and she said, "Joe Blow's or Joe Schmoe's." According to her, Dracula ruled the world and he's the son of Gutenberg, the guy who invented the printing press.

Being an heir of the '40s and '50s cultures, this kind of talk was fine with me. Gutenberg could have been some guy who stepped out of an old folk song, too. Practically speaking, the '50s culture was like a judge in his last days on the bench. It was about to go. Within ten years' time, it would struggle to rise and then come crashing to the floor. With folk songs embedded in my mind like a religion, it wouldn't matter. Folk songs transcended the immediate culture.

Before I moved into a place of my own, I'd stayed pretty much all over the Village. Sometimes for a night or two, sometimes for weeks or more. I stayed a lot at Van Ronk's. I probably stayed at Vestry Street off and on longer than anywhere. I liked it at Ray and Chloe's. I felt comfortable there. Ray had an elite background, even studied at Camden Military Academy in South Carolina, which he had left with "sincere and utter hatred." He'd also been "expelled with gratitude" from Wake Forest Divinity School, a religious college. He had parts of Byron's *Don Juan* memorized and could quote it—also some of the beautiful lines of "Evangeline," the Longfellow poem. He was working in a tool-and-die factory in Brooklyn, but before that had drifted around, had been employed at the Studebaker plant in South Bend and also at an Omaha slaughterhouse on the kill floor. Once I asked him what that was like. "You ever heard of Auschwitz?" Sure I had, who hadn't? It was one of the Nazi death camps in Europe and Adolf Eichmann, the chief Nazi Gestapo organizer who'd managed them, had been put on trial recently in Jerusalem. He'd escaped after the war and was captured by the Israelis at a bus stop in Argentina. His trial was a big deal. On the witness stand Eichmann declared he was merely following orders, but his prosecutors had no problem proving that he had carried out his mission with monstrous zeal and relish. Eichmann had been convicted and his fate was now being decided. There was a lot of talk about sparing his life, even sending him back to Argentina, but that would have been foolish. Even if he was set free he probably wouldn't last an hour. The State of Israel claimed the right to act as heir and executor of all who perished in the final solution. The trial reminds the whole world of what led to the formation of the Israeli state.

I was born in the spring of 1941. The Second World War was already raging in Europe, and America would soon be in it. The world was being blown apart and chaos was already driving its fist into the face of all new visitors. If you were born around this time or were living and alive, you could feel the old world go and the new one beginning. It was like putting the clock back to when B.C. became A.D. Everybody born around my time was a part of both. Hitler, Churchill, Mussolini, Stalin, Roosevelt—towering figures that the world would never see the likes of again, men who relied on their own resolve, for better or worse, every one of them prepared to act alone, indifferent to approval—indifferent to wealth or love, all presiding over the destiny of mankind and reducing the world to rubble. Coming from a long line of Alexanders and Julius Caesars, Genghis Khans, Charlemagnes and Napoleons, they carved up the world like a really dainty dinner. Whether they parted their hair in the middle or wore a Viking helmet, they would not be denied and were impossible to reckon with—rude barbarians stampeding across the earth and hammering out their own ideas of geography.

My father was stricken with polio and it kept him out of the war, but my uncles had all gone and come back alive. Uncle Paul, Uncle Maurice, Jack, Max, Louis, Vernon, and others had gone off to the Philippines, Anzio, Sicily, North Africa, France and Belgium. They brought back mementos and keepsakes—a straw Japanese cigarette case, German bread bag, a British enameled mug, German dust goggles, British fighting knife, a German Luger pistol—all kinds of junk. They returned to civilian life as if nothing ever happened, never said a word about what they did or what they saw.

In 1951 I was going to grade school. One of the things we were trained to do was to hide and take cover under our desks when the air-raid sirens blew because the Russians could attack us with bombs. We were also told that the Russians could be parachuting from planes over our town at any time. These were the same Russians that my uncles had fought alongside only a few years earlier. Now they had become monsters who were coming to slit our throats and incinerate us. It seemed peculiar. Living under a cloud of fear like this robs a child of his spirit. It's one thing to be afraid when someone's holding a shotgun on you, but it's another thing to be afraid of something that's just not quite real. There were a lot of folks around who took this threat seriously, though, and it rubbed off on you. It was easy to become a victim of their strange fantasy. I had the same teachers in school that my mother did. They were young in her time and elderly in mine. In American history class, we were taught that commies couldn't destroy America with guns or bombs alone, that they would have to destroy the Constitution—the document that this country was founded upon. It didn't make any difference, though. When the drill sirens went off, you had to lay under your desk facedown, not a muscle quivering and not make any noise. As if this could save you from the bombs dropping. The threat of annihilation was a scary thing. We didn't know what we did to anybody to make them so mad. The Reds were everywhere, we were told, and out for bloodlust. Where were my uncles, the defenders of the country? They were busy making a living, working, getting what they could and making it stretch. How could they know what was going on in the schools, what kind of fear was being roused?

All that was over now. I was in New York City, communists or no communists. There were probably plenty around. Plenty of fascists, too. Plenty of would-be left-wing dictators and right-wing dictators. Radicals of all stripes. It was said that World War II spelled the end of the Age of Enlightenment, but I wouldn't have known it. I was still in it. Somehow I could still remember and feel the light of something about it. I'd read that stuff. Voltaire, Rousseau, John Locke, Montesquieu, Martin Luther—visionaries, revolutionaries . . . it was like I knew those guys, like they'd been living in my backyard.

I walked across the floor over to the cream colored drapes, pulled up the venetian blinds, seeing into the snowy streets. The furniture in the place was nice, some of it even hand built. That was nice, too—inlaid industrial dresser cabinets with highly stylized carvings with florid latches—floor-to-ceiling ornamental bookcases, a long narrow rectangular table with metal elements with geometrics that seemed to follow some unguided rule—one amusing piece, an organically shaped console table resembled a big toe. There were electric plates ingeniously placed in closet shelves. The small kitchen was like a forest. Kitchen herb boxes stuffed with pennyroyal, woodruff, lilac leaves, other things. Chloe, a Southern girl with Northern blood, was skilled in the use of bathroom clotheslines and sometimes I'd find one of my shirts hanging in there. I usually came in before dawn and slid onto the sofa, which came out into a folding bed in the high portico living room. I often fell asleep to the sounds of the night train rumbling and grumbling through Jersey, the iron horse with steam for blood.

I'd seen and heard trains from my earliest childhood days and the sight and sound of them always made me feel secure. The big boxcars, the iron ore cars, freight cars, passenger trains, Pullman cars. There was no place you could go in my hometown without at least some part of the day having to stop at intersections and wait for the long trains to pass. Tracks crossed the rural roads and ran alongside them as well. The sound of trains off in the distance more or less made me feel at home, like nothing was missing, like I was at some level place, never in any significant danger and that everything was fitting together.

Across the street from where I stood looking out the window was a church with a bell tower. The ringing of bells made me feel at home, too. I'd always heard and listened to the bells. Iron, brass, silver bells—the bells sang. On Sunday, for services, on holidays. They clanged when somebody important died, when people were getting married. Any special occasion would make the bells ring. You had a pleasant feeling when you heard the bells. I even liked doorbells and the NBC chimes on the radio. I looked out through the leaded glass window across to the church. The bells were silent now and snow swirled off the rooftops. A blizzard was kidnapping the city, life spinning around on a drab canvas. Icy and cold.

Across the way a guy in a leather jacket scooped frost off the windshield of a snow-packed black Mercury Montclair. Behind him, a priest in a purple cloak was slipping through the courtyard of the church through an opened gate on his way to perform some sacred duty. Nearby, a bareheaded woman in boots tried to manage a laundry bag up the street. There were a million stories, just everyday New York things if you wanted to focus in on them. It was always right out in front of you, blended together, but you'd have to pull it apart to make any sense of it. St. Valentine's Day, lovers' day, had come and gone and I hadn't noticed. I had no time for romance. I turned away from the window, from the wintry sun, crossed through the room, went to the stove and made and poured myself a cup of hot chocolate and then clicked on the radio.

I was always fishing for something on the radio. Just like trains and bells, it was part of the soundtrack of my life. I moved the dial up and down and Roy Orbison's voice came blasting out of the small speakers. His new song, "Running Scared," exploded into the room. Lately I'd been listening for songs with folk connotations. There had been some in the past: "Big Bad John," "Michael Row the Boat Ashore," "A Hundred Pounds of Clay." Brook Benton had made "Boll Weevil" a contemporary hit. The Kingston Trio and Brothers Four were getting radio play. I liked The Kingston Trio. Even though their style was polished and collegiate, I liked most of their stuff anyway. Songs like "Getaway John," "Remember the Alamo," "Long Black Rifle." There was always some kind of folk type song breaking through. "Endless Sleep," the Jodie Reynolds song that had been popular years before, had even been folk in character. Orbison, though, transcended all the genres—folk, country, rock and roll or just about anything. His stuff mixed all the styles and some that hadn't even been invented yet. He could sound mean and nasty on one line and then sing in a falsetto voice like Frankie Valli in the next. With Roy, you didn't know if you were listening to mariachi or opera. He kept you on your toes. With him, it was all about fat and blood. He sounded like he was singing from an Olympian mountaintop and he meant business. One of his early songs, "Ooby Dooby," had been popular way previously, but this new song of his was nothing like that. "Ooby Dooby" was deceptively simple, but Roy had progressed. He was now singing his compositions in three or four octaves that made you want to drive your car over a cliff. He sang like a professional criminal. Typically, he'd start out in some low, barely audible range, stay there a while and then astonishingly slip into histrionics. His voice could jar a corpse, always leave you muttering to yourself something like, "Man, I don't believe it." His songs had songs within songs. They shifted from major to minor key without any logic. Orbison was deadly serious—no pollywog and no fledgling juvenile. There wasn't anything 'else on the radio like him. I'd listen and wait for another song, but next to Roy the playlist was strictly dullsville . . . gutless and flabby. It all came at you like you didn't have a brain. Outside of maybe George Jones, I didn't like country music either. Jim Reeves and Eddy Arnold, it was hard to know what was country about that stuff. All the wildness and weirdness had gone out of country music. Elvis Presley. Nobody listened to him either. It had been years since he had done his hip thing and taken songs to other planets. I still kept turning the radio on, probably more out of mindless habit than anything else. Sadly, whatever it played reflected nothing but milk and sugar and not the real Jekyll and Hyde themes of the times. The *On the Road*, *Howl* and *Gasoline* street ideologies that were signaling a new type of human existence weren't there, but how could you have expected it to be? 45 records were incapable of it.

I agonized about making a record, but I wouldn't have wanted to make singles, 45s—the kind of songs they played on the radio. Folksingers, jazz artists and classical musicians made LPs, long-playing records with heaps of songs in the grooves—they forged identities and tipped the scales, gave more of the big picture. LPs were like the force of gravity. They had covers, back and front, that you could stare at for hours. Next to them, 45s were flimsy and uncrystallized. They just stacked up in piles and didn't seem important. I had no song in my repertoire for commercial radio anyway. Songs about debauched bootleggers, mothers that drowned their own children, Cadillacs that only got five miles to the gallon, floods, union hall fires, darkness and cadavers at the bottom of rivers weren't for radiophiles. There was nothing easygoing about the folk songs I sang. They weren't friendly or ripe with mellowness. They didn't come gently to the shore. I guess you could say they weren't commercial. Not only that, my style was too erratic and hard to pigeonhole for the radio, and songs, to me, were more important than just light entertainment. They were my preceptor and guide into some altered consciousness of reality, some different republic, some liberated republic. Greil Marcus, the music historian, would some thirty years later call it "the invisible republic." Whatever the case, it wasn't that I was anti–popular culture or anything and I had no ambitions to stir things up. I just thought of mainstream culture as lame as hell and a big trick. It was like the unbroken sea of frost that lay outside the window and you had to have awkward footgear to walk on it. I didn't know what age of history we were in nor what the truth of it was. Nobody bothered with that. If you told the truth, that was all well and good and if you told the un-truth, well, that's still well and good. Folk songs had taught me that. As for what time it was, it was always just beginning to be daylight and I knew a little bit about history, too—the history of a few nations and states—and it was always the same pattern. Some early archaic period where society grows and develops and thrives, then some classical period where the society reaches its maturation point and then a slacking off period where decadence makes things fall apart. I had no idea which one of these stages America was in. There was nobody to check with. A certain rude rhythm was making it all sway, though. It was pointless to think about it. Whatever you were thinking could be dead wrong.

I cut the radio off, crisscrossed the room, pausing for a moment, to turn on the black-and-white TV. *Wagon Train* was on. It seemed to be beaming in from some foreign country. I shut that off, too, and went into another room, a windowless one with a painted door—a dark cavern with a floor-to-ceiling library. I switched on the lamps. The place had an overpowering presence of literature and you couldn't help but lose your passion for dumbness. Up until this time I'd been raised in a cultural spectrum that had left my mind black with soot. Brando. James Dean. Milton Berle. Marilyn Monroe. Lucy. Earl Warren and Khrushchev, Castro. Little Rock and Peyton Place. Tennessee Williams and Joe DiMaggio. J. Edgar Hoover and Westinghouse. The Nelsons. Holiday Inns and hot-rod Chevys. Mickey Spillane and Joe McCarthy. Levittown.

Standing in this room you could take it all for a joke. There were all types of things in here, books on typography, epigraphy, philosophy, political ideologies. The stuff that could make you bugged-eyed. Books like *Fox's Book of Martyrs*, *The Twelve Caesars*, Tacitus lectures and letters to Brutus. Pericles' *Ideal State of Democracy*, Thucydides' *The Athenian General*—a narrative which would give you chills. It was written four hundred years before Christ and it talks about how human nature is always the enemy of anything superior. Thucydides writes about how words in his time have changed from their ordinary meaning, how actions and opinions can be altered in the blink of an eye. It's like nothing has changed from his time to mine.

There were novels by Gogol and Balzac, Maupassant, Hugo and Dickens. I usually opened up some book to the middle, read a few pages and if I liked it went back to the beginning. *Materia Medica* (the causes and cures for diseases)—that was a good one. I was looking for the part of my education that I never got. Sometimes I'd open up a book and see a handwritten note scribbled in the front, like in Machiavelli's *The Prince*, there was written, "The spirit of the hustler." "The cosmopolitan man" was written on the title page in Dante's *Inferno*. The books weren't arranged in any particular order or subject matter. Rousseau's *Social Contract* was next to *Temptation of St. Anthony*, and Ovid's *Metamor-*

*phoses*, the scary horror tale, was next to the autobiography of Davy Crockett. Endless rows of books—Sophocles' book on the nature and function of the gods—why there are only two sexes. Alexander the Great's march into Persia. When he conquered Persia, in order to keep it conquered, he had all of his men marry local women. After that, he never had any trouble with the population, no uprisings or anything. Alexander knew how to get absolute control. There was Simón Bolívar's biography, too. I wanted to read all these books, but I would have to have been in a rest home or something in order to do that. I read some of *The Sound and the Fury,* didn't quite get it, but Faulkner was powerful. I read some of the Albertus Magnus book . . . the guy who mixed up scientific theories with theology. It was lightweight compared to Thucydides. Magnus seemed like a guy who couldn't sleep, writing this stuff late at night, clothes stuck to his clammy body. A lot of these books were too big to read, like giant shoes fitted for large-footed people. I read the poetry books, mostly. Byron and Shelley and Longfellow and Poe. I memorized Poe's poem "The Bells" and strummed it to a melody on my guitar. There was a book there on Joseph Smith, the authentic American prophet who identifies himself with Enoch in the Bible and says that Adam was the first man-god. This stuff pales in comparison to Thucydides, too. The books make the room vibrate in a nauseating and forceful way. The words of "La Vita Solitaria" by Leopardi seemed to come out of the trunk of a tree, hopeless, uncrushable sentiments.

There was a book by Sigmund Freud, the king of the subconscious, called *Beyond the Pleasure Principle.* I was thumbing through it once when Ray came in, saw the book and said, "The top guys in that field work for ad agencies. They deal in air." I put the book back and never picked it up again. I did read a biography about Robert E. Lee, though, read about how his father had been disfigured in a riot, had lye poured into his eyes and then abandoned his family and went to the West Indies. Robert E. Lee had grown up without a father. Lee had made something out of himself, nevertheless. Not only that, but it was on his word and his word alone that America did not get into a guerrilla war that probably would have lasted 'til this day. The books were something. They were really something.

I read a lot of the pages aloud and liked the sound of the words, the language. Milton's protest poem, "Massacre in Piedmont." A political poem about the murder of innocents by the Duke of Savoy in Italy. It was like the folk song lyrics, even more elegant.

The Russian stuff on the shelves had an especially dark presence. There were the political poems of Pushkin, who was considered revolutionary. Pushkin was killed in a duel in 1837. There was a book by Count Leo Tolstoy, whose estate I'd visit more than twenty years later—his family estate, which he used to educate peasants. It was located outside of Moscow, and this was where he went later in life to reject all his writings and renounce all forms of war. One day when he was eighty-two years old he left a note for his family to leave him alone. He walked off into the snowy woods and a few days later they found him dead of pneumonia. A tour guide let me ride his bicycle. Dostoyevsky, too, had lived a dismal and hard life. The czar sent him to a prison camp in Siberia in 1849. Dostoyevsky was accused of writing socialist propaganda. He was eventually pardoned and wrote stories to ward off his creditors. Just like in the early '70s I wrote albums to ward off mine.

In the past, I'd never been that keen on books and writers but I liked stories. Stories by Edgar Rice Burroughs, who wrote about the mythical Africa—Luke Short, the mythical Western tales—Jules Verne—H. G. Wells. Those were my favorites but that was before I discovered the folksingers. The folksingers could sing songs like an entire book, but only in a few verses. It's hard to describe what makes a character or an event folk song worthy. It probably has something to do with a character being fair and honest and open. Bravery in an abstract way. Al Capone had been a successful gangster and was allowed to rule the underworld in Chicago, but nobody wrote any songs about him. He's not interesting or heroic in any kind of way. He's frigid. A sucker fish, seems like a man who never got out alone in nature for a minute in his life. He comes across as a thug or a bully, like in the song . . . "looking for that bully of the town." He's not even worthy enough to have a name—comes across as a heartless vamp. Pretty Boy Floyd, on the other hand, stirs up an adventurous spirit. Even his name has something to say. There's something unbound and not frozen in the muck about him. He'll never rule over any city, can't manipulate the machine or bend people to his will, yet he's the stuff of real flesh and blood, represents humanity in general and gives you an impression of power. At least before they trapped him in the boonies.

There was no noise in Ray's place, just if I'd turn the radio on or listen to records. If not, there was only a graveyard silence and I'd always return to the books . . . dig through them like an archeologist. I read the biography of Thaddeus Stevens, the radical Republican. He lived in the early part of the 1800s and was quite a character. He's from Gettysburg and he's got a clubfoot like Byron. He grew up poor, made a fortune and from then on championed the weak and any other group who wasn't able to fight equally. Stevens had a grim sense of humor, a sharp tongue and a white-hot hatred for the bloated aristocrats of his day. He wanted to confiscate the land of the slaveholding elite, once referred to a colleague on the floor of the chamber as "slinking in his own slime." Stevens was an anti-Mason and he denounced his foes as those whose mouths reeked from human blood. He got right in there, called his enemies a "feeble band of lowly reptiles who shun the light and who lurk in their own dens." Stevens was hard to forget. He made a big impression on me, was inspiring. Him and Teddy Roosevelt, maybe the strongest U.S. president ever. I read about Teddy, too. He was a cattle rancher and a crime buster, had to be restrained from declaring war on California—had a big run in with J. P. Morgan, a deity figure who owned most of the United States at the time. Roosevelt backed him down and threatened to throw him in jail.

Either one of those guys, Stevens or Roosevelt or even Morgan could have stepped out of a folk ballad. Songs like "Walkin' Boss," "The Prisoner's Song" or even one like "Ballad of Charles Guiteau." They're just in there somewhere, though maybe not in a specific way. They're even in early rock-and-roll songs if you want to add electricity and drums.

There were art books, too, on the shelves, books of Motherwell and early Jasper Johns, German impressionist pamphlets, Grunwald, Adolf von Menzel stuff. "How-to" books, how to repair a man's knee that's been bent backwards . . . how to deliver a baby, how to perform an appendectomy in the bedroom. The stuff could give you real hot dreams. There were other things laying around that would catch your eye—chalk sketches of Ferraris and Ducatis, books about Amazon women, Pharaonic Egypt, photo books of circus acrobats, lovers, graveyards. There weren't any big bookstores around, so it would have been hard to find these books in any one place. I liked the biographies a lot and read part of one about Frederick the Great, who, besides being King of Prussia, I was surprised to find out was also a composer. I also looked through *Vom Kriege,* the Clausewitz book. They called Clausewitz the premier philosopher of war. By the sound of his name you'd think he looked like Von Hindenburg, but he doesn't. In the book's portrait of him, he looks like Robert Burns, the poet, or Montgomery Clift, the actor. The book was published in 1832 and Clausewitz had been in the military since he'd been twelve. His armies were highly trained professionals, not young men who served only for a few years or more. His men were hard to replace and he talks a lot about how to maneuver into position where the other side can see there's no fighting chance and basically lay down their arms. In his time there was little to gain and much to lose by any serious fighting. For Clausewitz, flinging stones was not war—not idealized war, anyway. He talks a lot about psychological and accidental factors on the battlefield—the weather, air currents—playing a big part.

I had a morbid fascination with this stuff. Years earlier, before I knew I was going to be a singer and my mind was in full swing, I had even wanted to go to West Point. I'd always pictured myself dying in some heroic battle rather than in bed. I wanted to be a general with my own battalion and wondered how to get the key to open this wonderland. I asked my father how to get into West Point and he seemed shocked, said that my name didn't begin with a "De" or a "Von" and that you needed connections and proper credentials to get in there. His advice was that we should concentrate on how to acquire them. My uncle was even less forthcoming. He said to me, "You don't want to have to work for the government. A soldier is a housewife, a guinea pig. Go to work in the mines."

Mines or no mines, it was the connections and credentials thing that rattled me. I didn't like the sound of it, made me feel deprived of something. It wasn't long before I discovered what they were and how these things can sometimes interfere with your plans. When I put together my early bands, usually some other singer who was short of one would take it away. It seemed like this happened every time one of my bands was fully formed. I couldn't understand how this was possible seeing that these guys weren't any better at singing or playing than I was. What they did have was an open door to gigs where there was real money. Anybody who had a band could play at park pavilions, talent shows, county fairgrounds, auctions and store openings, but those gigs didn't pay except maybe for expenses and sometimes not even for that. These other crooners could perform at small conventions, private wedding parties, golden anniversaries in hotel ballrooms, Knights of Columbus functions, things like that—and there was cash involved. It was always the promise of money that lured my band away. I would always be moaning to my grandmother who lived with us, my one and only confidante, and she'd tell me not to take it personal. She'd say stuff like, "There are some people you'll never be able to win over. Just let it go—let it wear itself out." Sure, that's easy to say, but it didn't make me feel any less bad. Truth was, that the guys who took my bands away had family connections to someone up the ladder in the chamber of commerce or town council or merchants associations. These groups were connected to different committees throughout the counties. The family connection thing made a strong impression, left me feeling naked.

It went to the very root of things, gave unfair advantage to some and left others squeezed out. How could somebody ever reach the world this way? It seemed like it was the law of life, but even if it was, I wasn't going to sulk about it or, like my grandma said, take it personal. Family connections were legitimate. You couldn't blame anyone for having them. It got so that I almost always expected to lose my band and it didn't even shock me anymore if it happened. I kept forming them, though, because I was determined to play. There was a lot of halting and waiting, little acknowledgment, little affirmation, but sometimes all it takes is a wink or a nod from some unexpected place to vary the tedium of a baffling existence.

That happened to me when Gorgeous George the great wrestler came to my hometown. In the mid-'50s I was performing in the lobby of the National Guard Armory, the Veterans Memorial Building, the site where all the big shows happened—the livestock shows and hockey games, circuses and boxing shows, traveling preacher revivals, country-and-western jamborees. I'd seen Slim Whitman, Hank Snow, Webb Pierce and a lot of others there. Once a year or so, Gorgeous George would bring his whole troupe of performers to town: Goliath, The Vampire, The Twister, The Strangler, The Bone Crusher, The Holy Terror, midget wrestlers, a couple of lady wrestlers, and a whole lot more. I was playing on a makeshift platform in the lobby of the building with the usual wild activity of people milling about, and no one was paying much attention. Suddenly, the doors burst open and in came Gorgeous George himself. He roared in like the storm, didn't go through the backstage area, he came right through the lobby of the building and he seemed like forty men. It was Gorgeous George, in all his magnificent glory with all the lightning and vitality you'd expect. He had valets and was surrounded by women carrying roses, wore a majestic fur-lined gold cape and his long blond curls were flowing. He brushed by the makeshift stage and glanced towards the sound of the music. He didn't break stride, but he looked at me, eyes flashing with moonshine. He winked and seemed to mouth the phrase "You're making it come alive."

Whether he really said it or not, it didn't matter. It's what I thought I heard him say that mattered, and I never forgot it. It was all the recognition and encouragement I would need for years to come. Sometimes that's all it takes, the kind of recognition that comes when you're doing the thing for the thing's sake and you're on to something—it's just that nobody recognizes it yet. Gorgeous George. A mighty spirit. People said that he was as great as his race. Maybe he was. Inevitably, I would soon lose the band that was playing with me in the lobby of the Veterans building. Someone else had seen them and took them. I'd have to work on my connections. It was beginning to dawn on me that I would have to learn how to play and sing by myself and not depend on a band until the time I could afford to pay and keep one. Connections and credentials would have to become an irrelevancy, but I did feel good for a moment. Crossing paths with Gorgeous George was really something.

Clausewitz's book seemed outdated, but there's a lot in it that's real, and you can understand a lot about conventional life and the pressures of environment by reading it. When he claims that politics has taken the place of morality and politics is brute force, he's not playing. You have to believe it. You do exactly as you're told, whoever you are. Knuckle under or you're dead. Don't give me any of that jazz about hope or nonsense about righteousness. Don't give me that dance that God is with us, or that God supports us. Let's get down to brass tacks. There isn't any moral order. You can forget that. Morality has nothing in common with politics. It's not there to transgress. It's either high ground or low ground. This is the way the world is and nothing's gonna change it. It's a crazy, mixed up world and you have to look it right in the eye. Clausewitz in some ways is a prophet. Without realizing it, some of the stuff in his book can shape your ideas. If you think you're a dreamer, you can read this stuff and realize you're not even capable of dreaming. Dreaming is dangerous. Reading Clausewitz makes you take your own thoughts a little less seriously.

I read *The White Goddess* by Robert Graves, too. Invoking the poetic muse was something I didn't know about yet. Didn't know enough to start trouble with it, anyway. In a few years' time I would meet Robert Graves himself in London. We went out for a brisk walk around Paddington Square. I wanted to ask him about some of the things in his book, but I couldn't remember much about it. I liked the French writer Balzac a lot, read *Luck and Leather,* and *Le Cousin Pons.* Balzac was pretty funny. His philosophy is plain and simple, says basically that pure materialism is a recipe for madness. The only true knowledge for Balzac seems to be in superstition. Everything is subject to analysis. Horde your energy. That's the secret of life. You can learn a lot from Mr. B. It's funny to have him as a companion. He wears a monk's robe and drinks endless cups of coffee. Too much sleep clogs up his mind. One of his teeth falls out, and he says, "What does this mean?" He questions everything. His clothes catch fire on a candle. He wonders if fire is a good sign. Balzac is hilarious.

There was nothing upscale about the Gaslight, no ringside tables or anything, but it was always packed from start to finish—some people sitting at tables, some standing and crowded up along the walls—bare brick walls, low level lighting and pipes exposed. Even on cold winter nights there was a line to get in, clusters of people huddled in the doorway, twin entrances downstairs. There were always so many people inside, it was hard to breathe. I don't know how many it could hold, but it always seemed like ten thousand or more. The fire marshals would always be coming in and out, always a lot of anticipation, apprehension in the air, a lot of audacity. You got the feeling that something, someone, was always coming to blow away the fog.

I played twenty minute sets. Played the folk songs that I possessed and paid attention to what was going on in the moment. It was hot in there and too claustrophobic to hang around after playing, so performers would often hang out upstairs in one of the back rooms, which you got to by going out back through the kitchen, into the small courtyard and up the icy fire escape. There'd always be a card game going on. Van Ronk, Stookey, Romney, Hal Waters, Paul Clayton,

Luke Faust, Len Chandler and some others would play poker continuously through the night. You could come and go as you pleased. A small radio speaker in the room let you know who was performing downstairs so you knew when it was your turn to go back. Bets were usually nickels and dimes and quarters, although sometimes the pot could get up as high as twenty dollars. I usually folded my cards if I didn't have a pair by the second or third draw. Chandler told me once, "You gotta learn how to bluff. You'll never make it in this game if you don't. Sometimes you even have to get caught bluffing. It helps later if you got a winning hand and want some other players to think you might be bluffing."

I didn't spend too much time downstairs because it was too crowded and stifling. I'd either be up in the card room or at the Kettle of Fish Tavern next door. That place was usually packed, too, on any given night of the week. A frantic atmosphere—all kinds of characters talking fast, moving fast—some debonair, some rakish. Literary types with black beards, grim-faced intellectuals—eclectic girls, non-homemaker types. The kind of people who come from out of nowhere and go right back into it—a pistol-packing rabbi, a snaggle-toothed girl with a big crucifix between her breasts—all kinds of characters looking for the inner heat. I felt like I was seeing it all sitting on the crest of a cliff. Some people even had titles—"The Man Who Made History," "The Link Between the Races"—that's how they'd want to be referred to. Comedians from comedy shows, like Richard Pryor, used to hang around in there, too. You could sit on a bar stool and look out the windows to the snowy streets and see heavy people going by, David Amram bundled up, Gregory Corso, Ted Joans, Fred Hellerman.

One night a guy named Bobby Neuwirth came through the

door with a couple of friends and caused a lot of commotion. Bobby and I would meet again sometime later at a folk festival. Right from the start, you could tell that Neuwirth had a taste for provocation and that nothing was going to restrict his freedom. He was in a mad revolt against something. You had to brace yourself when you talked to him. Neuwirth was about the same age as me, from Akron, played clawhammer banjo and knew some songs. He was going to art school in Boston and could paint, too—said he was going back to Ohio in the spring to his folks' house to take down the storm windows and put up the screens. That was his customary thing to do and it had been mine, too. I wasn't planning on going back, though. Later we'd become pretty tight and travel around together. Like Kerouac had immortalized Neal Cassady in *On the Road,* somebody should have immortalized Neuwirth. He was that kind of character. He could talk to anybody until they felt like all their intelligence was gone. With his tongue, he ripped and slashed and could make anybody uneasy, also could talk his way out of anything. Nobody knew what to make of him. If there ever was a renaissance man leaping in and out of things, he would have to be it. Neuwirth was a bulldog. He didn't provoke me, though, not in any way. I got a kick out of everything he did and liked him. Neuwirth had talent, but he wasn't ambitious. We liked pretty much all the same things, even the same songs on the jukebox.

The jukebox in the place showed mostly jazz records. Zoot Simms, Hampton Hawes, Stan Getz, and some rhythm-and-blues records—Bumble Bee Slim, Slim Galliard, Percy Mayfield. The Beats tolerated folk music, but they really didn't like it. They listened exclusively to modern jazz, bebop. A couple of times I dropped a coin right into the slot and played "The Man That Got Away" by Judy Garland. The song always did something to me, not in any stupefying, tremendous kind of way. It didn't summon up any strange thoughts. It just was nice to hear. Judy Garland was from Grand Rapids, Minnesota, a town about twenty miles away from where I came from. Listening to Judy was like listening to the girl next door. She was way before my time, and like the Elton John song says, "I would have liked to have known you, but I was just a kid." Harold Arlen had written "The Man That Got Away" and the cosmic "Somewhere Over the Rainbow," another song by Judy Garland. He had written a lot of other popular songs, too—the powerful "Blues in the Night," "Stormy Weather," "Come Rain or Come Shine," "Get Happy." In Harold's songs, I could hear rural blues and folk music. There was an emotional kinship there. I couldn't help but notice it. The songs of Woody Guthrie ruled my universe, but before that, Hank Williams had been my favorite songwriter, though I thought of him as a singer, first. Hank Snow was a close second. But I could never escape from the bittersweet, lonely intense world of Harold Arlen. Van Ronk could sing and play these songs. I could, too, but never would have dreamed of it. They weren't in my script. They weren't in my future. What was the future? The future was a solid wall, not promising, not threatening—all bunk. No guarantees of anything, not even the guarantee that life isn't one big joke.

You'd never know who you were liable to run into at the Kettle of Fish. Everyone seemed like somebody and nobody at the same time. Once, me and Clayton were sitting, drinking wine at a table with some people and one of the guys there had sometime back provided sound effects for radio shows. Radio shows had been a big part of my consciousness back in the Midwest, back when it seemed like I was living in perpetual youth. *Inner Sanctum*, *The Lone Ranger*, *This Is Your FBI*, *Fibber McGee and Molly*, *The Fat Man*, *The Shadow*, *Suspense*. *Suspense* always had a creaking door more horrible-sounding than any door you could imagine—nerve-wracking, stomach-turning tales week after week. *Inner Sanctum*, with its horror and humor all mixed up. *Lone Ranger,* with the sounds of buckboards and spurs clinking out of your radio. *The Shadow*, the man of wealth and student of science out to right the world's wrongs. *Dragnet* was a cop show with the musical theme that sounded like it was taken out of a Beethoven symphony. *The Colgate Comedy Hour* kept you in stitches.

There was no place too far. I could see it all. All I needed to know about San Francisco was that Paladin lived in a hotel there and that his gun was for hire. I knew that "stones" were jewels and that villains rode in convertibles and that if you wanted to hide a tree, hide it in the forest where nobody could find it. I was raised on that stuff, used to quiver with excitement listening to these shows. They gave me clues to how the world worked and they fueled my daydreams, made my imagination work overtime. Radio shows were a strange craft.

Before I had ever gone into any department store, I was already an imaginary consumer. I used Lava Soap, shaved with Gillette Blue Blades, was on Boliva Time, putting Vitalis in my hair, used laxatives and pills for acid indigestion— Feenamint and Dr. Lyon's tooth powder. I had the Mike

Hammer attitude, my own particular brand of justice. The courts were too slow and too complicated, don't take care of business. My sentiment was that the law is fine but this time, I'm the law—the dead can't speak for themselves. I'm speaking for 'em. Okay? I asked the guy who made the sound effects for the radio shows how he got the sound of the electric chair and he said it was bacon sizzling. What about broken bones? The guy took out a LifeSaver and crushed it between his teeth.

I can't say when it occurred to me to write my own songs. I couldn't have come up with anything comparable or halfway close to the folk song lyrics I was singing to define the way I felt about the world. I guess it happens to you by degrees. You just don't wake up one day and decide that you need to write songs, especially if you're a singer who has plenty of them and you're learning more every day. Opportunities may come along for you to convert something—something that exists into something that didn't yet. That might be the beginning of it. Sometimes you just want to do things your way, want to see for yourself what lies behind the misty curtain. It's not like you see songs approaching and invite them in. It's not that easy. You want to write songs that are bigger than life. You want to say something about strange things that have happened to you, strange things you have seen. You have to know and understand something and then go past the vernacular. The chilling precision that these old-timers used in coming up with their songs was no small thing. Sometimes you could hear a song and your mind jumps ahead. You see similar patterns in the ways that you were thinking about things. I never looked at songs as either "good" or "bad," only different kinds of good ones.

Some of them can be true to life cases. I'd been hearing a song around called "I Dreamed I Saw Joe Hill." I knew that Joe Hill was real and important. I didn't know who he was, so I asked Izzy at the Folklore Center. Izzy pulled out some pamphlets on him from the back room and gave them to me to read. What I read could have come out of a mystery novel. Joe Hill was a Swedish immigrant who fought in the Mexican War. He had led a bare and meager life, was a union organizer out West in about 1910, a Messianic figure who wanted to abolish the wage system of capitalism—a mechanic, musician and poet. They called him the workingman's Robert Burns.

Joe wrote the song "Pie in the Sky" and was the forerunner of Woody Guthrie. That's all I needed to know. He'd been convicted on circumstantial evidence for a murder crime and shot by a firing squad in Utah. His life story is heavy and deep. He was an organizer for the Wobblies, the fighting section of the American working class. Hill is tried for killing a grocery store owner and his son in a petty holdup and his only defense is to say, "Prove it!" The grocer's son, before he dies, fires off a shot at somebody, but there's no evidence that the bullet ever hits anything. Yet Joe's got a bullet wound and it looks pretty incriminating. Five people on the same night have bullet wounds and are treated in the same hospital, released, and they all disappear. Joe says he was somewhere else at the time of the crime, but he won't say where or with whom. He won't name any names, not even to save his own skin. There's a general belief that a woman was involved, a woman who Joe does not want to shame. It gets weirder and more complicated. Another guy, a good friend of Joe's, disappears the day after.

It's all pretty twisted. Joe's beloved by all workingmen nationwide—miners and meat cutters, sign painters and blacksmiths, plasterers, steamfitters, ironworkers—whoever they were, he united them and he fought for the rights of them all, risked his life to make things better for all the under-classed, the disadvantaged—the most poorly paid and mistreated workers in the country. If you read his history, his character comes through and you know he's not the type who would rob and murder a grocery clerk at random. He just wouldn't have that in him. It's impossible he would have done something like that for a bit of change. Everything in his life speaks of honor and fairness. He was a drifter and protector and at all times on foot patrol. To the politicians and industrialists who hated him, though, he was a hardened criminal and an enemy to society. For years they waited for an opportunity to get rid of him. Joe was judged guilty even before the trial began.

The history of it all is amazing. In 1915 there were marches and rallies on his behalf that filled the streets in all the big American cities—Cleveland, Indianapolis, St. Louis, Brooklyn, Detroit, many more—wherever there were workers and unions. That's how much he was known and loved. Even the president of the United States, Woodrow Wilson, tried to get Utah officials to look at the case again, but the governor of Utah thumbed his nose at the president. In his final hour, Joe says, "Scatter my ashes anyplace but Utah."

Sometime after that, the song "Joe Hill" was written. As far as protest songs went, I had heard a few. The Leadbelly song "Bourgeois Blues," Woody's "Jesus Christ" and "Ludlow Massacre," "Strange Fruit," the Billie Holiday song, some others—and they were all better than this one. Protest songs are difficult to write without making them come off as preachy and one-dimensional. You have to show people a side of themselves that they don't know is there. The song "Joe Hill" doesn't even come close, but if there ever was someone who could inspire a song, it was him. Joe had the light in his eyes.

I fantasized that if I had written the song, I would have immortalized him in a different way—more like Casey Jones or Jesse James. You would have had to. I thought about it two ways. One way was to title the song "Scatter My Ashes Anyplace but Utah" and make that line the refrain. The other way to do it was like the song "Long Black Veil," a song where a man talks from the grave . . . a song from the underworld. This is a ballad where a man gives up his life not to disgrace a certain woman and has to pay for somebody else's crime because of what he can't say. The more I thought about it, "Long Black Veil" seemed like it could have been a song written by Joe Hill himself, his very last one.

I didn't compose a song for Joe Hill. I thought about how I would do it, but didn't do it. The first song I'd wind up writing of any substantial importance was written for Woody Guthrie.

It was freezing winter with a snap and sparkle in the air, nights full of blue haze. It seemed like ages ago since I'd lay in the green grass and it smelled of true summer—glints of light dancing off the lakes and yellow butterflies on the black tarred roads. Walking down 7th Avenue in Manhattan in the early hours, you'd sometimes see people sleeping in the backseats of cars. I was lucky I had places to stay—even people who lived in New York sometimes didn't have one. There's a lot of things that I didn't have, didn't have too much of a concrete identity either. "I'm a rambler—I'm a gambler. I'm a long way from home." That pretty much summed it up.

In the world news, Picasso at seventy-nine years old had just married his thirty-five-year-old model. Wow. Picasso wasn't just loafing about on crowded sidewalks. Life hadn't flowed past him yet. Picasso had fractured the art world and cracked it wide open. He was revolutionary. I wanted to be like that.

There was an art movie house in the Village on 12th Street that showed foreign movies—French, Italian, German. This made sense, because even Alan Lomax himself, the great folk archivist, had said somewhere that if you want to get out of America, go to Greenwich Village. I'd seen a couple of Italian Fellini movies there—one called *La Strada,* which means "The Street," and another one called *La Dolce Vita.* It was about a guy who sells his soul and becomes a gossip hound. It looked like life in a carnival mirror except it didn't show any monster freaks—just regular people in a freaky way. I watched it intently, thinking that I might not see it again. One of the actors in it, Evan Jones, was also a dramatist and I would meet him in a few years when I went to London to perform in a play he had written. I knew he looked familiar when I saw him. I never forget a face.

A lot was changing in America. The sociologists were saying that TV had deadly intentions and was destroying the minds and imaginations of the young—that their attention spans were being dragged down. Maybe that's true but the three minute song also did the same thing. Symphonies and operas are incredibly long, but the audience never seems to lose its place or fail to follow along. With the three minute song, the listener doesn't have to remember anything as far back as twenty or even ten minutes ago. There's nothing you have to be able to connect. Nothing to remember. A lot of the songs I was singing were indeed long, maybe not as long as an opera or a symphony, but still long . . . at least lyrically. "Tom Joad" had at least sixteen verses, "Barbara Allen" about twenty. "Fair Ellender," "Lord Lovell," "Little Mattie Groves" and others had numerous verses and I didn't find it troubling at all to remember or sing the story lines.

I had broken myself of the habit of thinking in short song cycles and began reading longer and longer poems to see if I could remember anything I read about in the beginning. I trained my mind to do this, had cast off gloomy habits and learned to settle myself down. I read all of Lord Byron's *Don Juan,* and concentrated fully from start to finish. Also, Coleridge's *Kubla Khan.* I began cramming my brain with all kinds of deep poems. It seemed like I'd been pulling an empty wagon for a long time and now I was beginning to fill it up and would have to pull harder. I felt like I was coming out of the back pasture. I was changing in other ways, too. Things that used to affect me, didn't affect me anymore. I wasn't too concerned about people, their motives. I didn't feel the need to examine every stranger that approached.


Ray had told me to read Faulkner. "It's hard, what Faulkner does," he said. "It's hard putting deep feeling into words. It's easier to write *Das Kapital.*" Ray was an opium smoker, smoked opium in a bamboo pipe with a mushroom bowl.

They had cooked it up once in the kitchen, boiling little kilos of bricks until they became like gum. Boiling and reboiling and draining liquid through filtered cloth—the kitchen smelled like cat piss. They kept it in a crock jar. He wasn't like a slob junkie from the junkyard, though, not in any way, not like somebody who uses dope just to get normal—not a part time junkie, he's not even addicted. He's not someone who would rob anybody to pay for a habit. He's wasn't like that. There's a lot of things I didn't know about Ray. I didn't know what saved him from arrest, either.

One time Clayton and myself came in late and Ray was asleep in a big chair—he looked like he was asleep in the room with the light on his face—dark hollows under his eyes, face caked with sweat. It looked like he was dreaming a dead dream. We just stood there. Paul is tall, has dark hair, Vandyke beard, resembles Gauguin the painter. Paul takes a deep breath and seems to hold it forever and then he turns around and leaves.

Ray dressed in a variety of ways. Sometimes you'd see him in a striped suit with a wing-shaped collar, pleated pants that were pegged. Sometimes he's in a sweater, corduroy trousers, country boots. A lot of times he dressed in overalls like a garage mechanic. He wears a long coat. Tan. Camel's hair. Wore it over everything.

Within the first few months that I was in New York I'd lost my interest in the "hungry for kicks" hipster vision that Kerouac illustrates so well in his book *On the Road*. That book had been like a bible for me. Not anymore, though. I still loved the breathless, dynamic bop poetry phrases that flowed from Jack's pen, but now, that character Moriarty seemed out of place, purposeless—seemed like a character who inspired idiocy. He goes through life bumping and grinding with a bull on top of him.

Ray wasn't like that. He wasn't somebody who would leave any footprints on the sands of time, but there was something special about him. He had blood in his eyes, the face of a man who could do no wrong—total lack of viciousness or wickedness or even sinfulness in his face. He seemed like a man who could conquer and command anytime he wished to. Ray was mysterious as hell.

Through the narrow passageway, trailing through the apartment that led past one or two Victorian type rooms, there was another room—a larger one with a big window that backed up to an alley. The space was configured into a workshop with all kinds of paraphernalia piled up. Most things either on a table with a long wooden top, or on another one with a slate surface. There were some iron flowers on a spiral vine painted white leaning in the corner. All kinds of tools laying around—hammers, hacksaws, screwdrivers, electricians' pliers, wire cutters and levers, claw chisels, boxes with gear wheels—everything glistening in the backlight of the sun. Soldering equipment and sketch pads, paint tubes and gauges, electric drill—cans of stuff that could make things either waterproof or fireproof.

Everything in plain sight. A lot of firearms, too. You'd think that Ray was part of the police force or a licensed gunsmith or something. There were different parts of guns—of pistols, large frame, small frame, Taurus Tracker pistol, a pocket pistol, trigger guards, everything like in a compost heap—altered guns . . . guns with shortened barrels, different brands of guns—Ruger, Browning, a single-action Navy pistol, everything poised to work, shined out. You'd walk into this room and feel like you were under the vigilance of some unsleeping eye. It was weird. Ray was anything but a macho tough guy. I asked him once what he did with all this stuff back there, what it was for. "Tactical response," he said.

I'd seen guns before. My old hometown girlfriend, my Becky Thatcher had a father who wasn't anything like Judge Thatcher. He had had a lot of guns laying around, too. Mostly deer rifles and shotguns, some long-barreled pistols and that was pretty creepy. She lived in a log house past the edge of town, off the asphalt. It was always kind of dangerous over there because the old man had a reputation for being mean. It was funny because her mother was the kindest woman—like Mother Earth. Her dad, though, was a hard-scrabble guy, weather-beaten face, always unshaven—wore a hunter's cap, had calloused hands . . . nice enough when he'd been working, but when not, you'd have to look out. You'd never know which mood you'd catch him in. The kind of guy that's always thinking that somebody's out to take advantage of him. When he wasn't working, he'd be drinking and get wrecked and then things would turn evil. He'd come into the room and mutter something through locked teeth. Once he ran me and a friend of mine off with a shotgun. He shot at us in the dark down a gravel road. But other times, he could be considerate. You just never knew. One of the reasons I liked going there, besides puppy love, was that they had Jimmie Rodgers records, old 78s in the house. I used to sit there mesmerized, listening to the Blue Yodeler, singing, "I'm a Tennessee hustler, I don't have to work." I didn't want to have to work, either. I was looking at all the guns up at Ray's place and thought about my old-time girlfriend, wondered what she was doing. The last time I'd seen her, she was heading West. Everybody said she looked like Brigitte Bardot, and she did.

There was other stuff in the room, other delights. A Remington typewriter, the neck piece of a saxophone with a swanlike curve, aluminum constructed field glasses covered in Moroccan leather, things to marvel over—a little machine that put out four volts, a small Mohawk tape recorder, odd photos, one of Florence Nightingale with a pet owl on her shoulder, novelty postcards—a picture postcard from California with a palm tree.

I'd never been to California. It seemed like it was the place of some special, glamorous race. I knew that movies came from there and that there was a folk club in Los Angeles called the Ash Grove. At the Folklore Center I'd seen posters of folk shows at the Ash Grove and I used to dream about playing there. It seemed so far away. I never thought I'd ever get out there. As it turned out, not only did I get out there, but I bypassed the Ash Grove entirely and when I finally did arrive in California, my songs and my reputation had preceded me. I had records out on Columbia and I'd be playing at the Santa Monica Civic Auditorium and meeting all the performers who had recorded my songs—artists like The Byrds, who'd recorded "Mr. Tambourine Man," Sonny and Cher, who'd done "All I Really Want to Do," The Turtles, who recorded "It Ain't Me, Babe," Glen Campbell, who had released "Don't Think Twice," and Johnny Rivers, who had recorded "Positively 4th Street."

Of all the versions of my recorded songs, the Johnny Rivers one was my favorite. It was obvious that we were from the same side of town, had been read the same citations, came from the same musical family and were cut from the same cloth. When I listened to Johnny's version of "Positively 4th Street," I liked his version better than mine. I listened to it over and over again. Most of the cover versions of my songs seemed to take them out into left field somewhere, but Rivers's version had the mandate down—the attitude and melodic sense to complete and surpass even the feeling that I had put into it. It shouldn't have surprised me, though. He had done the same thing with "Maybellene" and "Memphis," two Chuck Berry songs. When I heard Johnny sing my song, it was obvious that life had the same external grip on him as it did on me.

It would be a few more years before I'd reach Sunland. I stared around the room, looked over towards the back window and saw that twilight was coming. Ice was stacked up, thick, all along the fire escape rail. I stared down into the alleyway and then up to the rooftops from tower to tower. Snow was beginning to fall again, covered the cement covered earth. If I was building any new kind of life to live, it really didn't seem that way. It's not as if I had turned in any old one to live it. If anything, I wanted to understand things and then be free of them. I needed to learn how to telescope things, ideas. Things were too big to see all at once, like all the books in the library—everything laying around on all the tables. You might be able to put it all into one paragraph or into one verse of a song if you could get it right.

Sometimes you know things have to change, are going to change, but you can only feel it—like in that song of Sam Cooke's, "Change Is Gonna Come"—but you don't know it in a purposeful way. Little things foreshadow what's coming, but you may not recognize them. But then something immediate happens and you're in another world, you jump into the unknown, have an instinctive understanding of it— you're set free. You don't need to ask questions and you already know the score. It seems like when that happens, it happens fast, like magic, but it's really not like that. It isn't like some dull boom goes off and the moment has arrived— your eyes don't spring open and suddenly you're very quick and sure about something. It's more deliberate. It's more like you've been working in the light of day and then you see one day that it's getting dark early, that it doesn't matter where you are—it won't do any good. It's a reflective thing. Somebody holds the mirror up, unlocks the door—something jerks it open and you're shoved in and your head has to go into a different place. Sometimes it takes a certain somebody to make you realize it.

Mike Seeger had that effect on me. I'd seen him recently up at Camilla Adams's place. Camilla was an exotic, dark haired lady, a full bodied woman who looked like Ava Gardner. I used to see her in Gerde's Folk City, the preeminent folk club in America. Gerde's was on Mercer Street near West Broadway at the edge of the Village, an uptown type club not unlike the Blue Angel, but it was downtown. It booked mostly nationally known folksingers with records out and you needed a union card plus a cabaret card to work there. On Monday nights, which were called Hootenanny Nights, unknown folksingers could perform. One of those nights, I was in there and I met Camilla. From then on, I knew her a little bit. She'd usually be with the type of guys that looked like private detectives. She was a superb picture of a woman, close friends with Josh White and also Cisco Houston. Cisco had a terminal disease and he would be doing some of his last few performances at Folk City and I was there to hear him. I'd heard him a lot on the Woody Guthrie records and also on his own records, all the cowboy songs, lumberjack and railroad songs and bad man ballads. He was a perfect counterpart to Woody and had a soothing baritone voice—had traveled extensively and worked all the towns with Woody, made records with him, went to sea with him on a merchant marine ship during World War II. Cisco, handsome and dashing with a pencil thin mustache, looked like a riverboat gambler, like Errol Flynn. People said he could have been a movie star, that he once turned down a starring role opposite Myrna Loy. Burl Ives, who did go on to become a movie star, and Cisco had played together at migrant camps during the Great Depression. Cisco also starred on his own TV show on CBS but it was during the McCarthy era and the network had to let him go. I knew all about him. Cisco was sitting with Camilla during a break in his set, and she introduced me to him, told Cisco that I was a young folksinger and sang a lot of Woody's songs. Cisco was gracious, had a dignified air about him, talked like he sang. He didn't need to say much—you knew he had been through a lot, achieved some great deed, praiseworthy and meritorious, yet unspoken about it. I'd watched him perform and even though he was a hair's breadth away from death, you suspected nothing. Camilla was having a get-together for him later in the week, a bon voyage party, and she invited me to come by. She lived in a large apartment on 5th Avenue near Washington Square Park on the top floor of a Romanesque mansion.

Though I didn't know it, later she might have been influential with the owners of Gerde's Folk City, Mike Porco and his brother John, in hiring me for a two-week booking, opposite John Lee Hooker. Because I was underaged, Mike signed for me as a guardian on my cabaret and union cards, so he became like a father to me—the Sicilian father that I never had. I showed up at Camilla's with my sort of part-time girlfriend, Delores Dixon, the girl singer from The New World Singers, a group I was pretty close with. Delores was from Alabama, an ex-reporter and an ex-dancer.

As we came through the door, I could see the rooms were already swarming with people, the bohemian crowd—a lot of old-timers. The air was thick with perfume and cigarette smoke and the smell of whiskey and a lot of people. The apartment was very Victorian, decorated with a lot of lovely things. Beaux Arts lamps, carved boudoir chairs, couches in plush velvet—heavy andirons connected with chains by the fireplace and the fireplace was flaming. I got up close to it, it made me think of hot dogs and marshmallows. Delores and I didn't feel out of place, not too much. I was wearing a thick flannel shirt under a sheepskin jacket, peaked cap, khaki pants and motorcycle boots. Delores was wearing a long beaver fur coat over a nightgown that looked like a dress. I saw a lot of people here that I'd meet again not too far off, a lot of the folk community hierarchy, who were all pretty indifferent towards me at the time and showed very little enthusiasm. They could tell I wasn't from the North Carolina mountains nor was I a very commercial, cosmopolitan singer either. I just didn't fit in. They didn't know what to make of me. Pete Seeger did, though, and he said hello. He was with Harold Leventhal who managed The Weavers. Harold spoke in a low, guttural whisper. You had to lean in close to hear what he was saying. He'd later promote a concert of mine at Town Hall.

Another guy there, Henry Sheridan, had been Mae West's boyfriend. Mae West would later record a song of mine. Everybody was there, avant-garde artists like Judith Dunne, a choreographer whose dance pieces were based on sports activities like wrestling and baseball, Ken Jacobs, the underground filmmaker who made *Blond Cobra*, and Peter Schumann, from the Bread and Puppet Theatre—his play *Christmas Story* portrayed King Herod smoking a big cigar and one puppet in a three-faced mask who played all the Magi. Moe Asch, who founded Folkways Records, was also there and so was Theodore Bikel, who played Sheriff Max Muller in the film *The Defiant Ones*. Theo was an accomplished actor who also sang folk songs in foreign languages. In a few years' time, I'd travel to Mississippi with both him and Pete to play at a voters' registration rally. At Camilla's place I met up with Harry Jackson, who I already knew from Folk City—Harry, the cowboy sculptor, painter, singer from Wyoming. Harry had a studio on Broome Street and would later make a painting of me, which I sat for. He also had a studio in Italy where he made statues for town piazzas. He was a rough, gruff guy—looked like General Grant, sang cowboy songs and was a heavy drinker.

Cisco brought all kinds of people together. There were union guys there—ex-union guys, labor organizers. Recently, there'd been some accounts in the national news of an AFL-CIO executive council meeting that had been held in Puerto Rico and it was pretty funny. It had been a weeklong affair, and the union bosses were photographed drinking

mammoth rum drinks, visiting casinos and nightclubs—
hanging around at hotel pools in flowing bathrobes, swimming the surf, wearing Hollywood-ish sunglasses—doing
handstands on the diving board. It looked pretty decadent.
They were supposedly there to discuss the march on Washington to dramatize the unemployment problem. Evidentially
they didn't know they were being photographed.

These guys at Camilla's place weren't like that, though,
they looked more like tugboat captains or baggy-pantsed out-
fielders or roustabouts. Mack Mackenzie had been an organizer on the Brooklyn waterfront. I met him and his wife,
Eve, who was an ex–Martha Graham dancer. They lived on
28th Street. Later on, I'd be their houseguest, too . . . sleep
on their living room couch. Some people were there from the
art world, too—people who knew and commented on what
was going on in Amsterdam, Paris and Stockholm. One of
them, Robyn Whitlaw, the outlaw artist, walked by in a mo-
tion like a slow dance. I said to her, "What's happening?"
"I'm here to eat the big dinner," she responded. Years later
Whitlaw would be arrested for breaking and entering and
stealing. Her defense was that she was an artist and that the
act was performance art and, incredulously, the charges
against her were dropped.

Irwin Silber, the editor of the folk magazine *Sing Out!* was
there, too. In a few years' time he would castigate me publicly
in his magazine for turning my back on the folk community. It
was an angry letter. I liked Irwin, but I couldn't relate to it.
Miles Davis would be accused of something similar when he
made the album *Bitches Brew*, a piece of music that didn't
follow the rules of modern jazz, which had been on the verge
of breaking into the popular marketplace, until Miles's

record came along and killed its chances. Miles was put down by the jazz community. I couldn't imagine Miles being too upset. Latin artists were breaking rules, too. Artists like João Gilberto, Roberto Menescal and Carlos Lyra were breaking away from the drum infested samba stuff and creating a new form of Brazilian music with melodic changes. They were calling it bossa nova. As for me, what I did to break away was to take simple folk changes and put new imagery and attitude to them, use catchphrases and metaphor combined with a new set of ordinances that evolved into something different that had not been heard before. Silber scolded me in his letter for doing this, as if he alone and a few others had the keys to the real world. I knew what I was doing, though, and wasn't going to take a step back or retreat for anybody.

There were Broadway and Off-Broadway actors at Camilla's place, too—Diana Sands, an electrifying actress who I might have been secretly in love with, and some others. A lot of musicians and singers—Lee Hayes, Erik Darling (Erik had just formed a group called The Rooftop Singers and they'd soon record an old Gus Cannon song called "Walk Right In" that hit the pop charts), Sonny Terry, Brownie McGhee, Logan English. I knew Logan from Folk City, too. Logan was from Kentucky, wore a black neckerchief and played the banjo . . . was an expert in playing Bascom Lamar Lunsford songs like "Mole in the Ground" and "Grey Eagle." Logan was like a psychology professor, a good performer, but originality not his long suit. There was something very formal and orthodox about him, but he had a twinkle in his eye and a passion for the old-time music, had a ruddy complexion, and there's always a drink in his hand— calls me Robert. Millard Thomas, who played guitar for

Harry Belafonte, was also there. Harry was the best balladeer in the land and everybody knew it. He was a fantastic
artist, sang about lovers and slaves—chain gang workers,
saints and sinners and children. His repertoire was full of
old folk songs like "Jerry the Mule," "Tol' My Captain,"
"Darlin' Cora," "John Henry," "Sinner's Prayer" and also a
lot of Caribbean folk songs all arranged in a way that appealed to a wide audience, much wider than The Kingston
Trio. Harry had learned songs directly from Leadbelly and
Woody Guthrie. Belafonte recorded for RCA and one of his
records, *Belafonte Sings of the Caribbean*, had even sold a
million copies. He was a movie star, too, but not like Elvis.
Harry was an authentic tough guy, not unlike Brando or Rod
Steiger. He was dramatic and intense on the screen, had a
boyish smile and a hard-core hostility. In the movie *Odds
Against Tomorrow*, you forget he's an actor, you forget he's
Harry Belafonte. His presence and magnitude was so wide.
Harry was like Valentino. As a performer, he broke all attendance records. He could play to a packed house at Carnegie
Hall and then the next day he might appear at a garment
center union rally. To Harry, it didn't make any difference.
People were people. He had ideals and made you feel you're
a part of the human race. There never was a performer who
crossed so many lines as Harry. He appealed to everybody,
whether they were steelworkers or symphony patrons or
bobby-soxers, even children—everybody. He had that rare
ability. Somewhere he had said that he didn't like to go on
television, because he didn't think his music could be repre-
sented well on a small screen, and he was probably right.
Everything about him was gigantic. The folk purists had a
problem with him, but Harry—who could have kicked the

shit out of all of them—couldn't be bothered, said that all folksingers were interpreters, said it in a public way as if someone had summoned him to set the record straight. He even said he hated pop songs, thought they were junk. I could identify with Harry in all kinds of ways. Sometime in the past, he had been barred from the door of the world famous nightclub the Copacabana because of his color, and then later he'd be headlining the joint. You've got to wonder how that would make somebody feel emotionally. Astoundingly and as unbelievable as it might have seemed, I'd be making my professional recording debut with Harry, playing harmonica on one of his albums called *Midnight Special*. Strangely enough, this was the only one memorable recording date that would stand out in my mind for years to come. Even my own sessions would become lost in abstractions. With Belafonte I felt like I'd become anointed in some kind of way. He did the same thing for me that Gorgeous George did. Harry was that rare type of character that radiates greatness, and you hope that some of it rubs off on you. The man commands respect. You know he never took the easy path, though he could have.

It was getting late and me and Delores were about to leave when I suddenly spotted Mike Seeger in the room. I hadn't noticed him before and I watched him walk from the wall to the table. When I saw him my brain became wide awake and I was instantly in a good mood. I'd seen Mike play previously with The New Lost City Ramblers at a schoolhouse on East 10th Street. He was extraordinary, gave me an eerie feeling. Mike was unprecedented. He was like a duke, the knight errant. As for being a folk musician, he was the supreme archetype. He could push a stake through Dracula's black heart. He was the romantic, egalitarian and revolutionary type all at once—had chivalry in his blood. Like some figure from a restored monarchy, he had come to purify the church. You couldn't imagine him making a big deal out of anything. I also heard him play on his own up in Alan Lomax's loft on 3rd Street. Lomax used to have parties twice a month where he'd bring in folksingers to play. They weren't really parties or concerts. I don't know what you'd call them . . . soirees? You might see Roscoe Holcomb or Clarence Ashley or Dock Boggs, Mississippi John Hurt, Robert Pete Williams or even Don Stover and The Lilly Brothers—sometimes, even real live section gang convicts that Lomax would get out of state penitentiaries on passes and bring to New York to do field hollers in his loft. The invitees to these gatherings would most likely be local doctors, city dignitaries, anthropologists, but there'd always be some regular folk there, too.

I'd been there once or twice and that's where I saw Mike play without The Ramblers. He played "The Five Mile Chase," "Mighty Mississippi," "Claude Allen Blues" and some other songs. He played all the instruments, whatever the song called for—the banjo, the fiddle, mandolin, autoharp, and the guitar, even harmonica in the rack. Mike was skin-stinging. He was tense, poker-faced and radiated telepathy, wore a snowy white shirt and silver sleeve bands. He played on all the various planes, the full index of the old-time styles, played in all the genres and had the idioms mastered—Delta blues, ragtime, minstrel songs, buck-and-wing, dance reels, play party, hymns and gospel—being there and seeing him up close, something hit me. It's not as if he just played everything well, he played these songs as good as it was possible to play them. I was so absorbed in listening to him that I wasn't even aware of myself. What I had to work at, Mike already had in his genes, in his genetic makeup. Before he was even born, this music had to be in his blood. Nobody could just learn this stuff, and it dawned on me that I might have to change my inner thought patterns . . . that I would have to start believing in possibilities that I wouldn't have allowed before, that I had been closing my creativity down to a very narrow, controllable scale . . . that things had become too familiar and I might have to disorientate myself.

I knew I was doing things right, was on the right road, was getting all the knowledge immediately and firsthand—memorizing words and melodies and changes, but now I saw that it could take me the rest of my life to make practical use of that knowledge and Mike didn't have to do that. He was just right there. He was too good and you can't be "too good," not in this world, anyway. In order to be as good as that, you'd just about have to be him, and nobody else. Folk songs are evasive—the truth about life, and life is more or less a lie, but then again that's exactly the way we want it to be. We wouldn't be comfortable with it any other way. A folk song has over a thousand faces and you must meet them all if you want to play this stuff. A folk song might vary in meaning and it might not appear the same from one moment to the next. It depends on who's playing and who's listening.

The thought occurred to me that maybe I'd have to write my own folk songs, ones that Mike didn't know. That was a startling thought. Up 'til then, I'd gone some places and thought I knew my way around. And then it struck me that I'd never been there before. You open a door to a dark room and you think you know what's there, where everything is arranged, but you really don't know until you step inside. I can't say I'd seen any performances that were like spiritual experiences until I went to Lomax's loft. I pondered it. I wasn't ready to act on any of it but knew somehow, though, that if I wanted to stay playing music, that I would have to claim a larger part of myself. I would have to overlook a lot of things—a lot of things that might even need attention—but that was all right. They were things that I probably felt totally powerless over, anyway. I had the map, could even draw it freehand if I had to. Now I knew I'd have to throw it away. Not today, not tonight, sometime soon, though.

At Camilla's apartment, Moe Asch was chatting with Mike. They were just standing there like people who knew what they were talking about. Moe's Folkways Records put out all The Ramblers stuff and that's the label that captured my attention the most. It would have been a dream come true if Moe would have signed me to the label. It was time for me and Delores to leave, so I said good-bye to Cisco, talked with him for a moment—told him that I'd been visiting Woody Guthrie in the hospital. Cisco smiled, said that Woody never tried to camouflage anything, did he, and told me to say hello to him next time I went. I nodded, said good-bye, walked out into the hallway and down the stairs . . . went out through the lobby.

Outside Delores and I stopped and looked up at the Romanesque pillars surmounted by carved mythological beasts. It was freezing cold. I put my hands in my pockets and we headed off towards 6th Avenue. There was a lot of action and people on the street and I watched them go by. T. S. Eliot wrote a poem once where there were people walking to and fro, and everybody taking the opposite direction was appearing to be running away. That's what it looked like that night and often would for some time to come. In *Beyond Good and Evil*, Nietzsche talks about feeling old at the beginning of his life . . . I felt like that, too. Somebody told me a few weeks later that Cisco had died.

America was changing. I had a feeling of destiny and I was riding the changes. New York was as good a place to be as any. My consciousness was beginning to change, too, change and stretch. One thing for sure, if I wanted to compose folk songs I would need some kind of new template, some philosophical identity that wouldn't burn out. It would have to come on its own from the outside. Without knowing it in so many words, it was beginning to happen.

Sometimes Paul Clayton and Ray would talk through the night. They called New York City the capital of the world. They would sit at two tables . . . either they'd lean back against the wall or forward on the table, drink coffee and glasses of brandy. Clayton, a good friend of Van Ronk's, was from New Bedford, Mass., the whaling town—he sang a lot of sea shanties, had a Puritan ancestry, but some of his old relatives had been from the early Virginia families. Clayton had a log cabin outside of Charlottesville, too, where he used to go from time to time. Later on, a few of us went down there and hung around for a week or so in the mountains. The place had no electricity or plumbing or anything; kerosene lamps lit the place at night with reflective mirrors.

Ray, who was from Virginia, had ancestors who had fought on both sides of the Civil War. I'd lean back against the wall and shut my eyes. Their voices drifting into my head like voices talking from another world. They talked about dogs and fishing and forest fires—love and monarchies, and the Civil War. Ray had said that New York City was the city that won the Civil War, came out on top—that the wrong side had lost, that slavery was evil and that the thing would have died out anyway, Lincoln or no Lincoln. I heard him say it and thought it was a mysterious and bad thing to say, but if he said it, he said it and that's all there is to it.

When I woke up later in the day, the place was empty. After a while I walked downstairs and left to go meet a singing pal of mine, Mark Spoelstra. We planned to meet up at a creepy but convenient little coffeehouse on Bleecker Street near Thompson run by a character called the Dutchman. The Dutchman resembled Rasputin, the Siberian mad monk. He held the lease on the place. It was mostly a jazz coffeehouse where Cecil Taylor played a lot. I played there with Cecil once. We played "The Water Is Wide," the old folk song. Cecil could play regular piano if he wanted to. I had also played with Billy Higgins and Don Cherry there. From the coffeehouse, Mark and I were going to walk over to Gerde's Folk City and run over some songs with Brother John Sellers, a Mississippi gospel blues singer who MC'd the shows there.

I was heading to meet Mark, walking along Carmine Street, past the garages, the barbershops and dry cleaners, hardware stores. Radio sounds came shifting out of cafes. Snowy streets full of debris, sadness, the smell of gasoline. The coffeehouses and folk music joints were only a few blocks away, but it seemed like miles would go by.

When I got to the place, Spoelstra was already there and so was the Dutchman. The Dutchman was lying dead in the doorway of his storefront. There were splotches of blood on the ice and red lines in the snow, like spiderwebs. The old man who owned the building had been waiting for him and had stuck a knife in him. The Dutchman was still wearing his fur hat, long brown overcoat and riding boots, and his head was propped up on the stoop under the pearl gray sky. The problem had something to do with the Dutchman refusing to pay his rent and being belligerent about it. A lot of times he'd force the old man out physically. The little old man had taken enough and snapped, he must have thrown himself through the air like Houdini. It must have taken much skill and faculty to stick a knife through the heavy brown over-coat. Seeing the Dutchman lying there, his long brown stringy hair and frosted beard, he looked like a mercenary who could have fallen at Gettysburg. The old man was sitting inside with the door open, facing the sidewalk surrounded by a couple of cops. His face was misshapen, looked queer formed, almost mutilated—like putty in color. His eyes were dead, and he had no idea where he was.

A few people were passing by and not even looking. Spoelstra and I walked away, headed towards Sullivan Street. "It's sad. Makes you sorry as hell, but what can you do?" he said, not like he expected any answer. "Sure it is," I said. But I wasn't sorry. The only thing that I was thinking was that it was unpleasant and sick and that I might not ever go back into this joint again, and probably never would.

The power of the scene somehow jarred my mind, though—maybe because I'd just heard talk about it the previous night, but it reminded me of some old still images I'd seen of the Civil War. How much did I know about that cataclysmic event? Probably close to nothing. There weren't any great battles fought out where I grew up. No Chancellorsvilles, Bull Runs, Fredericksburgs or Peachtree Creeks. What I knew about it, was that it was a war fought about states' rights and it ended slavery. It seemed odd, but I became curious to know more and so I asked Van Ronk, who was as politically minded as anybody, what he knew about states' rights. Van Ronk could talk all day about socialist heavens and political utopias—bourgeois democracies and Trotskyites and Marxists, and international workers' orders—he could grasp all that stuff firmly, but about states' rights he almost looked bemused. "The Civil War was fought to free the slaves," he said, "there's no mystery to it." But then again, Van Ronk would never let you forget that he had his own way of seeing things. "Look, my man, even if those elite Southern barons would have freed their captives, it wouldn't have done them any good. We still would have gone down there and annihilated them, invaded them for their land. It's called imperialism." Van Ronk took the Marxist point of view. "It was one big battle between two rival economic systems is what it was."

One thing about Van Ronk, what he said was never dull or muddy. We sang the same type of songs and all of these songs were originally sung by singers who seemed to be groping for words, almost in an alien tongue. I was beginning to feel that maybe the language had something to do with causes and ideals that were tied to the circumstances and blood of what happened over a hundred years ago over secession from the Union—at least to those generations who were caught in it. All of a sudden, it didn't seem that far back.

Once I was talking to the folks back home and my father got on the line, asked me where I was. I told him that I was in New York City, the capital of the world. He said, "That's a good joke." But it wasn't a joke. New York City was the magnet—the force that draws objects to it, but take away the magnet and everything will fall apart.

Ray had flowing, wavy, blond hair like Jerry Lee Lewis or Billy Graham, the evangelist—the kind of hair that preachers had. The kind that the early rock-and-roll singers used to imitate and want to look like. The kind that could create a cult. Ray wasn't a preacher, though, but he knew how to be one and he could be funny. He said if he preached to farmers, he'd tell them about plowing the furrows with seeds of love and then reaping the harvest of salvation. He could preach to businessmen, too. He would say stuff like, "Sisters and brothers, there's no profit in trading in sin! Everlasting life is not bought and sold." He had a sermon for just about anybody. Ray was a Southerner and made no bones about it, but he would have been antislavery as much as he would have been antiunion. "Slavery should have been outlawed from the start," he said. "It was diabolical. Slave power makes it impossible for free workers to make a decent living—it had to be destroyed." Ray was pragmatic. Sometimes it was as if he had no heart or soul.

There were about five or six rooms in the apartment. In one of them was this magnificent rolltop desk, sturdy looking, almost indestructible—oak wood with secret drawers and a double sided clock on the mantel, carved nymphs and a medallion of Minerva—mechanical devices to release hidden drawers, upper side panels and gilt bronze mounts emblematic of mathematics and astronomy. It was incredible. I sat down at it, firm footed, and pulled out a sheet of paper and dashed off a letter to my cousin Reenie. Reenie and I were pretty close growing up—we rode the same bicycle, one of those Schwinns with coaster brakes. Sometimes she'd come along with me when I played at different places, even embroidered a shirt for me to play in that was pretty flashy, and she sewed stripes of ribbon down the sides of a pair of pants.

One time she asked me why I was using a different name when I played, especially in the neighboring towns. Like, didn't I want people to know who I was? "Who's Elston Gunn?" she asked. "That's not you, is it?" "Ah," I said, "you'll see." The Elston Gunn name thing was only temporary. What I was going to do as soon as I left home was just call myself Robert Allen. As far as I was concerned, that was who I was—that's what my parents named me. It sounded like the name of a Scottish king and I liked it. There was little of my identity that wasn't in it. What kind of confused me later was seeing an article in a *Downbeat* magazine with a story about a West Coast saxophone player named David Allyn. I had suspected that the musician had changed the spelling of Allen to Allyn. I could see why. It looked more exotic, more inscrutable. I was going to do this, too. Instead of Robert Allen it would be Robert Allyn. Then sometime later, unexpectedly, I'd seen some poems by Dylan Thomas. Dylan and Allyn sounded similar. Robert Dylan. Robert Allyn. I couldn't decide—the letter *D* came on stronger. But Robert Dylan didn't look or sound as good as Robert Allyn. People had always called me either Robert or Bobby, but Bobby Dylan sounded too skittish to me and besides, there already was a Bobby Darin, a Bobby Vee, a Bobby Rydell, a Bobby Neely and a lot of other Bobbys.

## Bob Dylan

Bob Dylan looked and sounded better than Bob Allyn. The first time I was asked my name in the Twin Cities, I instinctively and automatically without thinking simply said, "Bob Dylan."

Now, I had to get used to people calling me Bob. I'd never been called that before, and it took me some time to respond to people who called me that. As far as Bobby Zimmerman goes, I'm going to give this to you right straight and you can check it out. One of the early presidents of the San Bernardino Angels was Bobby Zimmerman, and he was killed in 1964 on the Bass Lake run. The muffler fell off his bike, he made a U-turn to retrieve it in front of the pack and was instantly killed. That person is gone. That was the end of him.

I finished the letter to Reenie and signed it Bobby. That's how she knew me and always would. Spelling is important. If I would have had to choose between Robert Dillon or Robert Allyn, I would have picked Robert Allyn, because it looked better in print. The name Bob Allyn never would have worked—sounded like a used-car salesman. I'd suspected that Dylan must have been Dillon at one time and that that guy changed the spelling, too, but there was no way to prove it.

Speaking of Bobbys, my old friend and fellow performer Bobby Vee had a new song out on the charts called "Take Good Care of My Baby." Bobby Vee was from Fargo, North Dakota, raised not too far from me. In the summer of '59 he had a regional hit record out called "Suzie Baby" on a local label. His band was called The Shadows and I had hitchhiked out there and talked my way into joining his group as a piano player on some of his local gigs, one in the basement of a church. I played a few shows with him, but he really didn't need a piano player and, besides, it was hard finding a piano that was in tune in the halls that he played.

Bobby Vee and me had a lot in common, even though our paths would take such different directions. We had the same musical history and came from the same place at the same point of time. He had gotten out of the Midwest, too, and had made it to Hollywood. Bobby had a metallic, edgy tone to his voice and it was as musical as a silver bell, like Buddy Holly's, only deeper. When I knew him, he was a great rockabilly singer and now he had crossed over and was a pop star. He recorded for Liberty Records and was having one Top 40 hit after another. He'd still be having songs hit the charts even right alongside The Beatles when they invaded the country. His current song, "Take Good Care of My Baby," was as slick as ever.

I wanted to see him again, so I took the D train out to the Brooklyn Paramount Theater on Flatbush Avenue where he was appearing with The Shirelles, Danny and the Juniors, Jackie Wilson, Ben E. King, Maxine Brown, and some others. He was on the top of the heap now. It seemed like so much had happened to him in such a short time. Bobby came out to see me, was as down-to-earth as ever, was wearing a shiny silk suit and narrow tie, seemed genuinely glad to see me, didn't even act surprised. We talked for a little while. He asked me about New York, what it was like to be here. "Lot of walking. Got to keep your feet in good shape," I said.

I told him I was playing in the folk clubs, but it was impossible to give him any indication of what it was all about. His only reference would have been The Kingston Trio, Brothers Four, stuff like that. He'd become a crowd pleaser in the pop world. As for myself, I had nothing against pop songs, but the definition of pop was changing. They just didn't seem to be as good as they used to be. I loved songs like "Without a Song," "Old Man River," "Stardust" and hundreds of others. My favorite of all the new ones was "Moon River." I could sing that in my sleep. My Huckleberry friend, too, was up there, waiting 'round the bend maybe on 14th Street. At Ray's, where there weren't many folk records, I used to play the phenomenal "Ebb Tide" by Frank Sinatra a lot and it had never failed to fill me with awe. The lyrics were so mystifying and stupendous. When Frank sang that song, I could hear everything in his voice—death, God and the universe, everything. I had other things to do, though, and I couldn't be listening to that stuff much.

Standing there with Bobby, I didn't want to act selfishly on his time so we said good-bye and I walked down the side of the theater and out through one of the side doors. There were throngs of young girls waiting for him in the cold outside the building. I cut back out through them into the press of cabs and private cars plowing slowly through the icy streets and headed back to the subway station. I wouldn't see Bobby Vee again for another thirty years, and though things would be a lot different, I'd always thought of him as a brother. Every time I'd see his name somewhere, it was like he was in the room.

Greenwich Village was full of folk clubs, bars and coffeehouses, and those of us who played them all played the old-timey folk songs, rural blues and dance tunes. There were a few who wrote their own songs, like Tom Paxton and Len

Chandler and because they used old melodies with new words they were pretty much accepted. Both Len and Tom wrote topical songs—songs where you'd pick articles out of newspapers, fractured, demented stuff—some nun getting married, a high school teacher taking a flying leap off the Brooklyn Bridge, tourists who robbed a gas station, Broadway beauty being beaten and left in the snow, things like that. Len could usually fashion some song out of all that, found some kind of angle. Tom's songs were topical, too, even though his most famous song, "Last Thing on My Mind," was a yearning romantic ballad. I wrote a couple and slipped them into my repertoire but really didn't think they were here nor there.

I had been singing a lot of topical songs, anyway. Songs about real events were always topical. You could usually find some kind of point of view in it, though, and take it for what it was worth, and the writer doesn't have to be accurate, could tell you anything and you're going to believe it.

Billy Gashade, the man who presumably wrote the Jesse James ballad, makes you believe that Jesse robbed from the rich and gave to the poor and was shot down by a "dirty little coward." In the song, Jesse robs banks and gives the money to the destitute and in the end is betrayed by a friend. By all accounts, though, James was a bloodthirsty killer who was anything but the Robin Hood sung about in the song. But Billy Gashade has the last word and he spins it around.

Topical songs weren't protest songs. The term "protest singer" didn't exist any more than the term "singer-songwriter." You were a performer or you weren't, that was about it—a folksinger or not one. "Songs of dissent" was a term people used but even that was rare. I tried to explain later that I didn't think I was a protest singer, that there'd been a screwup. I didn't think I was protesting anything any more than I thought that Woody Guthrie songs were protesting anything. I didn't think of Woody as a protest singer. If he is one, then so is Sleepy John Estes and Jelly Roll Morton. What I was hearing pretty regularly, though, were rebellion songs and those really moved me. The Clancy Brothers—Tom, Paddy and Liam—and their buddy Tommy Makem sang them all the time.

I got to be friends with Liam and began going after-hours to the White Horse Tavern on Hudson Street, which was mainly an Irish bar frequented mostly by guys from the old country. All through the night they would sing drinking songs, country ballads and rousing rebel songs that would lift the roof. The rebellion songs were a really serious thing. The language was flashy and provocative—a lot of action in the words, all sung with great gusto. The singer always had a merry light in his eye, had to have it. I loved these songs and could still hear them in my head long after and into the next day. They weren't protest songs, though, they were rebel ballads . . . even in a simple, melodic wooing ballad there'd be rebellion waiting around the corner. You couldn't escape it. There were songs like that in my repertoire, too, where something lovely was suddenly upturned, but instead of rebellion showing up it would be death itself, the Grim Reaper. Rebellion spoke to me louder. The rebel was alive and well, romantic and honorable. The Grim Reaper wasn't like that.

I was beginning to think I might want to change over. The Irish landscape wasn't too much like the American landscape, though, so I'd have to find some cuneiform tablets—some archaic grail to lighten the way. I had grasped the idea of what kind of songs I wanted to write, I just didn't know how to do it yet.

I did everything fast. Thought fast, ate fast, talked fast and walked fast. I even sang my songs fast. I needed to slow my mind down if I was going to be a composer with anything to say.

I couldn't exactly put in words what I was looking for, but I began searching in principle for it, over at the New York Public Library, a monumental building with marble floors and walls, vacuous and spacious caverns, vaulted ceiling. A building that radiates triumph and glory when you walk inside. In one of the upstairs reading rooms I started reading articles in newspapers on microfilm from 1855 to about 1865 to see what daily life was like. I wasn't so much interested in the issues as intrigued by the language and rhetoric of the times. Newspapers like the *Chicago Tribune*, the *Brooklyn Daily Times*, and the *Pennsylvania Freeman*. Others, too, like the *Memphis Daily Eagle*, the *Savannah Daily Herald* and *Cincinnati Enquirer*. It wasn't like it was another world, but the same one only with more urgency, and the issue of slavery wasn't the only concern. There were news items about reform movements, antigambling leagues, rising crime, child labor, temperance, slave-wage factories, loyalty oaths and religious revivals. You get the feeling that the newspapers themselves could explode and lightning will burn and everybody will perish. Everybody uses the same God, quotes the same Bible and law and literature. Plantation slavecrats of Virginia are accused of breeding and selling their own children. In the Northern cities, there's a lot of discontent and debt is piled high and seems out of control. The plantation aristocracy run their plantations like city-states. They are like the Roman republic where an elite group of characters rule supposedly for the good of all. They've got sawmills, gristmills, distilleries, country stores, et cetera. Every state of mind opposed by another . . . Christian piety and weird mind philosophies turned on their heads. Fiery orators, like William Lloyd Garrison, a conspicuous abolitionist from Boston who even has his own newspaper. There are riots in Memphis and in New Orleans. There's a riot in New York where two hundred people are killed outside of the Metropolitan Opera House because an English actor has taken the place of an American one. Anti–slave labor advocates inflaming crowds in Cincinnati, Buffalo and Cleveland, that if the Southern states are allowed to rule, the Northern factory owners would then be forced to use slaves as free laborers. This causes riots, too. Lincoln comes into the picture in the late 1850s. He is referred to in the Northern press as a baboon or giraffe, and there were a lot of caricatures of him. Nobody takes him seriously. It's impossible to conceive that he would become the father figure that he is today. You wonder how people so united by geography and religious ideals could become such bitter enemies. After a while you become aware of nothing but a culture of feeling, of black days, of schism, evil for evil, the common destiny of the human being getting thrown off course. It's all one long funeral song, but there's a certain imperfection in the themes, an ideology of high abstraction, a lot of epic, bearded characters, exalted men who are not necessarily good. No one single idea keeps you contented for too long. It's hard to find any of the neoclassical virtues, either. All that rhetoric about chivalry and honor—that must have been added later. Even the Southern womanhood thing. It's a shame what happened to the women. Most of them were abandoned to starve on farms with their children, unprotected and left to fend for themselves as victims to the elements. The suffering is endless, and the punishment is going to be forever. It's all so unrealistic, grandiose and sanctimonious at the same time. There was a difference in the concept of time, too. In the South, people lived their lives with sun-up, high noon, sunset, spring, summer. In the North, people lived by the clock. The factory stroke, whistles and bells. Northerners had to "be on time." In some ways the Civil War would be a battle between two kinds of time. Abolition of slavery didn't even seem to be an issue when the first shots were fired at Fort Sumter. It all makes you feel creepy. The age that I was living in didn't resemble this age, but yet it did in some mysterious and traditional way. Not just a little bit, but a lot. There was a broad spectrum and commonwealth that I was living upon, and the basic psychology of that life was every bit a part of it. If you turned the light towards it, you could see the full complexity of human nature. Back there, America was put on the cross, died and was resurrected. There was nothing synthetic about it. The godawful truth of that would be the all-encompassing template behind everything that I would write.

I crammed my head full of as much of this stuff as I could stand and locked it away in my mind out of sight, left it alone. Figured I could send a truck back for it later.

Down in the Village nothing seemed wrong. Life was not complex. Everybody was looking for openings. Some would get 'em and then they'd be gone and others never did. Mine was coming, but not just yet.

Len Chandler, a classically trained musician from Ohio, was on the bill with me at the Gaslight and we got to be friends. We'd usually hang out either up in the card room between sets or sometimes over at the Metro Diner near 6th Avenue. Len was educated and serious about life, was even working with his wife downtown to start a school for under-privileged children. His thing was writing topical songs, and his inspiration would come from the newspapers. He usually put new words to old melodies but sometimes created his own melodies.

One of his most colorful songs had been about a negligent school bus driver in Colorado who accidentally drove a bus full of kids down a cliff. It had an original melody and because I liked the melody so much, I wrote my own set of lyrics to it. Len didn't seem to mind. We'd drink coffee and look through the daily newspapers left behind on the counter to see if there was song material in any of it. After seeing the newspapers at the New York Public Library, these papers seemed almost threadbare and dull.

France was in the news and had exploded an atom bomb in the Sahara Desert. France had just been booted out of North Vietnam by Ho Chi Minh after one hundred years of colonial rule. Ho had seen enough of the French. They had turned Hanoi, the capital city, into the "brothel-studded Paris of the orient." Ho kicked them out and would now be going to get his supplies from Bulgaria and Czechoslovakia. The French had been plundering the country for years. The press reported Hanoi was grubby and cheerless, that the people dressed in Chinese shapeless jackets and you couldn't tell the difference between the men and the women—everybody rode a bicycle and did calisthenics in public three times a day. The newspapers made it sound as if it were a weird place. The Vietnamese might have to be straightened out—might have to send some Americans over there.

Anyway, France had now brought themselves into the atomic age and there were movements springing up to ban the bombs, French, American, Russian and otherwise, but this movement also had its detractors. Reputable psychiatrists were saying that some of these people who claimed to be so against nuclear testing are secular last judgment types—that if nuclear bombs are banned, it would deprive them of their highly comforting sense of doom. Len and I couldn't believe this stuff. There'd be articles about things like new modern-day phobias, all with fancy Latin names, like fear of flowers, fear of the dark, of height, fear of crossing bridges, of snakes, fear of getting old, fear of clouds. Just any old thing could be frightening. My big fear was that my guitar would go out of tune. Women were speaking out in the news, too, challenging the status quo. Some were complaining that they were told that they needed and deserved equal rights. Then when they got them, they were accused of becoming too much like men. Some women wanted to be called "a woman" when they reached twenty-one. Some sales girls, or women, didn't want to be referred to as "salesladies." In churches, too, things were shaking up. Some white ministers didn't want to be labeled "the Reverend." They wanted to be called just plain "Reverend."

Semantics and labels could drive you crazy. The inside story on a man was that if he wanted to be successful, he must become a rugged individualist, but then he should make some adjustments. After that, he needed to conform. You could go from being a rugged individualist to a conformist in the blink of an eye.

Len and I thought this stuff was idiotic. Reality was not so simple and everybody had their own take on it. Jean Genet's play *The Balcony* was being performed in the Village and it portrayed the world as a mammoth cathouse where chaos rules the universe, where man is alone and abandoned in a meaningless cosmos. The play had a strong sense of focus, and from what I'd seen about the Civil War period, it could have been written one hundred years ago. The songs I'd write would be like that, too. They wouldn't conform to modern ideas. I hadn't begun yet writing streams of songs as I would, but Len was, and everything around us looked absurd—there was a certain consciousness of madness at work. Even the photos of Jackie Kennedy going in and out of revolving doors at the Carlyle Hotel uptown, carrying shopping bags of clothes, looked disturbing. Nearby at the Biltmore, the Cuban Revolutionary Council was meeting. The Cuban government in exile. They had recently given a news conference, said that they needed bazookas and recoilless rifles and demolition experts and that those things cost money. If they could get enough donations, they could take back Cuba, the old Cuba, land of plantations, sugarcane, rice, tobacco—patricians. The Roman Republic. In the sports pages the New York Rangers had beaten the Chicago Blackhawks 2 to 1, and Vic Hadfield had scored both goals. Our tall Texan vice president, Lyndon Johnson, was quite a character, too. He'd flipped out and got angry at the U.S. Secret Service—told them to stop fencing him in, stop shadowing him, following him around. Johnson grabs guys by the lapels and squeezes the back of their heads to make a point. He reminded me of Tex Ritter—seemed simple and down to earth. Later, when he became president, he used the phrase "We shall overcome" in a speech to the American people. "We Shall Overcome" was the spiritual marching anthem of the civil rights movement. It had been the rallying cry for the oppressed for many years. Johnson interpreted the idea to suit himself, rather than eradicate it. He was not as homespun as it seemed. The dominant myth of the day seemed to be that anybody could do anything, even go to the moon. You could do whatever you wanted—in the ads and in the articles, ignore your limitations, defy them. If you were an indecisive person, you could become a leader and wear lederhosen. If you were a housewife, you could become a glamour girl with rhinestone sunglasses. Are you slow witted? No worries—you can be an intellectual genius. If you're old, you can be young. Anything was possible. It was almost like a war against the self. The art world was changing, too, being turned on its head. Abstract painting and atonal music were hitting the scene, mangling recognizable reality. Goya himself would have been lost at sea if he tried to sail the new wave of art. Len and I would look at all this stuff for what it was worth, and not one cent more.

One guy who kept reappearing in the news was Caryl Chessman, a notorious rapist whom they called the Red-Light Bandit. He was on death row in California after being tried and convicted of raping young women. He had a creative way of doing it—strapped a flashing red light to the top of his automobile and then pulled the girls over to the side of the road, ordering them out, hauling them into the woods, robbing and raping them. He'd been on death row for quite a while making appeal after appeal, but his last appeal had been final and he was scheduled to go into the gas chamber. Chessman had become a cause célèbre and luminaries had taken up his plight. Norman Mailer, Ray Bradbury, Aldous Huxley, Robert Frost, even Eleanor Roosevelt were calling for his life to be spared. An anti–death penalty group had asked Len to write a song about Chessman.

"How do you write a song about a pariah who rapes young women, what would be the angle?" he asked me as if his imagination was actually on fire.

"I don't know, Len, I guess you'd have to build it slowly . . . maybe start with the red lights."

Len never did write the song, but I think someone else did. One thing about Chandler was that he was fearless. He didn't suffer fools, and no one could get in his way. He was powerfully built, like a linebacker, could kick your silly ass from here to Chinatown, could probably break anybody's nose. He had studied economics and science, and had it down. Len was brilliant and full of goodwill, one of those guys who believed that all of society could be affected by one solitary life.

Besides being a songwriter, he was also a daredevil. One freezing winter's night I sat behind him on his Vespa motor scooter riding full throttle across the Brooklyn Bridge and my heart just about shot up in my mouth. The bike was speeding on the crisscrossed grid in high winds, and I felt like I could have gone overboard at any time—weaving in and out of the night's traffic, it scared the lights out of me—sliding all over on the iced-up steel. I was on edge the whole way, but I could feel that Chandler was in control, his eyes unblinking and centered steadfast. No doubt about it, heaven was on his side. I've only felt like that about a few people.

When I wasn't staying at Van Ronk's, I'd usually stay at Ray's place, get back sometime before dawn, mount the dark stairs and carefully close the door behind me. I shoved off into the sofa bed like entering a vault. Ray was not a guy who had nothing on his mind. He knew what he thought and he knew how to express it, didn't make room in his life for mistakes. The mundane things in life didn't register with him. He seemed to have some golden grip on reality, didn't sweat the small stuff, quoted the Psalms and slept with a pistol near his bed. At times he could say things that had way too much edge. Once he said that President Kennedy wouldn't last out his term because he was a Catholic. When he said it, it made me think about my grandmother, who said to me that the Pope is the king of the Jews. She lived back in Duluth on the top floor of a duplex on 5th Street. From a window in the back room you could see Lake Superior, ominous and foreboding, iron bulk freighters and barges off in the distance, the sound of foghorns to the right and left. My grandmother had only one leg and had been a seamstress. Sometimes on weekends my parents would drive down from the Iron Range to Duluth and drop me off at her place for a couple of days. She was a dark lady, smoked a pipe. The other side of my family was more light-skinned and fair. My grandmother's voice possessed a haunting accent—face always set in a half-despairing expression. Life for her hadn't been easy. She'd come to America from Odessa, a seaport town in southern

Russia. It was a town not unlike Duluth, the same kind of temperament, climate and landscape and right on the edge of a big body of water.

Originally, she'd come from Turkey, sailed from Trabzon, a port town, across the Black Sea—the sea that the ancient Greeks called the Euxine—the one that Lord Byron wrote about in *Don Juan*. Her family was from Kagizman, a town in Turkey near the Armenian border, and the family name had been Kirghiz. My grandfather's parents had also come from that same area, where they had been mostly shoemakers and leatherworkers.

My grandmother's ancestors had been from Constantinople. As a teenager, I used to sing the Ritchie Valens song "In a Turkish Town" with the lines in it about the *"mystery Turks and the stars above,"* and it seemed to suit me more than "La Bamba," the song of Ritchie's that everybody else sang and I never knew why. My mother even had a friend named Nellie Turk and I'd grown up with her always around.

There were no Ritchie Valens records up at Ray's place, "Turkish Town" or otherwise. Mostly, it was classical music and jazz bands. Ray had bought his entire record collection from a shyster lawyer who was getting divorced. There were Bach fugues and Berlioz symphonies—Handel's *Messiah* and Chopin's A-Major Polonaise. Madrigals and religious pieces, Darius Milhaud violin concertos—symphonic poems by virtuoso pianists, string serenades with themes that sound like polka dances. Polka dances always got my blood pumping. That was the first type of loud, live music I'd ever heard. On Saturday nights the taverns were filled with polka bands. I also liked the Franz Liszt records—liked the way one piano could sound like a whole orchestra. Once I put on Beethoven's *Pathetique* Sonata—it was melodic, but then again, it sounded like a lot of burping and belching and other bodily functions. It was funny—sounded almost like a cartoon. Reading the record jacket, I learned that Beethoven had been a child prodigy and he'd been exploited by his father and that Beethoven distrusted all people for the rest of his life. Even so, it didn't stop him from writing symphonies.

I'd listen to a lot of jazz and bebop records, too. Records by George Russell or Johnny Cole, Red Garland, Don Byas, Roland Kirk, Gil Evans—Evans had recorded a rendition of "Ella Speed," the Leadbelly song. I tried to discern melodies and structures. There were a lot of similarities between some kinds of jazz and folk music. "Tattoo Bride," "A Drum Is a Woman," "Tourist Point of View" and "Jump for Joy"—all by Duke Ellington—they sounded like sophisticated folk music. The music world was getting bigger every day. There were records by Dizzy Gillespie, Fats Navarro, Art Farmer and amazing ones by Charlie Christian and Benny Goodman. If I needed to wake up real quick, I'd put on "Swing Low Sweet Cadillac" or "Umbrella Man" by Dizzy Gillespie. "Hot House" by Charlie Parker was a good record to wake up to. There were a few souls around who had heard and seen Parker play and it seemed like he had transmitted some secret essence of life to them. "Ruby, My Dear" by Monk was another one. Monk played at the Blue Note on 3rd Street with John Ore on bass and the drummer Frankie Dunlop.

Sometimes he'd be in there in the afternoon sitting at the piano all alone playing stuff that sounded like Ivory Joe Hunter—a big half-eaten sandwich left on top of his piano. I dropped in there once in the afternoon, just to listen—told him that I played folk music up the street. "We all play folk music," he said. Monk was in his own dynamic universe even when he dawdled around. Even then, he summoned magic shadows into being.

I liked modern jazz a lot, liked to listen to it in the clubs . . . but I didn't follow it and I wasn't caught up in it. There weren't any ordinary words with specific meanings, and I needed to hear things plain and simple in the King's English, and folk songs are what spoke to me most directly. Tony Bennett sang in the King's English and one of his records was laying around—the one called *Hit Songs of Tony Bennett,* which had "In the Middle of an Island," "Rags to Riches" and the Hank Williams song "Cold, Cold Heart."

The first time I heard Hank he was singing on the *Grand Ole Opry,* a Saturday night radio show broadcast out of Nashville. Roy Acuff, who MC'd the program, was referred to by the announcer as "The King of Country Music." Someone would always be introduced as "the next governor of Tennessee" and the show advertised dog food and sold plans for old-age pensions. Hank sang "Move It On Over," a song about living in the doghouse and it struck me really funny. He also sang spirituals like "When God Comes and Gathers His Jewels" and "Are You Walking and a-Talking for the Lord." The sound of his voice went through me like an electric rod and I managed to get a hold of a few of his 78s—"Baby, We're Really in Love" and "Honky Tonkin'" and "Lost Highway"— and I played them endlessly.

They called him a "hillbilly singer," but I didn't know what that was. Homer and Jethro were more like what I thought a hillbilly was. Hank was no burr head. There was nothing clownish about him. Even at a young age, I identified fully with him. I didn't have to experience anything that Hank did to know what he was singing about. I'd never seen a robin weep, but could imagine it and it made me sad. When he sang "the news is out all over town," I knew what news that was, even though I didn't know. The first chance I got, I was going to go to the dance and wear out my shoes, too. I'd learn later that Hank had died in the backseat of a car on New Year's Day, kept my fingers crossed, hoped it wasn't true. But it was true. It was like a great tree had fallen. Hearing about Hank's death caught me squarely on the shoulder. The silence of outer space never seemed so loud. Intuitively I knew, though, that his voice would never drop out of sight or fade away—a voice like a beautiful horn.

Much later, I'd discover that Hank had been in tremendous pain all his life, suffered from severe spinal problems—that the pain must have been torturous. In light of that, it's all the more astonishing to hear his records. It's almost like he defied the laws of gravity. The *Luke the Drifter* record, I just about wore out. That's the one where he sings and recites parables, like the Beatitudes. I could listen to the *Luke the Drifter* record all day and drift away myself, become totally convinced in the goodness of man. When I hear Hank sing, all movement ceases. The slightest whisper seems sacrilege.

In time, I became aware that in Hank's recorded songs were the archetype rules of poetic songwriting. The architectural forms are like marble pillars and they had to be there. Even his words—all of his syllables are divided up so they make perfect mathematical sense. You can learn a lot about the structure of songwriting by listening to his records, and I listened to them a lot and had them internalized. In a few years' time, Robert Shelton, the folk and jazz critic for the

*New York Times,* would review one of my performances and would say something like, "resembling a cross between a choirboy and a beatnik . . . he breaks all the rules in song-writing, except that of having something to say." The rules, whether Shelton knew it or not, were Hank's rules, but it wasn't like I ever meant to break them. It's just that what I was trying to express was beyond the circle.

One night, Albert Grossman, the manager of Odetta and Bob Gibson, came into the Gaslight to talk to Van Ronk. Whenever he came in, you couldn't help but notice him. He looked like Sidney Greenstreet from *The Maltese Falcon,* had an enormous presence, dressed always in a conventional suit and tie, and he sat at a corner table. Usually when he talked, his voice was loud, like the booming of war drums. He didn't talk so much as growl. Grossman was from Chicago, had a non–show business background but didn't let that stand in his way. Not your usual shopkeeper, he had owned a night-club in the Windy City and had to deal with district bosses and various fixes and ordinances and carried a .45. Grossman was no hayseed. Van Ronk told me later that Grossman had discussed with him the possibility of Dave playing in a new super folk group that he was putting together. Grossman had no illusions or doubts that the group was going to go straight to the top, be immensely popular.

Eventually, Dave passed on the opportunity. It wasn't his cup of tea, but Noel Stookey would accept the offer. Grossman changed Stookey's name to Paul and the group that Grossman had created was Peter, Paul and Mary. I had met Peter earlier back in Minneapolis when he was the guitarist for a dance troupe that came through town, and I'd known Mary ever since I first got into the Village.

It would have been interesting if Grossman had asked me to be in the group. I would have had to change my name to Paul, too. Grossman did hear me play from time to time, but I didn't know what he made of me. It was premature for that anyway. I wasn't yet the poet musician that I would become, Grossman couldn't get behind me just yet. He would, though.

I woke up around midday to the smell of frying steak and onions on a gas burner. Chloe was standing over the stove and the pan was sizzling. She wore a Japanese kimono over a red flannel shirt, and the smell was assaulting my nostrils. I felt like I needed a face mask.

I had planned to go see Woody Guthrie earlier, but when I woke up the weather was too stormy. I had tried to visit Woody regularly, but now it was getting harder to do. Woody had been confined to Greystone Hospital in Morristown, New Jersey, and I would usually take the bus there from the Port Authority terminal, make the hour-and-a-half ride and then walk the rest of the half mile up the hill to the hospital, a gloomy and threatening granite building—looked like a medieval fortress. Woody always asked me to bring him cigarettes, Raleigh cigarettes. Usually I'd play him his songs during the afternoon. Sometimes he'd ask for specific ones— "Rangers Command," "Do Re Me," "Dust Bowl Blues," "Pretty Boy Floyd," "Tom Joad," the song he'd written after seeing the movie *The Grapes of Wrath*. I knew all those songs and many more. Woody was not celebrated at this place, and it was a strange environment to meet anybody, least of all the true voice of the American spirit.

The place was really an asylum with no spiritual hope of any kind. Wailing could be heard in the hallways. Most of the patients wore ill-fitting striped uniforms and they would file in and out walking aimlessly about while I played Woody songs. One guy's head would be constantly falling forward on his knees. Then he'd raise up and he would fall forward again. Another guy thought he was being chased by spiders and he twirled in circles, hands slapping his arms and legs. Someone else who imagined he was the president wore an Uncle Sam hat. Patients rolled their eyes, tongues, sniffed the air. One guy, continually licking his lips. An orderly in a white gown told me that the guy eats communists for breakfast. The scene was frightful, but Woody Guthrie was oblivious to all of it. A male nurse would usually bring him out to see me and then after I'd been there a while, would lead him away. The experience was sobering and psychologically draining.

On one of my visits, Woody had told me about some boxes of songs and poems that he had written that had never been seen or set to melodies—that they were stored in the basement of his house in Coney Island and that I was welcome to them. He told me that if I wanted any of them to go see Margie, his wife, explain what I was there for. She'd unpack them for me. He gave me directions on how to find the house.

In the next day or so, I took the subway from the West 4th Street station all the way to the last stop, like he said, in Brooklyn, stepped out on the platform and went hunting for the house. Woody had said it was easy to find. I saw what looked to be a row of houses across a field, the kind he described, and I walked towards it only to discover I was walking out across a swamp. I sunk into the water, knee level, but kept going anyway—I could see the lights as I moved forward, didn't really see any other way to go. When I came out on the other end, my pants from the knees down were drenched, frozen solid, and my feet almost numb but I found the house and knocked on the door. A babysitter opened it slightly, said that Margie, Woody's wife, wasn't there. One of Woody's kids, Arlo, who would later become a professional singer and songwriter in his own right, told the babysitter to let me in. Arlo was probably about ten or twelve years old and didn't know anything about any manuscripts locked in the basement. I didn't want to push it—the babysitter was uncomfortable, and I stayed just long enough to warm up, said a quick good-bye and left with my boots still waterlogged, trudged back across the swamp to the subway platform.

Forty years later, these lyrics would fall into the hands of Billy Bragg and the group Wilco and they would put melodies to them, bring them to full life and record them. It was all done under the direction of Woody's daughter Nora. These performers probably weren't even born when I had made that trip out to Brooklyn.

I wouldn't be going to see Woody today. I was sitting in Chloe's kitchen, and the wind was howling and whistling by the window. I could look out on the street and see in both directions. Snow was falling like white dust. Up the street, towards the river, I watched a blonde lady in a fur coat with a guy in a heavy overcoat who walked with a limp. I watched them for a while and then looked over to the calendar on the wall.

March was coming in like a lion and once more I wondered

what it would take to get into a recording studio, to get signed by a folk record label—was I getting any closer? "No Happiness for Slater," a song off The Modern Jazz Quartet's record, played in the apartment.

One of Chloe's hobbies was to put fancy buckles on old shoes and she suggested wanting to do it to mine.

"Those clodhoppers could use some buckles," she said.

I told her, no thanks, I didn't need any buckles.

She said, "You got forty-eight hours to change your mind." I wasn't going to change my mind. Sometimes Chloe tried to give me motherly advice, especially about the opposite sex . . . that people get into their own fixes and not to care about anybody more than they care about themselves. The apartment was a good place to hibernate.

Once I was in the kitchen listening to Malcolm X talking on the radio. He was lecturing on why not to eat pork or ham, said that a pig is actually one third cat, one third rat, one third dog—it's unclean and you shouldn't eat it. It's funny how things stick with you. About ten years later I was having dinner at Johnny Cash's house outside of Nashville. There were a lot of songwriters there. Joni Mitchell, Graham Nash, Harlan Howard, Kris Kristofferson, Mickey Newberry and some others. Joe and Janette Carter were also there. Joe and Janette were the son and daughter of A.P. and Sarah Carter and cousins to June Carter, Johnny's wife. They were like the royalty of country music.

Johnny's big fireplace was blazing and crackling. After dinner, everybody sat around in the rustic living room with high wooden beams and wide plate-glass windows that overlooked a lake. We sat in a circle and each songwriter would play a song and pass the guitar to the next player. Usually,

there'd be comments made like "You really nailed that one."
Or "Yeah, man, you said it all in them few lines." Or maybe
something like "That song's got a lot of history in it." Or
"You put all yourself into that tune." Mostly just complimen-
tary stuff. I played "Lay, Lady, Lay" and then I passed the
guitar to Graham Nash, anticipating some kind of response.
I didn't have to wait long. "You don't eat pork, do you?" Joe
Carter asked. That was his comment. I waited for a second
before replying. "Uh, no sir, I don't," I said back. Kristofferson almost swallowed his fork. Joe asked, "Why not?" It's
then that I remembered what Malcolm X had said. "Well, sir,
it's kind of a personal thing. I don't eat that stuff, no. I don't
eat something that's one third rat, one third cat and one
third dog. It just doesn't taste right." There was an awkward
momentary silence that you could have cut with one of the
knives off the dinner table. Johnny Cash then almost doubled over. Kristofferson just shook his head. Joe Carter was
quite a character.

There weren't any Carter Family records up at the apartment, either. Chloe slapped some steak and onions on my
plate and said, "Here, it's good for you." She was cool as pie,
hip from head to toe, a Maltese kitten, a solid viper—always
hit the nail on the head. I don't know how much weed she
smoked, but a lot. She also had her own ideas about the nature of things, told me that death was an impersonator, that
birth is an invasion of privacy. What could you say? You
couldn't say anything back when she said stuff like that. It's
not like you could prove her wrong. New York City didn't
faze her at all. "A bunch of monkeys in this town," she'd say.
Talking to her you'd get the idea right away. I put on my hat
and coat, grabbed my guitar and started bundling up. Chloe

knew that I was trying to get places. "Maybe someday your name will get around the country like wildfire," she'd say. "If you ever get a couple of hundred bucks, buy me something."

I shut the door behind me and went out into the hallway and down the spiral cascading staircase, got to the marble-floored landing at the bottom and went out through the narrow courtyard entryway. The walls smelled of chloride. I walked leisurely through the door and up to the sidewalk through the latticed iron gate, threw a scarf around my face and headed for Van Dam Street. On the corner, I passed a horse-drawn wagon full of covered flowers, all under a plastic wrap, no driver in sight. The city was full of stuff like that.

Folk songs played in my head, they always did. Folk songs were the underground story. If someone were to ask what's going on, "Mr. Garfield's been shot down, laid down. Nothing you can do." That's what's going on. Nobody needed to ask who Mr. Garfield was, they just nodded, they just knew. It was what the country was talking about. Everything was simple—seemed to make some kind of splendid, formulaic sense.

New York City was cold, muffled and mysterious, the capital of the world. On 7th Avenue I passed the building where Walt Whitman had lived and worked. I paused momentarily imagining him printing away and singing the true song of his soul. I had stood outside of Poe's house on 3rd Street, too, and had done the same thing, staring mournfully up at the windows. The city was like some uncarved block without any name or shape and it showed no favoritism. Everything was always new, always changing. It was never the same old crowd upon the streets.

I crossed over from Hudson to Spring, passed a garbage

can loaded with bricks and stopped into a coffee shop. The waitress at the lunch counter wore a close-fitting suede blouse. It outlined the well-rounded lines of her body. She had blue-black hair covered with a kerchief and piercing blue eyes, clear stenciled eyebrows. I was wishing she'd pin a rose on me. She poured the steaming coffee and I turned back towards the street window. The whole city was dangling in front of my nose. I had a vivid idea of where everything was. The future was nothing to worry about. It was awfully close.

# 3
# New
# Morning

I HAD JUST returned to Woodstock from the Midwest— from my father's funeral. There was a letter from Archibald MacLeish waiting for me on the table. MacLeish, Poet Laureate of America—one of them. Carl Sandburg, poet of the prairie and the city, and Robert Frost, the poet of dark meditations were the others. MacLeish was the poet of night stones and the quick earth. These three, the Yeats, Browning and Shelley of the New World, were gigantic figures, had defined the landscape of twentieth-century America. They put everything in perspective. Even if you didn't know their poems, you knew their names.

The previous week had left me drained. I had gone back to the town of my early years in a way I could never have imagined—to see my father laid to rest. Now there would be no way to say what I was never capable of saying before. Growing up, the cultural and generational differences had been insurmountable—nothing but the sound of voices, colorless unnatural speech. My father, who was plain speaking and straight talking had said, "Isn't an artist a fellow who paints?" when told by one of my teachers that his son had the nature of an artist. It seemed I'd always been chasing after something, anything that moved—a car, a bird, a blowing leaf—anything that might lead me into some more lit place, some unknown land downriver. I had not even the vaguest notion of the broken world I was living in, what society could do with you.

When I left home, I was like Columbus going off into the desolate Atlantic. I'd done that and I'd been to the ends of the earth—to the water's edge—and now I was back in Spain, back where it all started, in the court of the Queen with a half-glazed expression on my face, with even the wisp of a beard. "What's with the decoration?" one of the neighbors who had come to pay their respects said pointing to my face. In the short time I was there, it all came back to me, all the flimflam, the older order of things, the Simple Simons— but something else did, too—that my father was the best man in the world and probably worth a hundred of me, but he didn't understand me. The town he lived in and the town I lived in were not the same. All that aside, we had more in common now than ever—I, too, was a father three times over—there was a lot that I wanted to share, to tell him— and also now I was in a position to do a lot of things for him.

Archie's letter said that he'd like to meet with me to discuss the possibility of me composing some songs for a play that he was writing, called *Scratch*, based on a Stephen Vincent Benet short story. MacLeish had earlier won a Tony Award on Broadway for one of his plays called *JB*. My wife and I drove over to Conway, Massachusetts, where he lived, to meet with him about his new play. It seemed like a civilized thing to do. MacLeish wrote deep poems, was the man of godless sand. He could take real people from history, people like Emperor Charles or Montezuma and Cortés the Conquistador, and with the tender touch of a creator, deliver them right to your door. He praised the sun and the great sky. It was fitting that I'd go see him.

The events of the day, all the cultural mumbo jumbo were imprisoning my soul—nauseating me—civil rights and political leaders being gunned down, the mounting of the barricades, the government crackdowns, the student radicals and demonstrators versus the cops and the unions—the streets exploding, fire of anger boiling—the contra communes—the lying, noisy voices—the free love, the anti–money system movement—the whole shebang.

I was determined to put myself beyond the reach of it all. I was a family man now, didn't want to be in that group portrait.

MacLeish's place was up past a quaint village on a quiet mountain laurel road—bright maple leaves piled high around the walkway. It was easy walking across the small footbridge leading to a wood-shaded alcove and a reconstructed stone cottage with modern kitchen facilities, MacLeish's studio. A caretaker had led us in, and his wife placed a tray of tea on the table, said something cordial and then left. My wife went with her. I glanced around the room. There were gardening boots in the corner, photos on the desk and framed on the walls. Lace-cap flowers with dark stems—baskets of flowers, geraniums, dusty leaf flowers—white cloth, silver plates, bright fireplace—circular shadows . . . a gallery forest out the window in full bloom.

I discovered what MacLeish looked like through the photos. There was a snapshot of him as a young boy on a saddled pony, a woman in a bonnet holding the reins. Other photos— Archie at the head of his class at Harvard—photos of him at Yale and as a World War I captain in the artillery—in another photo he's with a small company of people in front of the Eiffel Tower—photos taken of him at the Library of Congress—in another photo he's at the table with a board of editors from *Fortune* magazine. In another, he's being given the Pulitzer Prize . . . there's a picture of him and some Boston lawyers. I heard his steps coming up the stone pathway, and he entered the room, came forward and extended his hand.

He had the aura of a governor, a ruler—every bit of him an officer—a gentleman of adventure who carried himself with the peculiar confidence of power bred of blood. He got right straight to it, starts right up the track. He reiterates a few things he said in his letter. (In his letter, he made mention of some lines in a song of mine that places T. S. Eliot and Ezra Pound symbolically fighting in a captain's tower.) "Pound and Eliot were too scholastic, weren't they?" he says. What I know about Pound is that he was a Nazi sympathizer in World War II and did anti-American broadcasts from Italy. I never did read him. I liked T. S. Eliot. He was worth reading. Archie says, "I knew them both. Hard men. We have to go through them. But I know what you mean when you say they are fighting in a captain's tower." MacLeish would do most of the talking, told me some remarkable stuff about the novelist Stephen Crane, who wrote *The Red Badge of Courage*. He said he was a sickly reporter always on the side of the underdog—wrote Bowery stories for magazines, and that he once wrote a piece defending a prostitute being shaken down by the vice squad only to have the vice squad come against him and haul him into court. He didn't go to cocktail parties or theater openings— went to Cuba to cover the Cuban War, drank a lot and died of tuberculosis at twenty-eight. MacLeish had more than a passing knowledge of Crane, said that he was a man who did things for himself and that I should check out *Red Badge of Courage*. It sounded like Crane was the Robert Johnson of literature. Jimmie Rodgers died of TB, too. I wondered if they ever crossed paths.

Archie said he liked a song of mine called "John Brown," a song about a boy that goes off to war. "I don't find the song to be about this boy at all. It's really more of a Greek drama, isn't it? It's about mothers," he tells me. "The different kinds of mothers—biological, honorary . . . all the mothers wrapped into one." I'd never thought of that, but it sounded right. He mentioned a line in one of my songs, that says that "goodness hides behind its gates," and asked if I really saw it that way and I said that sometimes it appears that way. At some point, I was going to ask him what he thought about the hip, cool Ginsberg, Corso and Kerouac, but it seemed like it would have been an empty question. He asked me if I had read Sappho or Socrates. I said, nope, that I hadn't, and then he asked me the same about Dante and Donne. I said, not much. He said the thing to remember about them was that you always come out where you went in.

MacLeish tells me that he considers me a serious poet and that my work would be a touchstone for generations after me, that I was a postwar Iron Age poet but that I had seemingly inherited something metaphysical from a bygone era. He appreciated my songs because they involved themselves with society, that we had many traits and associations in

common and that I didn't care for things the way he didn't
care for them. At one point he had to excuse himself momentarily, left the room. I glanced out the window. The afternoon sun was breaking, throwing a vague radiance to the
earth. A jackrabbit scampered past the scattered chips by
the woodpile. When he returned things fell back into place.
MacLeish picked up where he left off. MacLeish tells me that
Homer, who wrote the *Iliad*, was a blind balladeer and that
his name means "hostage." He also told me that there's a difference between art and propaganda and he told me the
difference between the effects. He asked me if I'd ever read
the French poet François Villon, and I told him that I did
read him and then he said he saw some slight influence in my
work. Archie spoke about blank verse, rhyme verse, ele-
giacs, ballads, limericks and sonnets. He asked me what I
had sacrificed to pursue my dreams. He said the worth of
things can't be measured by what they cost but by what they
cost you to get it, that if anything costs you your faith or
your family, then the price is too high and that there are
some things that will never wear out. MacLeish had been a
classmate of Douglas MacArthur at West Point and he talked
about him, too. He also talked about Michelangelo, said that
Michelangelo had no friends of any kind and didn't want
any, spoke to no one. Archie told me that a lot of things that
were happening when he was young had blown over. He tells
me about J. P. Morgan, the financier, that he was one of the
six or eight persons at the beginning of the century who
owned all of America. Morgan had said, "America is good
enough for me," and some senator commented that if he ever
changes his mind, he should give it back. There was no way
to measure the soul of a man like that.

MacLeish asked me who my boyhood heroes were and I told him, "Robin Hood and St. George the Dragon Slayer." "You wouldn't want to get on their bad side," he chuckled. He said that he'd forgotten the meaning of a lot of his earlier poems and that an authentic poet makes a style of his own, a few masterpieces last across the years. The play for which he wanted me to write songs was laying on his reading desk. He wanted songs in it that made some comment to go along with the scenes, and he began reading out loud some of the speeches and suggested some song titles—"Father of Night," "Red Hands," "Lower World" were a few of them.

After listening intently, I intuitively realized that I didn't think this was for me. After hearing a few lines from the script, I didn't see how our destinies could be intermixed. This play was dark, painted a world of paranoia, guilt and fear—it was all blacked out and met the atomic age head on, reeked of foul play. There really wasn't much to say or add to it. The play spelled death for society with humanity lying facedown in its own blood. MacLeish's play was delivering something beyond an apocalyptic message. Something like, man's mission is to destroy the earth. MacLeish was signaling something through the flames. The play was up to something and I didn't think I wanted to know. That being said, I told MacLeish I would think about it.

In 1968 The Beatles were in India. America was wrapped up in a blanket of rage. Students at universities were wrecking parked cars, smashing windows. The war in Vietnam was sending the country into a deep depression. The cities were in flames, the bludgeons were coming down. Hard-hat union guys were beating kids with baseball bats. The fictitious Don Juan, a mysterious medicine man from Mexico, had become the new consciousness craze, had brought in a new level of awareness or life force and was wielding it like a machete. Books about him were sailing off the shelves. Acid tests were in full swing, acid was giving people the right attitude. The new worldview was changing society and everything was moving fast—lickety-split. Strobes, black lights—freakouts, the wave of the future. Students trying to seize control of national universities, antiwar activists forcing bitter exchanges. Maoists, Marxists, Castroites—leftist kids who read Che Guevara instruction booklets were out to topple the economy. Kerouac had retired, and the organized press was stirring things up, fanning the flames of hysteria. If you saw the news, you'd think that the whole nation was on fire. It seemed like every day there was a new riot in another city, everything on the edge of danger and change—the jungles of America being cleared away. Things that had used to be in traditional black and white were now exploding in full, sunny color.

I had been in a motorcycle accident and I'd been hurt, but I recovered. Truth was that I wanted to get out of the rat race. Having children changed my life and segregated me from just about everybody and everything that was going on. Outside of my family, nothing held any real interest for me and I was seeing everything through different glasses. Even the horrifying news items of the day, the gunning down of the Kennedys, King, Malcolm X . . . I didn't see them as leaders being shot down, but rather as fathers whose families had been left wounded. Being born and raised in America, the country of freedom and independence, I had always cherished the values and ideals of equality and liberty. I was determined to raise my children with those ideals.

A few years earlier Ronnie Gilbert, one of The Weavers, had introduced me at one of the Newport Folk Festivals saying, "And here he is . . . take him, you know him, he's yours." I had failed to sense the ominous forebodings in the introduction. Elvis had never even been introduced like that. "Take him, he's yours!" What a crazy thing to say! Screw that. As far as I knew, I didn't belong to anybody then or now. I had a wife and children whom I loved more than anything else in the world. I was trying to provide for them, keep out of trouble, but the big bugs in the press kept promoting me as the mouthpiece, spokesman, or even conscience of a generation. That was funny. All I'd ever done was sing songs that were dead straight and expressed powerful new realities. I had very little in common with and knew even less about a generation that I was supposed to be the voice of. I'd left my hometown only ten years earlier, wasn't vociferating the opinions of anybody. My destiny lay down the road with whatever life invited, had nothing to do with representing any kind of civilization. Being true to yourself, that was the thing. I was more a cowpuncher than a Pied Piper.

People think that fame and riches translate into power, that it brings glory and honor and happiness. Maybe it does, but sometimes it doesn't. I found myself stuck in Woodstock, vulnerable and with a family to protect. If you looked in the press, though, you saw me being portrayed as anything but that. It was surprising how thick the smoke had become. It seems like the world has always needed a scapegoat—someone to lead the charge against the Roman Empire. But America wasn't the Roman Empire and someone else would have to step up and volunteer. I really was never any more than what I was—a folk musician who gazed into the gray mist with tear-blinded eyes and made up songs that floated in a luminous haze. Now it had blown up in my face and was hanging over me. I wasn't a preacher performing miracles. It would have driven anybody mad.

Early on, Woodstock had been very hospitable to us. I had actually discovered the place long before moving there. Once, at night, driving down from Syracuse after playing a show, I told my manager about the town. We were going to be driving right by it. He said he was looking for a place to buy a country house. We drove through the town, he spied a house he liked and bought it there and then. I had bought one later on, and it was in this same house that intruders started to break in day and night. Tensions mounted almost immediately and peace was hard to come by. At one time the place had been a quiet refuge, but now, no more. Roadmaps to our homestead must have been posted in all fifty states for gangs of dropouts and druggies. Moochers showed up from as far away as California on pilgrimages. Goons were breaking into our place all hours of the night. At first, it was merely the nomadic homeless making illegal entry—seemed harmless enough, but then rogue radicals looking for the Prince of Protest began to arrive—unaccountable-looking characters, gargoyle-looking gals, scarecrows, stragglers looking to party, raid the pantry. Peter LaFarge, a folksinger friend of mine, had given me a couple of Colt single-shot repeater pistols, and I also had a clip-fed Winchester blasting rifle around, but it was awful to think about what could be done with those things. The authorities, the chief of police (Woodstock had about three cops) had told me that if anyone was shot accidentally or even shot at as a warning, it would be me that would be going to the lockup. Not only that, but creeps thumping their boots across our roof could even take me to court if any of them fell off. This was so unsettling. I wanted to set fire to these people. These gate-crashers, spooks, trespassers, demagogues were all disrupting my home life and the fact that I was not to piss them off or they could press charges really didn't appeal to me. Each day and night was fraught with difficulties. Everything was wrong, the world was absurd. It was backing me into a corner. Even persons near and dear offered no relief.

Once in the midsummer madness I was riding in a car with Robbie Robertson, the guitar player in what later was to be called The Band. I felt like I might as well have been living in another part of the solar system. He says to me, "Where do you think you're gonna take it?"

I said, "Take what?"

"You know, the whole music scene." The whole music scene! The car window was rolled down about an inch. I rolled it down the rest of the way, felt a gust of wind blow into my face and waited for what he said to die away—it was like dealing with a conspiracy. No place was far enough away. I don't know what everybody else was fantasizing about but what I was fantasizing about was a nine-to-five existence, a house on a tree-lined block with a white picket fence, pink roses in the backyard. That would have been nice. That was my deepest dream. After a while you learn that privacy is something you can sell, but you can't buy it back. Woodstock had turned into a nightmare, a place of chaos. Now it was time to scramble out of there in search of some new silver lining and that's what we did. We moved to New York City for a while in hopes to demolish my identity, but it wasn't any better there. It was even worse. Demonstrators found our house and paraded up and down in front of it chanting and shouting, demanding for me to come out and lead them somewhere—stop shirking my duties as the conscience of a generation. Once the street was blocked off and our house was picketed by firebrands with city permits, demonstrators roaring and snorting. The neighbors hated us. To them it must have seemed like I was something out of a carnival show—some exhibition in the Palace of Wonders. They would stare at me when they saw me, like they'd stare at a shrunken head or a giant jungle rat. I pretended that I didn't care.

Eventually, we tried moving West—tried a few different places, but in short time reporters would come sniffing around in hopes to gain some secret—maybe I'd confess some sin. Our address would be printed in the local press and then the same thing would start up. Even if these reporters had been allowed in the house, what would they find? A whole lotta stuff—stacking toys, push and pull toys, child-sized tables and chairs—big empty cardboard boxes—science kits, puzzles and toy drums . . . I wasn't going to let anybody in the house. As for house rules, we didn't have many. If the kids wanted to play basketball in the kitchen, they played basketball in the kitchen. If they got into the pots and pans, we put all the pots and pans out on the floor. My house was chaotic inside as well as out.

Joan Baez recorded a protest song about me that was getting big play, challenging me to get with it—come out and take charge, lead the masses—be an advocate, lead the crusade. The song called out to me from the radio like a public service announcement. The press never let up. Once in a while I would have to rise up and offer myself for an interview so they wouldn't beat down the door. Usually the questions would start out with something like, "Can we talk further upon things that are happening?" "Sure, like what?" Reporters would shoot questions at me and I would tell them repeatedly that I was not a spokesman for anything or anybody and that I was only a musician. They'd look into my eyes as if to find some evidence of bourbon and handfuls of amphetamines. I had no idea what they were thinking. Later an article would hit the streets with the headline "Spokesman Denies That He's a Spokesman." I felt like a piece of meat that someone had thrown to the dogs. The *New York Times* printed quacky interpretations of my songs. *Esquire* magazine put a four-faced monster on their cover, my face along with Malcolm X's, Kennedy's and Castro's. What the hell was that supposed to mean? It was like I was on the edge of the earth. If anybody had any sound guidance or advice to offer, it wasn't forthcoming. My wife, when she married me, had no idea of what she was getting into. Me neither, actually, and now we were in a no win situation.

For sure my lyrics had struck nerves that had never been struck before, but if my songs were just about the words, then what was Duane Eddy, the great rock-and-roll guitarist, doing recording an album full of instrumental melodies of my songs? Musicians have always known that my songs were about more than just words, but most people are not musicians. What I had to do was recondition my mind and stop putting the blame on external forces. I had to educate myself, get rid of some baggage. The solitude of time was what I didn't have. Whatever the counterculture was, I'd seen enough of it. I was sick of the way my lyrics had been extrapolated, their meanings subverted into polemics and that I had been anointed as the Big Bubba of Rebellion, High Priest of Protest, the Czar of Dissent, the Duke of Disobedience, Leader of the Freeloaders, Kaiser of Apostasy, Archbishop of Anarchy, the Big Cheese. What the hell are we talking about? Horrible titles any way you want to look at it. All code words for *Outlaw*.

It was tough moving around—like the Merle Haggard song, ". . . I'm on the run, the highway is my home." I don't know if Haggard ever had to get his family out with him, but I know I did. It's a little different when you have to do that. The landscape burned behind us. The press was in no hurry to retract their judgment and I couldn't just lie there, had to take the bull by the horns myself and remodel the image of me, change the perception of it anyway. There aren't any rules to cover an emergency of this kind. This was a new thing for me and I wasn't used to thinking this way. I'd have to send out deviating signals, crank up the wrecking train—create some different impressions.

At first I was only able to do little things, local things. Tactics, really. Unexpected things like pouring a bottle of whiskey over my head and walking into a department store and act pie-eyed, knowing that everyone would be talking amongst themselves when I left. I was hoping that the news would spread. What mattered to me most was getting breathing room for my family. The whole spectral world could go to hell. My outer image would have to be something a bit more confusing, a bit more humdrum. It's hard to live like this. It takes all your effort. The first thing that has to go is any form of artistic self-expression that's dear to you. Art is unimportant next to life, and you have no choice. I had no hunger for it anymore, anyway. Creativity has much to do with experience, observation and imagination, and if any one of those key elements is missing, it doesn't work. It was impossible now for me to observe anything without being observed. Even when I walked to the corner store someone would spot me and sneak away to find a phone. In Woodstock I'd be out in the yard and a car would come rolling up, some guy would jump out of the passenger side, point in my direction and then walk away—and a bunch of sightseers would then come down the hill. Citizens would see me coming down the street and cross it, didn't want to get caught—guilt by association. Sometimes in a restaurant (my name was widely known but my face not so at the time) one of the eaters who recognized me would go up to the cashier, point in my direction and whisper, "That's him over there." The cashier would tell someone and the news would go from table to table. It was like lightning struck the place. Necks would stretch. Folks chewing their food would spit it out, look at one another and say, "That him?" "You mean that guy that was sitting over there at that table with the bunch of kids?" It was like moving a mountain. My house was being battered, ravens constantly croaking ill omens at our door. What kind of alchemy, I wondered, could create a perfume that would make reaction to a person lukewarm, indifferent and apathetic? I wanted to get some. I had never intended to be on the road of heavy consequences and I didn't like it. I wasn't the toastmaster of any generation, and that notion needed to be pulled up by its roots. Liberty for myself and my loved ones had to be secured. I had no time to kill and I didn't like what was being thrown at me. This main meal of garbage had to be mixed up with some butter and mushrooms and I'd have to go great lengths to do it. You gotta start somewhere.

I went to Jerusalem, got myself photographed at the Western Wall wearing a skullcap. The image was transmitted worldwide instantly and quickly all the great rags changed me overnight into a Zionist. This helped a little. Coming back I quickly recorded what appeared to be a country-western record and made sure it sounded pretty bridled and housebroken. The music press didn't know what to make of it. I used a different voice, too. People scratched their heads. I started a rumor with my record company that I would be quitting music and going to college, the Rhode Island School of Design—which eventually leaked out to the columnists. "He won't last a month," some people said. Journalists began asking in print, "Whatever happened to the old him?" They could go to hell, too. Stories were printed about me trying to find myself, that I was on some eternal search, that I was suffering some kind of internal torment. It all sounded good to me. I released one album (a double one) where I just threw everything I could think of at the wall and whatever stuck, released it, and then went back and scooped up everything that didn't stick and released that, too. I missed out on Woodstock—just wasn't there. Altamont—sympathy for the devil—missed that, too. Eventually I would even record an entire album based on Chekhov short stories—critics thought it was autobiographical—that was fine. I played a part in a movie, wore cowboy duds and galloped down the road. Not much required there. I guess I was naïve.

The novelist Herman Melville's work went largely unnoticed after *Moby-Dick*. Critics thought that he crossed the literary line and recommended burning *Moby-Dick*. By the time of his death he was largely forgotten.

I had assumed that when critics dismissed my work, the same thing would happen to me, that the public would forget about me. How mad is that? Eventually, I would have to face the music—go back to performing—the long-awaited ballyhooed reunion tour—gypsy tours—changing ideologies like tires, like shoes, like guitar strings. What's the difference? As long as my own form of certainty stayed intact, I owed nobody nothing. I wasn't going to go deeper into the darkness for anybody. I was already living in the darkness. My family was my light and I was going to protect that light at all cost. That was where my dedication was, first, last and everything in-between. What did I owe the rest of the world? Nothing. Not a damn thing. The press? I figured you lie to it. For the public eye, I went into the bucolic and mundane as far as possible. In my real life I got to do the things that I loved the best and that was all that mattered—the Little League games, birthday parties, taking my kids to school, camping trips, boating, rafting, canoeing, fishing . . . I was living on record royalties. In reality I was imperceptible, my image, that is. Sometime in the past I had written and performed songs that were most original and most influential, and I didn't know if I ever would again and I didn't care.

The actor Tony Curtis once told me that fame is an occupation in itself, that it is a separate thing. And Tony couldn't be more right. The old image slowly faded and in time I found myself no longer under the canopy of some malignant influence. Eventually different anachronisms were thrust upon me—anachronisms of lesser dilemma—though they might seem bigger. Legend, Icon, Enigma (Buddha in European Clothes was my favorite)—stuff like that, but that was all right. These titles were placid and harmless, threadbare, easy to get around with them. Prophet, Messiah, Savior—those are tough ones.

Archibald MacLeish's play *Scratch* had a couple of characters, one of them whose name was the title of the play. Scratch utters the lines "I know there is evil in the world—essential evil, not the opposite of good or the defective of good but something to which good itself is an irrelevance—a fantasy. No one can live as long as I have, hear what I have heard and not know that. I know too—more precisely—I am ready to believe that there may be something in the world—someone, if you prefer—that purposes evil, that intends it . . . powerful nations suddenly, without occasion, without apparent cause . . . decay. Their children turn against them. Their women lose their sense of being women. Their families disintegrate." From there on, it only gets better. Writing songs for a play wouldn't have been far-fetched for me and I had already composed a couple of things for him just to see if I could do it. I'd always liked the stage and even more so, the theater. It seemed like the most supreme craft of all craft. Whatever the environment, a ballroom or a sidewalk, the dirt of a country road, the action always took place in the eternal "now."

My first appearances in a public spectacle had been on my

hometown school auditorium stage, no small music box theater but a professional concert hall like Carnegie Hall built with East Coast mining money, with curtains and props, trapdoors and orchestra pit. My first performances were seen in the *Black Hills Passion Play of South Dakota*, a religious drama depicting the last days of Christ. This play always came to town during the Christmas season with professional actors in the leading roles, cages of pigeons, a donkey, a camel and a truck full of props. There were always parts that called for extras. One year I played a Roman soldier with a spear and helmet—breastplate, the works—a nonspeaking role, but it didn't matter. I felt like a star. I liked the costume. It felt like a nerve tonic . . . as a Roman soldier I felt like a part of everything, in the center of the planet, invincible. That seemed a million years ago now, a million private struggles and difficulties ago.

I wasn't feeling so invincible at the moment. Defiant, maybe. Anything but content. Surrounded on all sides. As far as I could see, nothing was visible. Nothing but my own kitchen. Nothing but the hot dogs with English muffins and noodles, the Cheerios and cornflakes with heavy cream—stirring flour into a large bowl for corn pudding and beating eggs, changing diapers and making bottles. Somehow between all that and maneuvering unmolested through the neighborhood and taking the dog for a walk, I'd gone to the piano, composed a few things for the play bearing in mind the titles that were given to me. The play itself was conveying some devastating truth, but I was going to stay far away from that. Truth was the last thing on my mind, and even if there was such a thing, I didn't want it in my house. Oedipus went looking for the truth and when he found it, it ruined him. It was a cruel horror of a joke. So much for the truth. I was gonna talk out of both sides of my mouth and what you heard depended on which side you were standing. If I ever did stumble on any truth, I was gonna sit on it and keep it down. I had gone to New York earlier in the week and met with the play's producer, Stewart Ostrow. I'd taken the songs up to his office in the Brill Building in New York and recorded them. He then sent the acetates to Archie.

While in New York, my wife and I went to the Rainbow Room on top of Rockefeller Center to see Frank Sinatra Jr., who was singing with a full orchestra. Why him and not somebody on the hip circuit? No hassles and nobody chasing me, that's why . . . that and maybe because I felt a connection—I reckoned that we were about near the same age and that he was a contemporary of mine. Anyway Frank was a fine singer. I didn't care if he was as good as his old man or not—he sounded fine, and I liked his big blasting band. Afterwards he came by and sat with us at our table. Obviously it had surprised him that someone like me would come see him, but when he saw that I genuinely liked show tunes, he eased up and relaxed, said he liked a few of my songs, "Blowin' in the Wind" and "Don't Think Twice," asked me questions about what kind of places I played (I was retired and lived like a hermit but didn't say that). He talked about the civil rights movement, said his father had been active in civil rights and had always fought for the underdog—that his father felt like he was one himself. Frank Jr. seemed pretty smart, nothing faked or put-on or ritzy about him. There was a legitimacy about what he did, and he knew who he was. The conversation rolled along.

"How do you think it would make you feel," he said, "to

find out that the underdog had turned out to be a son of a bitch?"

"I don't know," I said, "probably not so good."

Gazing out through the wall of windows, you could see the spectacular city view. From sixty floors up, it was a different world.

After a while, I bought a red flower for my wife, one of the loveliest creatures in the world of women, and we got up on our feet and left, said good-bye to Frank.

A reply from MacLeish eventually arrived and he had some questions. I knew he would. He invited me to come back up to his place—we could tune up the compositions, integrate them and talk about them further. With little hesitation, I jumped behind the wheel of our long, four-door Ford station wagon sedan and headed up again across the New England countryside. Even behind the wheel with my eyes on the open road, I couldn't keep the clanging reverberations out of my mind. I felt like a caged bird—like a refugee—zigzagging up the winding highways—felt like someone who was transporting a corpse across state lines and could be pulled over at any time.

I clicked on the radio. Johnny Cash was singing "Boy Named Sue." Once upon a time Johnny had shot a man in Reno just to watch him die. Now he was saying that he was stuck with a girl's name that his father had given him. Johnny was trying to change his image, too. Aside from that, I didn't see much similarity between my situation and anybody else's—felt pretty isolated with just myself and my small but growing family facing a fantastic world of sorcery.

One intriguing thing that caught my eye was that in the boxing world Jerry Quarry had fought Jimmy Ellis in Oakland and it was a fired up affair. Jimmy Ellis was a "take the money and go home" kind of guy—boxing was a job to him, no more no less. He had a family to feed and didn't care about becoming a legend or breaking any records. Jerry Quarry, a white boxer, was being touted as the new Great White Hope—an odious designation. Jerry, whose father had come to California on a boxcar, wanted no part of it. The white vigilante groups who came to cheer him didn't move Quarry. Nor did the intense atmosphere—he wouldn't accept their bigoted allegiance and resisted the dementia swirling around him. He didn't need any gimmicks. I identified with both Ellis and Quarry and drew an analogy between our situations and responses to it. Like Quarry, I wasn't going to acknowledge being an emblem, symbol or spokesman either, and like Ellis, I too had a family to feed.

Rolling through the bright autumn day, the scenery had become a pale blur. For a minute I'd felt like I'd been moving around in circles. After a while, I cruised into Massachusetts and arrived again at Archie's. Same thing as before—I was escorted in across the wooden bridge—up the path—in the distance a long dead tree, branches shooting off from the main trunk—all very serene, very picturesque. I crossed over the eroded gully full of rotting leaves with distilled beams of light coming off of rock fragments, walked up the dry, rocky ridge that led to his door. I went past a sign leaning up against the building, a wooden Masonite board with a base coat of outdoor paint and auto enamel and plastic letters. Once again I waited and looked back out the window to a cool ravine and clear running brook and wildflowers. A lot of flowers were still arranged in the room—flowers of deep purple, fernlike flowers rough to the touch, blue flowers with

white centers—buds coiled at the tip and looking like a fiddle
. . . Archie walked into the room and greeted me warmly—it
was like seeing an old friend, and I wondered if he was going
to touch on serious topics again, but he didn't want to make
chitchat.

He wondered why the songs weren't darker than they
were, and he made suggestions . . . he revisited and explained certain characters, said the main character was,
among other things, envious, slanderous and baiting and that
should be brought out more. I felt myself sitting there and
degenerating into boorishness, felt like two parts of my self
were beginning to battle. MacLeish wanted clear answers. He
looked at me with his wise eyes. He possessed more knowledge of mankind and its vagaries than most men acquire in a
lifetime. I wanted to tell him things were muddled, that a
mob had been surrounding our house with bullhorns and
calling on me to come out into the streets and lead a march
on city hall, on Wall Street, on the Capitol . . . that mythological figures of the fates have been weaving and now cutting
my thread of life . . . that there were a hundred thousand
demonstrators in Washington and the police have surrounded the White House with transport busses bumper to
bumper to protect the executive mansion. The president was
inside watching a football game. People I've never heard of
were calling for me to be there and take command. It was all
making me want to throw up. In my dreams crowds were
chanting, challenging me, shouting, "Follow us and fit in." I
wanted to tell him that life itself has turned into a prowling
lion. I wanted to tell him that that I needed to escape the
blaze of bullshit. I glanced around the room. The book-
shelves were full of books and I noticed the novel *Ulysses*.

Goddard Lieberson, president of Columbia Records, had given me this as a gift, a first-edition copy of the book and I couldn't make hide nor hair of it. James Joyce seemed like the most arrogant man who ever lived, had both his eyes wide open and great faculty of speech, but what he say, I knew not what. I wanted to ask MacLeish to explain James Joyce to me, to make sense of something that seemed so out of control, and I knew that he would have, but I didn't. Deep down, I knew that I couldn't have anything to add to the message of his play. He didn't need my help anyway. He wanted only to talk about the songs for his play and that's why I was here, but there was no hope and there was nothing to be done and soon that became obvious.

The sun had set and the solemn night was establishing itself. I was asked to stay for dinner, but politely declined. He'd been patient with me. Suddenly on my way out, my mind sprang back to another time, the time I'd seen the Leopard Girl. Sometimes you just think of things you've seen, old memories that you've salvaged from the rubble of your life. The Leopard Girl. A carnie barker had explained about her, how her mother who was pregnant with her in North Carolina saw a leopard on a dark road at night and the animal had marked her unborn child. Then I saw the Leopard Girl and when I did, my emotions got weak.

I wondered, now, whether all of us—MacLeish, me and everyone else—had been inscribed and marked before birth, given a sticker, some secret sign. If that's true, then none of us could change anything. We're all running a wild race. We play the game the way it's set up or we don't play. If the secret sign thing is true, then it wouldn't be fair to judge anybody . . . and I hoped MacLeish wouldn't be judging me.

It was time to go. If I'd have stayed any longer at Archie's I would have had to take up residence in his house. I asked him, just out of curiosity, why he didn't want to write the songs himself. He said he wasn't a songwriter and that his play needed another voice, another angle—that sometimes we become too content. Walking back over the small stream, it seemed like I was seeing the small ringlets of a river. Archie's play was so heavy—so full of midnight murder. There was no way I could make its purpose mine, but it was great meeting him, a man who had reached the moon when most of us scarcely make it off the ground. In some ways, he taught me how to swim the Atlantic. I wanted to thank him but found it difficult. We waved at each other from the roadway and I knew I'd never see him again.

Bob Johnston, my record producer, was on the line. He was calling me from Nashville and had reached me in East Hampton. We were living in a rented house on a quiet street with majestic old elms—a Colonial house with plantation-shuttered windows. It was hidden from the street by elevated hedges. There was a large backyard and a key to a gated dune which led to the pristine Atlantic sandy beach. The house belonged to Henry Ford. East Hampton, which was originally settled by farmers and fishermen, was now a refuge for artists and writers and wealthy families. Not really a place but a "state of mind." If your balance had been severely disrupted, this was a place where you could get it back. Some folks there traced their families back three hundred years and some houses dated back to 1700—there'd been witch trials there in the past. Wainscott, Springs, Amagansett—green expanses—English style windmills—year round charm and a unique kind of light approximate to the woods and oceans.

I started painting landscapes there. There was plenty to do. We had five kids and often went to the beach, boated on the bay, dug for clams, spent afternoons at a lighthouse near Montauk, went to Gardiner's Island—hunted for Captain Kidd's buried treasure—rode bikes, go-carts and pulled wagons—went to the movies and the outdoor markets, walked around on Division Street—drove over to Springs a lot, a painter's paradise where De Kooning had his studio. We had rented the house under my mother's maiden name and had no trouble getting around. My face wasn't that well known, although the name would have made people uncomfortable.

Earlier in the week we had gotten back from Princeton, New Jersey, where I had been given a Honorary Doctorate degree. It had been a weird adventure. Somehow, I had motivated David Crosby to come along. Crosby was part of a new supergroup, but I knew him from when he was in The Byrds, part of the West Coast music scene. They'd recorded a song of mine, "Mr. Tambourine Man," and the record made it to the top of the charts. Crosby was a colorful and unpredictable character, wore a Mandrake the Magician cape, didn't get along with too many people and had a beautiful voice—an architect of harmony. He was tottering on the brink of death even then and could freak out a whole city block all by himself, but I liked him a lot. He was out of place in The Byrds. He could be an obstreperous companion.

We pulled off of Route 80 in a '69 Buick Electra, found the university on a hot and cloudless day. In short time the officials led me into a crowded room and put me in a robe, and soon I was looking out over a crowd of well-dressed peo-

ple in the sun. There were also others on the stage getting
honorary degrees and I needed mine as much as they needed
theirs but for different reasons. Walter Lippmann, the lib-
eral columnist, Coretta Scott King, some others—but all eyes
were on me. I stood there in the heat staring out at the
crowd, daydreaming, had attention-span disorder.

When my turn came to accept the degree, the speaker in-
troducing me said something like how I distinguished myself
in *carminibus canendi* and that I now would enjoy all the
university's individual rights and privileges wherever they
pertain, but then he added, "Though he is known to millions,
he shuns publicity and organizations preferring the solidar-
ity of his family and isolation from the world, and though he
is approaching the perilous age of thirty, he remains the authentic expression of the disturbed and concerned conscience
of Young America." Oh Sweet Jesus! It was like a jolt. I
shuddered and trembled but remained expressionless. The
disturbed conscience of Young America! There it was again. I
couldn't believe it! Tricked once more. The speaker could
have said many things, he could have emphasized a few
things about my music. When he said to the crowd that I preferred isolation from the world, it was like he told them that
I preferred being in an iron tomb with my food shoved in on
a tray.

The sunlight was blocking my vision, but I could still see
the faces gawking at me with such strange expressions. I was
so mad I wanted to bite myself. Lately the public perception
of me had begun to shift and move around like a yo-yo, but
this kind of thing could set it back a thousand years. Didn't
they know what was happening? Even the Russian newspaper *Pravda* had called me a money-hungry capitalist. Even

the Weathermen, a notorious group who made homemade bombs in basements to blow up public buildings, who had taken their name from a line in one of my songs, had recently changed their name from the Weathermen to the Weather Underground. I was losing all kinds of credibility. There were all kinds of things going on. I was glad I came to get the degree, though. I could use it. Every look and touch and scent of it spelled respectability and had something of the spirit of the universe in it. After whispering and mumbling my way through the ceremony, I was handed the scroll. We piled back into the big Buick and drove away. It had been a strange day. "Bunch of dickheads on auto-stroke," Crosby said.

Johnston asked over the phone if I was thinking about recording. Of course I was. As long as my records were still selling, why wouldn't I be thinking about recording? I didn't have a whole lot of songs, but what I did have were the MacLeish pieces—and I figured I could add to them—make up more in the studio if I had to and Johnston was raring to go . . . working with him was like a drunken joyride. Bob was an interesting cat—originally from West Texas, living in Tennessee, built like a wrestler, thick wrists and big forearms, barreled chest, short but with a personality that makes him seem bigger than he really is—a musician and songwriter who had even written a couple of songs that Elvis recorded.

Johnston was trying to get us to move to Nashville, and every time we were there he tried to sell it to us as being very laid-back and having everything you need. It's been reformed, he told us. People do their own thing here. Nobody cares who anybody is. You can stand on the street 'til morning and no one will see you.

I'd been there a few times to make some records—first time I recorded there was in '66. The town was like being in a soap bubble. They nearly ran Al Kooper, Robbie Robertson and me out of town for having long hair. All the songs coming out of the studios then were about slut wives cheating on their husbands or vice versa.

Slowly driving around Nashville in his red Eldorado convertible, Johnston pointed out the sights. "There's Eddy Arnold's house." He'd point to another one. "That house is where Waylon lives. That one over there is Tom T. Hall's. That's Faron Young's." He'd turn the corner and then signal somewhere else. "Porter Wagoner's place is up that street." I'd lean back in the big leather cushioned seat, gaze around from east to west. Johnston had fire in his eyes. He had that thing that some people call "momentum." You could see it in his face and he shared that fire, that spirit. Columbia's leading folk and country producer, he was born one hundred years too late. He should have been wearing a wide cape, a plumed hat and riding with his sword held high. Johnston disregarded any warning that might get in his way. His idea for producing a record was to keep the machines oiled, turn 'em on and let 'er rip . . . there was no telling who he'd bring to the studio and there was always heavy traffic, and yet he seemed to have a place for everybody. If a song wasn't going right or things were fluttering, he'd come out into the studio and say stuff like, "Gentlemen, we just have too many men on the floor." That was his way of sorting things out. Johnston lived on low country barbeque, and he was all charm—

referred to one of his judge friends in Nashville as that "bob-tailed politician." "You gotta meet him," he said, "I gotta get you two together sometime." Johnston was unreal. We wouldn't be recording in Nashville this time, though. We were going to be recording in New York City and he was going to have to book the musicians and either bring them with him or else find them here.

I was wondering who he was going to bring to the sessions this time and was hoping he'd bring Charlie Daniels. He'd brought Charlie before, but he'd failed to bring him a few times, too. I felt I had a lot in common with Charlie. The kind of phrases he'd use, his sense of humor, his relationship to work, his tolerance for certain things. Felt like we had dreamed the same dream with all the same distant places. A lot of his recollections seemed to coincide with mine. Charlie would fiddle with stuff and make sense of it. I had no band at the time and relied on the A&R man or producer to throw one together. When Charlie was around, something good would usually come out of the sessions. Johnston had moved Daniels to Nashville from North Carolina to play guitar and be a side-man on other artists' records. Charlie played fiddle, too, but Johnston didn't allow him to play it when he was on my sessions. Years earlier Charlie had a band in his hometown called The Jaguars who had made a few surf rockabilly records, and although I hadn't made any records in my hometown, I had a band, too, about the same time. I felt our early histories were somewhat similar. Charlie eventually struck it big. After hearing the Allman Brothers and the side-winding Lynyrd Skynyrd, he'd find his groove and prove himself with his own brand of dynamics, coming up with a new form of hillbilly boogie that was pure genius. Atomic fueled—with surrealistic double fiddle playing and great tunes like "Devil Went Down to Georgia." For a time there, Charlie had it all.

Al Kooper, who had happened to discover Lynyrd Skynyrd, had played on some of my best records, so I asked Johnston to call him. That was my only suggestion to Johnston as to who to book. I thought Al might be in New York anyway. Kooper was from Brooklyn or Queens and had been in the teen group The Royal Teens growing up. The group had a big hit with a song called "Short Shorts." Kooper played a variety of instruments and was good at them all. He had the right feel. He was a songwriter, too, out of the New York scene. Gene Pitney had recorded a song of his. Kooper put together groups like Blood, Sweat and Tears, The Blues Project, even a supergroup with Steven Stills and Michael Bloomfield, but he'd walked away from them all. He was a talent scout, too, he was the Ike Turner of the white world. All he needed was a dynamo chick singer. Janis Joplin would have been the perfect front singer for Al. I mentioned this once to Albert Grossman, the man who had managed me and now was managing Janis's career. Grossman said it was the stupidest thing he ever heard. I didn't think it was so stupid, though, I thought it was visionary. Sadly, Janis would soon breathe no more and Kooper would be in eternal musical limbo. I should have been a manager.

Within a week I was in the New York Columbia studios with Johnston at the helm, and he's thinking that everything I'm recording is fantastic. He always does. He's thinking that something is gonna strike pay dirt, that everything is totally together. On the contrary. Nothing was ever together. Not even after a song had been finished and recorded was it ever together. For one of these sets of lyrics, Kooper played some Teddy Wilson riffs on the piano. There were three girl singers in the room, who sounded like they'd been plucked from a choir and one of them did some improvisational scat singing. The whole thing was done in just one take and called "If Dogs Run Free."

I recorded some of the earlier stuff from the MacLeish play that did have melodies and that seemed to go well. Whatever else fit—fragments, tunes, offbeat phrases. It didn't matter. My reputation was firm in hand—at least these songs wouldn't make any gory headlines. Message songs? There weren't any. Anybody listening for them would have to be disappointed. As if I was going to make a career out of that anyway. Regardless, you could still feel the anticipation in the air. When will the old him be back? When will the door burst open and the goose appear? Not today. I felt like these songs could blow away in cigar smoke, which suited me fine. That my records were still selling surprised even me. Maybe there were good songs in the grooves and maybe there weren't—who knows? But they weren't the kind where you hear an awful roaring in your head. I knew what those kind of songs were like and these weren't them. It's not like I hadn't any talent, I just wasn't feeling the full force of the wind. No stellar explosions. I was leaning against the console and listening to one of the playbacks. It sounded okay.

Johnston had asked me earlier, "What do you think you'll call this record?" Titles! Everybody likes titles. There's a lot to be said in a title. I didn't know, though, and hadn't thought about it. But one thing I did know was that there'd be a photo of me and Victoria Spivey on the cover. The photo had been taken a few years earlier in a small recording studio. I knew that this photo would be on the cover even before I recorded the songs. Maybe I was even making this record because I had the cover in mind and needed something to go into the sleeve. It could be. *"Down and Out on the Scene, how does that sound?"* Johnston stared at me and made out of it what he would. "Oh shit, that's gonna defang 'em all." I didn't know who the "them all" were that he was referring to, probably the executives at Columbia Records. He was always at war with them for some reason or another. He thought of them all as a bunch of rattlesnakes. "On what scene, where?" he asked. "It should be big." Johnston liked places. He had produced the *Johnny Cash at San Quentin* record. He liked naming places, thought they created atmospheres. "Oh, I don't know, someplace on top the world. Paris, Barcelona, Athens . . . one of those places." Johnston looked up. "Oh shit man, I gotta get me a travel poster. That's great!" But it wasn't great. It was too soon to be talking about a title, anyway.

I gazed around the room, got up and nervously paced around a few times, watched the clock on the wall—it seemed to be running backwards. I sat back down feeling lines plowing into my face and the whites of my eyes turning yellow. Al Kooper was clowning around, telling shaggy dog stories. I was listening to Daniels practicing scales on the fiddle, thumbing through some magazines that were left on the table, *Collier's, Billboard, Look* magazine. Running across an article in *Male* magazine about a guy, James Lally, a radio man in World War II who had crashed with his pilot in the Philippines, I got sidetracked for a second. It was a gut crunching article, unfiltered. Armstrong, the pilot, was killed in the crash, but Lally was taken prisoner by the

Japanese, who took him to a camp and beheaded him with a samurai sword and then used his head for bayonet practice. I pushed the magazine away. Russ Kunkel, the drummer on the sessions, was sitting on a couch with his eyes halfway shut, tapping two sticks together—gazing through the glass darkly. I couldn't stop thinking about Lally and felt like moaning in the wind.

Buzzy Feiten, one of the guitar players, was laying the groundwork for a tune maybe we'd cut tomorrow or the next day or maybe never get to it at all. Johnston came in, cheerful as always and he had a lot of zest. Few people have it for long, but he's got a never-ending supply and it's not faked. I had just heard the song "New Morning," on the playback and thought it had come out pretty good. *New Morning* might make a good title, I thought and then said it to Johnston. "Man, you were reading my mind. That'll put 'em in the palm of your hand—they'll have to take one of them mind-training courses that you do while you sleep to get the meaning of that." Exactly. And I would have to take one of them mind-reading courses to know what Johnston meant by saying what he just said. It didn't matter, I knew where Bob must have gotten that from, though. I'd brought a book, *Secret of Mind Power* by Harry Lorayne, to the studio and had left it laying on one of the couches. I thought that the book might help me to continue freeze-framing my image, help me in learning how to suggest only shadows of my possible self.

Harry Lorayne, however, was no match for Machiavelli. A few years earlier, I'd read *The Prince* and had liked it a lot. Most of what Machiavelli said made sense, but certain things stick out wrong—like when he offers the wisdom that it's better to be feared than loved, it kind of makes you wonder if

Machiavelli was thinking big. I know what he meant, but sometimes in life, someone who is loved can inspire more fear than Machiavelli ever dreamed of.

The record that we were working on was eventually indeed called *New Morning* (the title of one of the songs I'd composed for the MacLeish play) and it did have the photo of me and Vickie on it. The twelve-song record was released and the flow of reports came streaming in. Some critics would find the album to be lackluster and sentimental, soft in the head. Oh well. Others would triumph it as finally the old him is back. At last. That wasn't saying much either. I took it all as a good sign. To be sure, the album itself had no specific resonance to the shackles and bolts that were strapping the country down, nothing to threaten the status quo. All this was in what the critics would later refer to as my "middle period" and in many camps this record was referred to as a comeback album—and it was. It would be the first of many.

The MacLeish play *Scratch* opened on Broadway at the St. James Theatre on May 6, 1971, and closed two days later on May 8.

# 4

# Oh Mercy

IT WAS 1987 and my hand, which had been ungodly injured in a freak accident, was in the state of regeneration. It had been ripped and mangled to the bone and was still in the acute stage—it didn't even feel like it was mine. I didn't know what had befallen me, and this was a bizarre shift of fate. All potentialities had gone to pieces. With a hundred show dates scheduled for me starting in the spring it was uncertain that I would be able to perform. This was a sobering experience. It was now only January, but my hand was going to need plenty of time to heal and be rehabilitated. Staring out French windows into an overgrown garden, with a cast on my hand that went nearly to my elbow, I realized that my playing days might well have faded out. In some sense, it would have been fitting, for up 'til then I had been kidding myself, exploiting whatever talent I had beyond the breaking point. I'd known it for a while. Recently, though, the picture had changed and now the historical implications of the situation bothered me.

The public had been fed a steady diet of my complete

recordings on disc for years, but my live performances never seemed to capture the inner spirit of the songs—had failed to put the spin on them. The intimacy, among a lot of other things, was gone. For the listeners, it must have been like going through deserted orchards and dead grass. My audience or future audience now would never be able to experience the newly plowed fields that I was about to enter. There were many reasons for this, reasons for the whiskey to have gone out of the bottle. Always prolific but never exact, too many distractions had turned my musical path into a jungle of vines. I'd been following established customs and they weren't working. The windows had been boarded up for years and covered with cobwebs, and it's not like I didn't know it.

Prior to this, things had changed and not in an abstract way. A few months earlier something out of the ordinary had occurred and I became aware of a certain set of dynamic principles by which my performances could be transformed. By combining certain elements of technique which ignite each other I could shift the levels of perception, time-frame structures and systems of rhythm which would give my songs a brighter countenance, call them up from the grave— stretch out the stiffness in their bodies and straighten them out. It was like parts of my psyche were being communicated to by angels. There was a big fire in the fireplace and the wind was making it roar. The veil had lifted. A tornado had come into the place at Christmastime, pushed all the fake Santa Clauses aside and swept away the rubble. It was mystifying why it had taken so long for this to happen. That it didn't happen earlier is a damn shame. I also knew that I had written perfect lyrics to complement the style of music that I played. The previous ten years had left me pretty whitewashed and wasted out professionally. Many times I'd come near the stage before a show and would catch myself thinking that I wasn't keeping my word with myself. What that word was, I couldn't exactly remember, but I knew it was back there somewhere. I tried to figure this out, but there didn't seem to be any formula. Maybe if I had seen it coming, I could have fixed it in its tracks, but I didn't. My performance days in heavy traffic had been grinding to a halt for a while, had almost come to a full stop. I had single-handedly shot myself in the foot too many times. It's nice to be known as a legend, and people will pay to see one, but for most people, once is enough. You have to deliver the goods, not waste your time and everybody else's. I hadn't actually disappeared from the scene, but the road had narrowed, almost was shut down and was supposed to be wide open. I hadn't gone away yet. I was lingering out on the pavement. There was a missing person inside of myself and I needed to find him. Now and again, I did try a few times, tried hard to force it. In nature there's a remedy for everything and that's where I'd usually go hunting for it. I'd find myself on a houseboat, a floating mobile home, hoping to hear a voice—crawling at slow speed—nosed up on a protective beach at night in the wilderness—moose, bear, deer around—the elusive timber wolf not so far off, calm summer evenings listening to the call of the loon. Think things out. But it was no use. I felt done for, an empty burned-out wreck. Too much static in my head and I couldn't dump the stuff. Wherever I am, I'm a '60s troubadour, a folk-rock relic, a wordsmith from bygone days, a fictitious head of state from a place nobody knows. I'm in the bottomless pit of cultural oblivion. You name it. I can't shake it. Stepping out of the woods, people see me coming. I knew what they were thinking. I have to take things for what they were worth.

I'd been on an eighteen month tour with Tom Petty and The Heartbreakers. It would be my last. I had no connection to any kind of inspiration. Whatever was there to begin with had all vanished and shrunk. Tom was at the top of his game and I was at the bottom of mine. I couldn't overcome the odds. Everything was smashed. My own songs had become strangers to me, I didn't have the skill to touch their raw nerves, couldn't penetrate the surfaces. It wasn't my moment of history anymore. There was a hollow singing in my heart and I couldn't wait to retire and fold the tent. One more big payday with Petty and that would be it for me. I was what they called over the hill. If I wasn't careful I could end up ranting and raving in shouting matches with the wall. The mirror had swung around and I could see the future—an old actor fumbling in garbage cans outside the theater of past triumphs.

I had written and recorded so many songs, but it wasn't like I was playing many of them. I think I was only up to the task of about twenty or so. The rest were too cryptic, too darkly driven, and I was no longer capable of doing anything radically creative with them. It was like carrying a package of heavy rotting meat. I couldn't understand where they came from. The glow was gone and the match had burned right to the end. I was going through the motions. Try as I might, the engines wouldn't start.

Benmont Tench, one of the musicians in Petty's band, would always be asking me, almost pleadingly, about including different numbers in the show. "Chimes of Freedom"—

can we try that? Or what about "My Back Pages"? Or "Spanish Harlem Incident"? And I'd always be making some lame excuse. Actually, I don't know who was making the excuse, for I had closed the door on my own self. The problem was that after relying so long on instinct and intuition, both these ladies had turned into vultures and were sucking me dry. Even spontaneity had become a blind goat. My haystacks weren't tied down and I was beginning to fear the wind.

The tour with Petty was broken up into parts and during one of the layoffs, one of the organizers, Elliot Roberts, had set up some shows for me to do with The Grateful Dead. I needed to go rehearse with the band for these shows, so I went to San Rafael to meet with The Dead. I thought it would be as easy as jumping rope. After an hour or so, it became clear to me that the band wanted to rehearse more and different songs than I had been used to doing with Petty. They wanted to run over all the songs, the ones they liked, the seldom seen ones. I found myself in a peculiar position and I could hear the brakes screech. If I had known this to begin with, I might not have taken the dates. I had no feelings for any of those songs and didn't know how I could sing them with any intent. A lot of them might have been only sung once anyway, the time that they'd been recorded. There were so many that I couldn't tell which was which—I might even get the words to some mixed up with others. I needed sets of lyrics to understand what they were talking about, and when I saw the lyrics, especially to the older, more obscure songs, I couldn't see how I could get this stuff off emotionally.

I felt like a goon and didn't want to stick around. The whole thing might have been a mistake. I'd have to go someplace for the mentally ill and think about it. After saying that

I'd left something at the hotel, I stepped back outside onto Front Street and started walking, put my head down against the drizzling rain. I wasn't planning on going back. If you have to lie, you should do it quickly and as well as you can. I started up the street—maybe four or five or six blocks went by and then I heard the sounds of a jazz combo playing up ahead. Walking past the door of a tiny bar, I looked in and saw that the musicians were playing at the opposite end of the room. It was raining and there were few people inside. One of them was laughing at something. It looked like the last stop on the train to nowhere and the air was filled with cigarette smoke. Something was calling to me to come in and I entered, walked along the long, narrow bar to where the jazz cats were playing in the back on a raised platform in front of a brick wall. I got within four feet of the stage and just stood there against the bar, ordered a gin and tonic and faced the singer. An older man, he wore a mohair suit, flat cap with a little brim and shiny necktie. The drummer had a rancher's Stetson on and the bassist and pianist were neatly dressed. They played jazz ballads, stuff like "Time on My Hands" and "Gloomy Sunday." The singer reminded me of Billy Eckstine. He wasn't very forceful, but he didn't have to be; he was relaxed, but he sang with natural power. Suddenly and without warning, it was like the guy had an open window to my soul. It was like he was saying, "You should do it this way." All of a sudden, I understood something faster than I ever did before. I could feel how he worked at getting his power, what he was doing to get at it. I knew where the power was coming from and it wasn't his voice, though the voice brought me sharply back to myself. I used to do this thing, I'm thinking. It was a long time ago and it had been automatic. No one had ever taught me. This technique was so elemental, so simple and I'd forgotten. It was like I'd forgotten how to button my own pants. I wondered if I could still do it. I wanted at least a chance to try. If I could in any way get close to handling this technique, I could get off this marathon stunt ride.

Returning to The Dead's rehearsal hall as if nothing had happened, I picked it up where we had left off, couldn't wait to get started—taking one of the songs that they wanted to do, seeing if I could sing it using the same method that the old singer used. I had a premonition something would happen. At first it was hard going, like drilling through a brick wall. All I did was taste the dust. But then miraculously something internal came unhinged. In the beginning all I could get out was a blood-choked coughing grunt and it blasted up from the bottom of my lower self, but it bypassed my brain. That had never happened before. It burned, but I was awake. The scheme wasn't sewed up too tight, would need a lot of stitches, but I grasped the idea. I had to concentrate like mad because I was having to maneuver more than one stratagem at the same time, but now I knew I could perform any of these songs without them having to be restricted to the world of words. This was revelatory. I played these shows with The Dead and never had to think twice about it. Maybe they just dropped something in my drink, I can't say, but anything they wanted to do was fine with me. I had that old jazz singer to thank.

I rejoined Petty for what was to be the final run of a long, drawn-out tour and told Tom's band that if they wanted to play anything, just tell me and we would do it. We started up in the Middle East on that run with two shows in Israel, one in Tel Aviv and one in Jerusalem, the next one in Switzerland and the next one in Italy. In these first four shows I sang eighty different songs, never repeating one, just to see if I could do it. It seemed easy. The angles I was using were unwieldy but highly effective. Because of this different formulaic approach to the vocal technique, my voice never got blown out and I could sing forever without fatigue.

Night after night it was like I was on cruise control. Regardless of all this, I was still planning to quit . . . retire from the scene. I hadn't planned to take it any further, hadn't talked myself out of that—I didn't figure I had much of an audience anyway. Even on this tour, as big as the crowds were, Petty was drawing most of the people. Before the Petty shows I hadn't been going on the road consistently anyway. It was tedious having to assemble and disassemble bands for a thirty- or forty-show run. It had become monotonous. My performances were an act, and the rituals were boring me. Even at the Petty shows I'd see the people in the crowd and they'd look like cutouts from a shooting gallery, there was no connection to them—just subjects at random. I was sick of it—sick of living in a mirage. It was time to break it off. The thought of retirement didn't bother me at all. I'd shaken hands with the idea and had gotten comfortable with it. The only thing that had changed from then 'til now was that performing now wasn't taking anything out of me. I was sailing along.

Then suddenly, one night in Locarno, Switzerland, at the Piazza Grande Locarno, it all fell apart. For an instant I fell into a black hole. The stage was outdoors and the wind was blowing gales, the kind of night that can blow everything away. I opened my mouth to sing and the air tightened up—vocal presence was extinguished and nothing came out. The techniques weren't working. I couldn't believe it. I thought I had it down so well, yet it was just another trick. There's no pleasure in getting caught in a situation like this. You can get a panic attack. You're in front of thirty thousand people and they're staring at you and nothing is coming out. Things can really get stupid. Figuring I had nothing to lose and not needing to take any precautions, I conjured up some different type of mechanism to jump-start the other techniques that weren't working. I just did it automatically out of thin air, cast my own spell to drive out the devil. Instantly, it was like a thoroughbred had charged through the gates. Everything came back, and it came back in multidimension. Even I was surprised. It left me kind of shaky. Immediately, I was flying high. This new thing had taken place right in front of everybody's eyes. A difference in energy might have been perceived, but that was about all. Nobody would have noticed that a metamorphosis had taken place. Now the energy was coming from a hundred different angles, completely unpredictable ones. I had a new faculty and it seemed to surpass all the other human requirements. If I ever wanted a different purpose, I had one. It was like I'd become a new performer, an unknown one in the true sense of the word. In more than thirty years of performing, I had never seen this place before, never been here. If I didn't exist, someone would have to have invented me.

The shows with Petty finished up in December, and I saw that instead of being stranded somewhere at the end of the story, I was actually in the prelude to the beginning of another one. I could put my decision to retire on hold. It might be interesting to start up again, put myself in the service of the public. I also knew that it would take years to perfect and refine this idiom, but because of my fame and reputation, the opportunity would be there. It seemed like the right time for it. After the tour, I was sitting in London at the St. James's Club with Elliot Roberts, who had engineered both the Petty shows and the Dead shows. I told him I needed to work two hundred show dates the next year. Elliot was pragmatic, said that I should take a couple of years off and then come back.

"The picture is perfect like it is," he said. "Let it be."

"No," I said. "It's not perfect and I have to correct it."

I poured the beer from the last bottle into two glasses and listened to him say that it might be more practical to wait at least 'til spring, give him more of a chance to get it together.

"All right," I told him. "That's good."

"I'll get you the band, too," he said.

"Sure, I don't mind." I thought that was fantastic. The thought hadn't even crossed my mind, that somebody else would find me the band. That would take a big weight off. I also told him that I needed him to book a similar amount of shows in the same towns the following year and also the year after that—a three-year schedule of more or less the same towns. I figured it would take me at least three years to get to the beginning, to find the right audience, or for the right audience to find me. The reason I thought it would take three years was that after the first year a lot of the older people wouldn't be coming back, but younger fans would bring their friends the second year so attendance would be just about equal. And in the third year, those people would also bring their friends and it would form the nucleus of my future audience. The fact that some of my songs were more than twenty years old wouldn't matter. I'd have to start at the bottom and I wasn't even on the bottom yet. There was nothing evolutionary about what I was about to do, no one could have expected it. Without knowing as much, I had a gut feeling that I had created a new genre, a style that didn't exist as of yet and one that would be entirely my own. All the cylinders were working and the vehicle was for hire. I definitely needed a new audience because my audience at that time had more or less grown up on my records and was past the point of accepting me as a new artist and this was understandable. In many ways, this audience was past its prime and its reflexes were shot. They came to stare and not participate. That was okay, but the kind of crowd that would have to find me would be the kind of crowd who didn't know what yesterday was. My fame was immense, could fill a football stadium, but it was like having some weird diploma that won't get you into any college. Promoters didn't want to touch me, either. They'd been burned often in the past and the anger hadn't gone out of them. "I'm all for you," they might say, "but I can't do it." In reality I was just above a club act. Could hardly fill small theaters. There weren't any alchemic shortcuts—critics could dismiss me easily, too, so I wouldn't be able to depend on them to tell my tale. Most music journalists had become nothing more than a public relations staff anyway. I would have to rely on word of mouth. I'd rely on that like my life depended on it. Word of mouth spreads like wildfire, doesn't take "no" for an answer. I wished I was at least twenty years younger, wished that I had just dropped on the scene all over again. But what could you do? I would have liked some help, but I didn't expect any. I'd been around too long for things like that. I was going to do like Roberts had said—wait until spring. I'd go home knowing that I was on the threshold of something— maybe not as pure as heaven's rain, but something anyway, and that whatever I was on the threshold of was going to deepen as the years went on.

Spring seemed like a long time to wait, but I can be patient. Maybe I should bring something to read. There were plenty of days coming when it would all come together. My destiny was shining silver in the sun. Life had lost its toxic effect. I had nothing more to bitch about . . . then it hit me.

Returning from the emergency room with my arm entombed in plaster I fell into a chair—something heavy had come against me. It was like a black leopard had torn into my tattered flesh. It was plenty sore. After being on the threshold of something bold, innovative and adventurous, I was now on the threshold of nothing, ruined. This could be the last turn of the screw. The trail had come to a halt. Only hours earlier things had been pretty wholesome and methodical. I was anticipating the spring, looking forward to stepping out on the stage where I'd be entirely at once author, actor, prompter, stage manager, audience and critic combined. That would be different. Now I was staring into the dark where all things seemed to be coming from. Like Falstaff, I'd been heading from one play into the next, but now fate itself had played a nightmarish trick. I wasn't Falstaff anymore.

My bright eyes were dull and I could do nothing. All I could do was groan. Here's why. Besides my devotion to a new vocal technique, something else would go along with helping me re-create my songs. It seemed like I had always

accompanied myself on the guitar. I played in the casual
Carter Family flat-picking style and the playing was more or
less out of habit and routine. It always had been clear and
readable but didn't reflect my psyche in any way. It didn't
have to. The style had been practical, but now I was going to
push that away from the table, too, and replace it with something more active with more definition of presence.

I didn't invent this style. It had been shown to me in the
early '60s by Lonnie Johnson. Lonnie was the great jazz and
blues artist from the '30s who was still performing in the
'60s. Robert Johnson had learned a lot from him. Lonnie
took me aside one night and showed me a style of playing
based on an odd- instead of even-number system. He had me
play chords and he demonstrated how to do it. This was just
something he knew about, not necessarily something he used
because he did so many different kinds of songs. He said,
"This might help you," and I had the idea that he was showing me something secretive, though it didn't make sense to
me at that time because I needed to strum the guitar in order
to get my ideas across. It's a highly controlled system of playing and relates to the notes of a scale, how they combine nu-
merically, how they form melodies out of triplets and are
axiomatic to the rhythm and the chord changes. I never used
this style, didn't see that there'd be any purpose to it. But
now all of a sudden it came back to me, and I realized that
this way of playing would revitalize my world. The method
works on higher or lower degrees depending on different patterns and the syncopation of a piece. Very few would be con-
verted to it because it had nothing to do with technique and
musicians work their whole lives to be technically superior
players. You probably wouldn't pay any attention to this

method if you weren't a singer. It was easy for me to pick this up. I understood the rules and critical elements because Lonnie had showed them to me so crystal clear. It would be up to me now to expel everything that wasn't natural to it. I would have to master that style and sing to it.

The system works in a cyclical way. Because you're thinking in odd numbers instead of even numbers, you're playing with a different value system. Popular music is usually based on the number 2 and then filled in with fabrics, colors, effects and technical wizardry to make a point. But the total effect is usually depressing and oppressive and a dead end which at the most can only last in a nostalgic way. If you're using an odd numerical system, things that strengthen a performance automatically begin to happen and make it memorable for the ages. You don't have to plan or think ahead. In a diatonic scale there are eight notes, in a pentatonic scale there are five. If you're using the first scale, and you hit 2, 5 and 7 to the phrase and then repeat it, a melody forms. Or you can use 2 three times. Or you can use 4 once and 7 twice. It's infinite what you can do, and each time would create a different melody. The possibilities are endless. A song executes itself on several fronts and you can ignore musical customs. All you need is a drummer and a bass player, and all shortcomings become irrelevant as long as you stick to the system. With any type of imagination you can hit notes at intervals and between backbeats, creating counterpoint lines and then you sing off of it. There's no mystery to it and it's not a technical trick. The scheme is for real. For me, this style would be most advantageous, like a delicate design that would arrange the structure of whatever piece I was performing. The listener would recognize and feel the dynamics immediately. Things could explode or retreat back at any time and there would be no way to predict the consciousness of any song. And because this works on its own mathematical formula, it can't miss. I'm not a numerologist. I don't know why the number 3 is more metaphysically powerful than the number 2, but it is. Passion and enthusiasm, which sometimes can be enough to sway a crowd, aren't even necessary. You can manufacture faith out of nothing and there are an infinite number of patterns and lines that connect from key to key—all deceptively simple. You gain power with the least amount of effort, trust that the listeners make their own connections, and it's very seldom that they don't. Miscalculations can also cause no serious harm. As long as you recognize it, you can turn the dynamic around architecturally in a second.

This is definitely a style that benefits the singer. In folk oriented and jazz-blues songs, it's perfect. I needed to play this way though I didn't need to be conspicuous about it because what I'd be playing was primarily orchestral, and if it's orchestral it would make sense that there should be a combination of instruments playing the part. I didn't have the time to put into that. I wouldn't be able to get that. I had to be more subtle. If my instrument was buried in the mix, where only I could hear it, I was thinking that it might be more effective. It wasn't like I was trying to play lead guitar and wow anybody. What I needed to do was phrase my singing off the bone structure of what I played. Ideally, I would have liked to have taken a song, played it more than a few times for a musicologist who would then write the basic parts for an orchestrated version. The orchestra could even play the vocal line. I wouldn't even have to be there.

What was different about this was that in the past on my

records there is no kinetic arrangement to any piece. In the studio the songs had only been sketched out but never brought from the shadows. There'd always been too many problems—wrestling with lyric phrasing, changing lyrics, switching melody lines, keys, tempos, any number of things all the while searching for a song's stylistic identity. Those who had followed me for years and thought they knew my songs might be a little confounded by the way they now were about to be played. The total effect would be physiological, and triplet forms would fashion melodies at intervals. This is what would drive the song—not necessarily the lyrical content. I had perfect faith in this system and knew it would work. Playing this way appealed to me. A lot of folks would say that the songs were altered and others would say that this was the way they should have sounded in the first place. You could take your pick.

Once I understood what I was doing, I realized that I wasn't the first one to do it, that Link Wray had done the same thing in his classic song "Rumble" many years earlier. Link's song had no lyrics, but he had played with the same numerical system. It would never have occurred to me where the song's power had come from because I had been hypnotized by the tone of the piece. I'd also thought I'd seen Martha Reeves do the same thing. I'd seen her in New York a few years earlier where she'd been playing with the Motown Revue. Her band couldn't keep up with her, had no idea what she was doing and just plodded along. She beat a tambourine in triplet form, up close to her ear and she phrased the song as if the tambourine were her entire band. A tambourine makes no melody lines, but the concept was similar.

When Lonnie had showed this to me so many years earlier it was as if he was saying something to me in a foreign language. I understood the etymology of it, I just didn't get how it could be applicable in any way. Now it all clicked. Now I could start getting into it. With a new incantation code to infuse my vocals with manifest presence I could ride high, unconsciously drag endless skeletons from the closet. Thematic triplets making everything hypnotic. I could even hypnotize myself. I could do this night after night. No fatigue or weariness. I had all the technical theory I would need. My audience would stop being a shady army of faceless people. Of course, some of them would still only concentrate on the lyrics and they might be dismayed because the two-beat strum they'd been used to for so long would now be off rhythm, refocused and rushing the songs into the heart of unimagined territory. But that's okay, they could handle it.

I had too long been freeze frozen in the secular temple of a museum anyway. It's not a complicated thing. There are thousands if not millions of variations of these patterns so you never run out of ideas. You're always at some unexploited fix point. It's not a heavy theorized thing, it's geometrical. I'm not that good at math, but I do know that the universe is formed with mathematical principles whether I understand them or not, and I was going to let that guide me. My playing was going to be an impellent in equanimity to my voice and I would use different algorithms that the ear is not accustomed to. It should be, but it's not.

This was coming into my life at exactly the right time. The deal would be complete. My lyrics, some written as long as twenty years earlier, would now explode musicologically like an ice cloud. Nobody else played this way and I thought of it as a new form of music. Strict and orthodox. Not one thing improvisational about it. The opposite of improvisation. Improvisation wouldn't have done me any good, in fact, it would have taken me the other way. Also, you don't need to feel any certain way in order to play like this. It doesn't run on emotion. That was another good thing. I had been leaving a lot of my songs on the floor like shot rabbits for a long time. That wouldn't be happening anymore. The thing was, I needed two hands. If I couldn't play, I wouldn't be doing anything better than ever now. Nothing would be exactly right.

It was noontime and I was shuffling around in my old-fashion garden. Cutting across the vacant lot to a bank of field flowers where my dogs and horses were, the strangled cry of a gull came whipping through the wind. Walking back to the main house, I caught a glimpse of the sea through the leafy boughs of the pines. I wasn't near it, but could feel the power beneath its colors. Seemed like a net had fallen over me and if I'd tried to run, I'd only get more entangled. My hand had been gashed pretty good—no feeling in the nerves. Maybe it might not heal, never be the same, and the sooner I believed it, the better. Oh, the wicked ironies of life. I'd gotten a cosmic kick in the pants. I probably should have been wearing steel underwear.

Things changed a little, though, later in the week when I went to a school play that one of my daughters was in. The creative energy displayed onstage brought me to my senses. In the midst of this, another piece of sad news came in. My sixty-three-foot sailboat had hit a reef in Panama. During the night, the harbor lights had been misread. The boat was put into reverse and the rudder broke off. She couldn't come down off the reef and the wind blew the boat up further. She lay on her side for a week, but it was too late. A lot of lines snapped trying to pull her off. Eventually, the sea took her back and the boat was gone. In the ten years that I had her my family and I had sailed the entire Caribbean and spent time on every island from Martinique to Barbados. This loss paled somewhat compared to the use of my hand, but I had been grateful for the boat and the news came as an unwelcomed shock.

One night I turned on the TV and saw soul singer Joe Tex on *The Tonight Show with Johnny Carson*. Joe sang and left. Johnny didn't talk to him—not like he did to the other guests. Johnny just waved to him from his desk. Carson used to like to talk to his guests about golf and things like that, but he had nothing to say to Joe. I didn't think he would have anything to say to me either. All of his guests tried to be funny, put on a happy face, not come unglued, be like Gene Kelly and go singing in the rain even during a big downpour. If I did that I'd get pneumonia. You had to act as if everything was wonderful. Like Joe Tex, I'd never been much in the mainstream. I thought about how much more I was like him than like Carson. I shut the TV off.

Outside I heard a woodpecker tapping up against a tree in the dark. As long as I was alive I was going to stay interested in something. If my hand didn't heal, what was I going to do with the remainder of my days? Not be a part of the music business, that's for sure. Get as far away from it as possible. I fantasized about the business world. What could be more

simple or elegant than venturing into that? It might be interesting to try the conventional life for a while. I was thinking
ahead. I called a friend of mine who put me in touch with a
broker who bought and sold independent businesses. Starting one from scratch was out of the question. I told him that
I was thinking about selling all I had and trading for something. What do you have? He came by and brought
brochures on just about every enterprise going—facts and
figures all down to the minutest detail . . . self-contained
businesses all over the place—sugarcane, trucks and tractors, a wooden leg factory in North Carolina, furniture factory in Alabama, a fish farm, flower plantations and more. It
was overwhelming. Just looking at this stuff made the weight
press down above my eyes. How do you decide, especially if
you don't have any real interest in any of them? My trusty
aide and mechanic, who was always helpful in a functional
way, said, "Leave it to me, gov. I'll go look at 'em—find the
best one." I knew he could do it, go out in the world and find
something. I didn't want to go ahead too fast, though, do
anything that later I'd be sorry about. I told him I'd give him
a definite date some other time. I wasn't too anxious to do
any follow-up.

I began to see less and less of the daylight. I'd lay back in a
chair to rest my eyes and then two or three hours later wake
up—go off to get something and forget what I went there to
get. I'm glad my wife was around. In times like this, it's good
if you're with someone who desires the same things as you and
is open and not closed to your energy. She could make me feel
like I wasn't in some godforsaken hole. One day when she was
wearing metallic sunglasses I could see myself in miniature
and thought how small everything had become.

The one thing that I had no strong desire to do was to compose songs. I hadn't written any in a long while, anyway. I had stopped doing that, just wasn't crazy for it. My last couple of record albums didn't contain many of my own compositions, anyway. As far as being a songwriter went, I couldn't have had a more casual attitude. I'd written plenty and that was fine. I did whatever it took to get there, had reached my goal and had no more high ambitions for it. Had long ceased running towards it. When and if an idea would come, I would no longer try to get in touch with the base of its power. I could easily deny it and stay clear of it. Just couldn't make myself do it. I never expected to write anything ever again. Didn't need any more songs anyway.

One night when everyone was asleep and I was sitting at the kitchen table, nothing on the hillside but a shiny bed of lights—all that changed. I wrote about twenty verses for a song called "Political World" and this was about the first of twenty songs I would write in the next month or so. They came from out of the blue. Maybe I wouldn't have written them if I wasn't laid up like I was. Maybe, maybe not. They were easy to write, seemed to float downstream with the current. It's not like they'd been faint or far away—they were right there in my face, but if you'd look too steady at them, they'd be gone.

A song is like a dream, and you try to make it come true. They're like strange countries that you have to enter. You can write a song anywhere, in a railroad compartment, on a boat, on horseback—it helps to be moving. Sometimes people who have the greatest talent for writing songs never write any because they are not moving. I wasn't moving in any of these songs, not externally, anyway. Still, I got them all down as if I was. Sometimes things you see and hear outside of yourself can influence a song. The song "Political World" could have been triggered by current events. There was a heated presidential race underway, you couldn't avoid hearing about it. But I had no interest in politics as an art form, so I don't think that was all there was to it. The song is too broad. The political world in the song is more of an underworld, not the world where men live, toil and die like men. With the song, I thought I might have broken through to something. It was like you wake up from a deep and drugged slumber and somebody strikes a little silver gong and you come to your senses. There were about twice as many verses as were later recorded. Verses like, "We live in a political world. Flags flying into the breeze. Comes out of the blue—moves towards you—like a knife cutting through cheese."

From the far end of the kitchen a silver beam of moonlight pierced through the leaded panes of the window illuminating the table. The song seemed to hit the wall, and I stopped writing and swayed backwards in the chair, felt like lighting up a fine cigar and climbing into a warm bath. This was the first song I'd written in a while and it looked like a clawish hand had written it. I knew that if I ever was to record again, I could use it. I was aware that I wasn't in the song, but that was all right; I didn't feel like being in there. I put the words in a drawer, couldn't play them anyway, and snapped out of a trance.

The low growl of a motorcycle rumbled up the roadway alongside the garage and I cranked the window open wider— smelled the pomegranate blossoms blowing in a breezy fashion. I cast an embracing glance over the primordial land-scape. It had been a while since I had written a song from start to finish all at once. "Political World" reminded me of another song I had written a couple of years before called "Clean-Cut Kid." I wasn't in that one, either.

Later in the week we went out to see Eugene O'Neill's *Long Day's Journey into Night*. The play was hard to bear, family life at its worst, self-centered morphine addicts. I was glad when it was over. I felt sorry for these people, but none of them touched me. After that, we stopped into Harvelle's, a local blues club on 4th Street, to see Guitar Shorty and J. J. "Badboy" Jones. It's always a trip seeing Shorty. He plays guitar with everything but his hands. I wished I could have done that. Shorty sounds like Guitar Slim, but he does some wild gymnastics that you'd never imagine Guitar Slim doing. While strolling back to the car along 4th Street, a homeless guy holding his head in his hands was being ordered to move by a couple of cops. A tiny spaniel lay at the guy's feet, the dog's beady black eyes following the nervous movements of his master. I couldn't see that the officers took any pride in what they had to do.

Later that night back at the house I started writing the song "What Good Am I?" . . . wrote it in a small art studio on the property. It's more than an art studio. There's arc-welding equipment in there, and I'd made ornate iron gates out of junk scrap metal in the barnlike room. Most of the place has a cement floor, but there's another area covered with linoleum. There's a table there and a window with low-ered blinds that looks out over a gully. The entire song came to me all at once; don't know what could have brought it on. Maybe seeing the homeless guy, the dog, the cops, the dreary play and maybe even the antics of Guitar Shorty might have had something to do with it. Who knows? Sometimes you see things in life that make your heart turn rotten and your gut sick and nauseous and you try to capture that feeling without naming the specifics. There were extra verses for this, too. Here's one. "What good am I if I'm walking on eggs, if I'm wild with excitement and wet between the legs? If I'm right in the thick of it and I don't know why, what good am I?" I put this song away in the same drawer with "Political World"—I wondered what they'd have to say to each other. No melodies for either. I went to sleep.

My mother and my aunt Etta were staying with us and they'd be up early, so I wanted to be up early, too. The next day was overcast and a fog hung in the air. My aunt was in the kitchen and I sat down with her to talk and drink coffee. The radio was playing and morning news was on. I was startled to hear that Pete Maravich, the basketball player, had collapsed on a basketball court in Pasadena, just fell over and never got up. I'd seen Maravich play in New Orleans once, when the Utah Jazz were the New Orleans Jazz. He was something to see—mop of brown hair, floppy socks—the holy terror of the basketball world—high flyin'—magician of the court. The night I saw him he dribbled the ball with his head, scored a behind the back, no look basket—dribbled the length of the court, threw the ball up off the glass and caught his own pass. He was fantastic. Scored something like thirty-eight points. He could have played blind. Pistol Pete hadn't played professionally for a while, and he was thought of as forgotten. I hadn't forgotten about him, though. Some people seem to fade away but then when they are truly gone, it's like they didn't fade away at all.

I started and completed the song "Dignity" the same day I'd heard the sad news about Pistol Pete. I started writing it in the early afternoon, about the time the morning news began to wear away and it took me the rest of the day and into the night to finish it. It's like I saw the song up in front of me and overtook it, like I saw all the characters in this song and elected to cast my fortunes with them. I have a problem sometimes remembering someone's real name, so I give them another one, something that more accurately describes them, and I had a tendency to do that throughout this song. There were more verses with other individuals in different interplays. The Green Beret, The Sorceress, Virgin Mary, The Wrong Man, Big Ben, and The Cripple and The Honkey. The list could be endless. All kinds of identifiable characters that found their way into the song but somehow didn't survive. I heard the whole piece in my head— rhythm, tempo, melody line, the whole bit. I'd always be able to remember this song. The wind could never blow it out of my head. This song was a good thing to have. On a song like this, there's no end to things. You hold an electric torch up to someone's face and see what's there. Yet to me, it's amazingly simple, no complications, everything pans out. As long as the things you see don't go by in a blur of light and shade, you're okay. Love, fear, hate, happiness— all in unmistakable terms, a thousand and one subtle ramifications. This song is like that. One line brings up another, like when your left foot steps forward and your right drags up to it. If I'd have written this ten years earlier, I'd have gone immediately to the recording studio. But a lot had changed and I had no anxiety about that stuff anymore, didn't feel the urge and necessity of it. I didn't feel like recording anyway. It was tedious and I didn't like the current sounds—mine or anybody else's. I didn't know why an old Alan Lomax field recording sounded better to me, but it did. I didn't think I could make a good record if I tried for a hundred years.

One day I went to the clinic where the doctor examined my hand, said the healing was coming along fine and that the feeling in the nerves might have a chance of coming back soon. It was encouraging to hear that. I returned to the house where my eldest son was sitting around in the kitchen with his soon-to-be wife. There was a thick seafood stew brewing up on the stove as I walked by. I took the cover off the pot to check it out.

"What do you think?" my future daughter-in-law asked.

"What about the whiskey sauce?"

"It has to be arranged," she said.

I dropped the cover back on the pot and went out to the garage. The rest of the day went by like a puff of wind.

The song "Disease of Conceit" definitely has gospel overtones. Again, events might trigger a song—sometimes they might start the motor. Recently, the popular Baptist preacher Jimmy Swaggart had been defrocked by the Assembly of God leadership for refusing to stop preaching. Jimmy was Jerry Lee Lewis's first cousin and was a big TV star, and the news came as a shock. He'd been linked to a prostitute, caught on camera leaving her motel room in sweatpants. Swaggart was ordered to vacate the pulpit temporarily. He wept in public and asked forgiveness, but still was told to stop preaching for a while. He couldn't help himself, though, and quickly went back to preaching as if nothing had happened and they defrocked him. The story was strange. Swaggart clearly wasn't in good shape, hadn't looked at the road. The story didn't make any sense. The Bible is full of these things. A lot of those old kings and leaders had many wives and concubines and Hosea the Prophet was even married to a prostitute, and it didn't stop him from being a holy man. But these were different times and for Swaggart, it was the end of the line. Reality can be overwhelming. It can also be a shadow, depending on how you look at it. As for me, I wondered what this harlot might have looked like that lured this famous preacher into rolling in the muck. A damsel of tempting statuesque beauty? Probably. It would have to be. If you paid any amount of mind to all this Mickey Mouse stuff, the way these hoity-toity people's doors and windows aren't shut tight, you might end up in a private lunatic asylum. This incident might have had something to do with inspiring the song, but then again, it's hard to say. Conceit is not necessarily a disease. It's more of a weakness. A conceited person could be set up easily and brought down accordingly. Let's face it, a conceited person has a fake sense of self-worth, an inflated opinion of himself. A person like this can be controlled and manipulated completely if you know what buttons to push. So in a sense, that's what the lyrics are talking about. The song rose up until I could read the look in its eyes. In the quiet of the evening I didn't have to hunt far for it. As always, there were a few verses left behind. "There's a whole lot of people dreaming tonight about the disease of conceit, whole lot of people screaming tonight about the disease of conceit. I'll hump ya and I'll dump ya and I'll blow your house down. I'll slice into your cake before I leave town. Pick a number—take a seat, with the disease of conceit."

I finished the lyrics and left the studio, went back to the

main house. Wind was blowing through the tall bamboo. The heavy chrome bumper from my old battered Buick was shining in the moonlight. I hadn't driven that car in years, was thinking of taking it apart and using it for scrap metal sculpture. The dark gully was overgrown with brush and there was a fox or a coyote down there. The dogs were yapping and chasing something. The lights from the main house were glittering like the inside of a casino. I went in, shut 'em off and glanced at one of my guitars which I hadn't touched in a while. I was reluctant to touch it. Might as well get some rest, I thought, and then I crawled into bed.

The song "What Was It You Wanted?" was also a quickly written one. I heard the lyric and melody together in my head and it played itself in a minor key. You have to be economical writing a song like this. If you've ever been the object of curiosity, then you know what this song is about. It doesn't need much explanation. Folks who are soft and helpless sometimes make the most noise. They can obstruct you in a lot of ways. It's pointless trying to resist them or deal with them by force. Sometimes you just have to bite your upper lip and put sunglasses on. Songs like this are strange dogs. They don't make good companions. Again, there were extra verses. "What was it you wanted? Can I be of any use? Can I do something for you? Do I have enough juice? Wherever you're off to, one thing you should know. You still got seven hundred miles yet still to go." The song almost wrote itself. It just descended upon my head. Maybe a couple of years earlier I might have rejected it, never finished it. Not now, though.

Another song, "Everything Is Broken" was made up of quick choppy strokes. The semantic meaning is all in the sounds of the words. The lyrics are your dance partner. It works on a mechanical level. Everything is broken or it looks that way—chipped, cracked, in need of repair. Things are broken, then rebroken, made into something else, then broken again. Once when I was lying on the beach in Coney Island, I saw a portable radio in the sand . . . a beautiful General Electric, self charging—built like a battleship—and it was broken. I could have remembered that image at the top of the song. But I had seen a lot of other things broken, too—bowls, brass lamps, vessels and jars and jugs, buildings, busses, sidewalks, trees, landscapes—all these things, when they're broken, make you feel ill at ease. I thought of all the best things in the world, the things I had a great affection for. Sometimes it might be a place, a place to start an evening from and go all night, but then these places become broken, too, and can't be pieced back together. There's a smashing and crashing of furniture and glass. Something just breaks and gives no warning. Sometimes your dearest possession. It's beastly hard to fix anything. There were extra verses for this, too. "Broken strands of prairie grass. Broken magnifying glass. I visited the broken orphanage and rode upon the broken bridge. I'm crossin' the river goin' to Hoboken. Maybe over there, things ain't broken." That was my bit of optimism to go along with a song like this. These then, and some other songs, I wrapped up and put them away to stay where they lay, kept them in a drawer, but I could sense their presence.

In time, my hand got right and it was ironic. I stopped writing the songs. The doctor encouraged me to play my guitar—that stretching my hand was therapeutic, actually good for my hand, and I was now doing that a lot. I could begin the shows that were scheduled for me, starting in the spring and it seemed like I was back where I began.

One night, Bono, the singer from U2, was over for dinner with some other friends. Spending time with Bono was like eating dinner on a train—feels like you're moving, going somewhere. Bono's got the soul of an ancient poet and you have to be careful around him. He can roar 'til the earth shakes. He's also a closet philosopher. He brought a case of Guinness with him. We were talking about things that you talk about when you're spending the winter with somebody— talked about Jack Kerouac. Bono knows Kerouac's stuff pretty good. Kerouac, who celebrated American towns like Truckee, Fargo, Butte and Madora—towns that most Americans never heard of. It seems funny that Bono would know more about Kerouac than most Americans. Bono says things that can sway anybody. He's like that guy in the old movie, the one who beats up a rat with his bare hands and wrings a confession out of him. If Bono had come to America in the early part of the century he would have been a cop. He seems to know a lot about America and what he doesn't, he's curious about.

We talked about fame and both agreed that the funny thing about fame is that nobody believes it's you. Warhol's name got batted around, too. Warhol, the king of pop. One art critic in Warhol's time had said that he'd give you a million dollars if you could find one ounce of hope or love in any of his work, as if that was important. Names appear in conversation and slip away. Names that have a certain feel to them. Idi Amin, Lenny Bruce, Roman Polanski, Herman

Melville, Mose Allison, Soutine the painter, the Jimmy Reed of the art world. When Bono or me aren't exactly sure about somebody, we just make it up. We can strengthen any argument by expanding on something either real or not real. Neither of us are nostalgic, and nostalgia doesn't enter into anything and we're gonna make damn sure about that. Bono says something about the English coming here and settling Jamestown and that the Irish built New York City—talks about the rightness, the richness, glory, beauty, wonder and magnificence of America. I told him that if he wants to see the birthplace of America, he should go to Alexandria, Minnesota.

It was just me and Bono sitting around the table. Everyone else was scattered about. My wife came by and said she was going up to bed. "Go on up," I said. "I'm going up in a minute." It took me a while to get there, though, and the case of Guinness was almost gone. "Where's Alexandria?" Bono asked. I tell him that's where the Vikings came and settled in the 1300s, said that there's a wooden statue of a Viking in Alexandria and it doesn't look anything like a dignified founding father of America. He's bearded, wears a helmet, strapped knee-high boots, long dagger in a sheath, holding a spear at his side, wearing a kilt—holding a shield that says, "The birthplace of America." Bono asks me how to get there and I tell him to follow the river up through Winona, Lake City, Frontenac and get onto Highway 10 all the way to Wadena, make a left on 29 and you'll run right into it. You shouldn't have any trouble getting there. Bono asked me where I was originally from and I told him the Iron Trail, the Mesabi Iron Range. "What does Mesabi mean?" he asked. I told him it was an Ojibwa word, means Land of Giants.

The night wore on. Out at sea, the lights of a freighter moved by every so often. Bono asked me if I'd had any new songs, any unrecorded ones. It just so happened that I did. I went into the other room and pulled them out of the drawer, brought them back and showed them to him. He looked them over, said I should record them. I said that I wasn't so sure about that, thought that maybe I should pour lighter fluid over them—said that I had been having a hard time making records, making that work out. He said, "No, no," and he brought up the name of Daniel Lanois . . . said that U2 had worked with him and he had been a great partner—that he'd be perfect for me to work with—would have much to scramble into the mix. Lanois had musical ideas that were compatible to mine. Bono picked up the phone and dialed the man, put him on the phone with me and we spoke for a moment. Basically, what Lanois said was that he was working out of New Orleans and told me that if I was ever there, I should look him up. I said that I would do that. To be sure, I was in no hurry to record. Performing was what was on my mind first and foremost. If I ever did make another record, it would have to have something in common with that purpose. I had a clear road ahead and didn't want to blow the chance to regain my musical freedom. I needed to let things straighten out and not get mixed up anymore.

It was autumn in New Orleans and I was staying at the Marie Antoinette Hotel, sitting around by the pool in the courtyard with G. E. Smith, the guitar player in my band. I was waiting for the arrival of Daniel Lanois. The air was sticky humid. Branches of trees hung overhead near a wooden trellis that climbed a garden wall. Water lilies floated in the dark squared fountain and the stone floor was inlaid with swirling marble squares. We were sitting at a table near a small statue of Cleo with a clipped nose. The statue seemed to know we were there. The courtyard door swung back and Danny came in. G.E., who surveyed the world with a set of unblinking steel-blue eyes, looked up warily and met the gaze of Lanois with a glance. "See ya in a moment," G.E. said, got up and left. The courtyard was haunted with friendly spirits and with a vague aroma of perfumed roses and lavender. Lanois sat down. He was *noir* all the way—dark sombrero, black britches, high boots, slip-on gloves—all shadow and silhouette—dimmed out, a black prince from the black hills. He was scuff proof. He orders a beer and I get an aspirin and Coke. He got right down to business, asked what kind of songs I had, what kind of record I had in mind. It wasn't a real question—just a way to start the conversation.

Over the course of an hour or so, I knew I could work with this guy, had a conviction about him. I didn't know what kind of record I had in mind. Didn't even know if the songs were any good. Hadn't looked at the songs since I'd shown them to Bono, who liked them a lot, but who knows if he really did. Most of them didn't even have melodies. Danny says to me, "You can make a great record, you know, if you really want to." I flatly said, "Of course I'll need your help," and he nodded. He wanted to know if I had any musicians in mind. When I told him I didn't, he asked about the band he had heard me play with the night before. "Not this time," I said. He told me that hit records don't matter to him, "Miles Davis never made any." That was fine with me.

At this point, we weren't thinking of any fixed time to start, we were just putting our heads together in order to see if they were both on the same page—both right side up. We talked most of the afternoon and the purple sunset began to fade. He asked me if I wanted to hear the record he was making with The Neville Brothers and I said, sure. We went over to the makeshift recording studio that he'd set up in a Victorian mansion on St. Charles Avenue, a boulevard lined with enormous oaks where streetcars, olive green, run a thirteen-mile route. The Neville Brothers' record *Yellow Moon* was nearly completed and we sat down to listen to some of the playbacks. One of The Neville Brothers was resting in the room, hands together in his lap, head tipped back, cap down over his eyes and his feet were up over one of the chairs. It surprised me to hear two of my songs, "Hollis Brown" and "With God on Our Side" sung by Aaron Neville. What a coincidence. Aaron is one of the world's great singers, a figure of rugged power, built like a tank but has the most angelic singing voice, a voice that could almost redeem a lost soul. It seems so incongruous. So much for appearances. There's so much spirituality in his singing that it could even bring sanity back in a world of madness. It always surprises me to hear a song of mine done by an artist like this who is on such a high level. Over the years, songs might get away from you, but a version like this always brings it closer again.

After hearing Aaron's renditions of my songs, I faintly remembered the reason we were there. Danny asked me if any of my new songs were like these. I told him, not much, I didn't think so, but we'll see. I liked the atmosphere and the setup a lot. Lanois said he could rent another house in the district and we could record in it. I played some fragmented melodies on the piano to go with some of the songs and we called it a day. I didn't realize he'd remember the spontaneous melodies and it would later come back to haunt me. We both agreed to try and meet up next spring. I liked Lanois. He didn't have any colossal ego, seemed disciplined—nothing wheeler-dealer about him, and he had an extraordinary passion for music. If anybody had the light, I figured Danny did and he might turn it on. He seemed like the kind of cat who, when he works on something, he did it like the fate of the world hinged on its outcome. We'd meet up again in March, like something foretold in the scriptures.

I showed up in New Orleans in early spring, moved into a large rented house near Audubon Park, a comfortable place, all the rooms fair sized, furnished quite simply, wardrobe cupboards in just about every room. We couldn't have come to a better place for me. It was really perfect. You could work slow here. They were waiting at the studio, but I didn't feel like jumping into anything. Sooner or later I'd have to get to the point but I could try it on another day. I brought a lot of the songs with me, I was pretty sure they would hold up well.

Right now, I strolled into the dusk. The air was murky and intoxicating. At the corner of the block, a giant, gaunt cat crouched on a concrete ledge. I got up close to it and stopped and the cat didn't move. I wished I had a jug of milk. My eyes and ears were open, my consciousness fully alive. The first thing you notice about New Orleans are the burying grounds—the cemeteries—and they're a cold proposition, one of the best things there are here. Going by, you try to be as quiet as possible, better to let them sleep. Greek, Roman, sepulchres—palatial mausoleums made to order, phantomesque, signs and symbols of hidden decay—ghosts of women and men who have sinned and who've died and are now living in tombs. The past doesn't pass away so quickly here. You could be dead for a long time. The ghosts race towards the light, you can almost hear the heavy breathing— spirits, all determined to get somewhere. New Orleans, unlike a lot of those places you go back to and that don't have the magic anymore, still has got it. Night can swallow you up, yet none of it touches you. Around any corner, there's a promise of something daring and ideal and things are just getting going. There's something obscenely joyful behind every door, either that or somebody crying with their head in their hands. A lazy rhythm looms in the dreamy air and the atmosphere pulsates with bygone duels, past-life romance, comrades requesting comrades to aid them in some way. You can't see it, but you know it's here. Somebody is always sinking. Everyone seems to be from some very old Southern families. Either that or a foreigner. I like the way it is.

There are a lot of places I like, but I like New Orleans better. There's a thousand different angles at any moment. At any time you could run into a ritual honoring some vaguely known queen. Bluebloods, titled persons like crazy drunks, lean weakly against the walls and drag themselves through the gutter. Even they seem to have insights you might want to listen to. No action seems inappropriate here. The city is one very long poem. Gardens full of pansies, pink petunias, opiates. Flower-bedecked shrines, white myrtles, bougainvillea and purple oleander stimulate your senses, make you feel cool and clear inside.

Everything in New Orleans is a good idea. Bijou Temple–type cottages and lyric cathedrals side by side. Houses and mansions, structures of wild grace. Italianate, Gothic, Romanesque, Greek Revival standing in a long line in the rain. Roman Catholic art. Sweeping front porches, turrets, cast-iron balconies, colonnades—thirty-foot columns, gloriously beautiful—double pitched roofs, all the architecture of the whole wide world and it doesn't move. All that and a town square where public executions took place. In New Orleans you could almost see other dimensions. There's only one day at a time here, then it's tonight and then tomorrow will be today again. Chronic melancholia hanging from the trees. You never get tired of it. After a while you start to feel like a ghost from one of the tombs, like you're in a wax museum below crimson clouds. Spirit empire. Wealthy empire. One of Napoleon's generals, Lallemand, was said to have come here to check it out, looking for a place for his commander to seek refuge after Waterloo. He scouted around and left, said that here the devil is damned, just like everybody else, only worse. The devil comes here and sighs. New Orleans. Exquisite, old-fashioned. A great place to live vicariously. Nothing makes any difference and you never feel hurt, a great place to really hit on things. Somebody puts something in front of you here and you might as well drink it. Great place to be intimate or do nothing. A place to come and hope you'll get smart—to feed pigeons looking for handouts. A great place to record. It has to be—or so I thought.

Lanois had set things up in one of his patented "pick up and move" studios—this one in a Victorian mansion on Soniat

Street not far from Lafayette Cemetery No.1—parlor windows, louvered shutters, high Gothic ceilings, walled-in courtyard, bungalows and garages in the back. Heavy blankets soundproofed the windows.

Dan had recruited an eclectic alliance of musicians. They included the Fort Worth guitarist and singer Mason Ruffner who played in Bourbon Street clubs like the Old Absinthe Bar. Ruffner was a regional star, had a high pompadour, a gold tooth smile with a tiny guitar inlaid. He had a few records out and had bags of explosive licks with funky edges, rockabilly tremolo–influenced, wrote songs, too, said that he'd hung around in Texas libraries reading Rimbaud and Baudelaire to get his language down. He also told me that as a teenager he'd played with Memphis Slim. I thought I had something in common with him there. I'd played with Big Joe Williams when I was just a kid. Mason had some fine songs. One of them had the line, "You do good things for people and it just makes them bad." I might have thought about recording it if I didn't have my own originals. The other guitar player, Brian Stoltz, from Slidell, also played in a funky and blistering way, but he was more laid-back and he had articulate schemes—been playing with the Nevilles for years. Brian's licks were thought out like piano patterns. He could play James Booker piano riffs on the guitar. Tony Hall was the electric bass player. Willie Green was on the bass drum and snare with Cyril Neville, who played percussion. Malcolm Burns, Lanois's recording engineer, played keyboards, and Danny himself played a variety of instruments—mandolins, mandolas, cello-looking guitars and other fretted stuff, plastic novelty instruments resembling toys. Danny had all the equipment needed.

With this group, I didn't see how you could go wrong unless you went a little crazy. The first song I took out of my note case was "Political World" and we started looking for quick, searching ways in how to do it. I didn't bring my own equipment, so I picked up one of Lanois's antiquated Telecasters—wicked sounding if you're on a cement floor beneath a corrugated tin roof, but in some cases, it could be too brittle. I liked playing it, so I stuck with it anyway. We tried "Political World" a few different ways and it didn't seem to be going anywhere. The sensation was always the same. The first way we tried was as good as the last, but someplace along the line as the night wore on, Lanois got committed to a funk style—he heard one of Mason's licks and decided to put the whole song on it. By then, I was hearing the song differently than I had when I started. Playing it out had brought me to different conclusions, that the lyrics might work better in fragmented rhythms and that I could lose a lot of the verses and add a differently arranged part, but at the time I didn't know what the part could be.

I was trying to figure out the realities of what Danny had in his mind, what he had to work with. I couldn't do that in just one day or just one session. To make a record anywhere, anytime with anyone is possible, but the reality is rare. You have to be surrounded by musicians of like purpose. There were methods I would have instinctively used in the past with a song like this but here, they wouldn't have worked. Long time ago, good; now, no good.

After a while I started to zone out, yawned heavily and left, took a tape of the song with me to study and headed back to the house. Passing the cemetery, I felt like going to pray at one of the tombs. Later that night, listening to what we'd done, I thought I'd figured it out. The following day, I went back to the studio and the song was played for me again, except this time it was even more funked up. A lot of work had continued after I'd left the night before. Ruffner had overdubbed torpedo licks over my very minimalistic Tele rhythms. My guitar was taken out of the mix entirely. My voice was out there in the middle of nowhere in some corridor of sonic atmosphere. The song got shanghaied. You could tap your foot to it, clap your hands or jig your head up and down, but it didn't open up the world of the real. It sounded like I was singing from the midst of the herd, a lot of artillery and tanks in the background. The longer it went, the worse it got.

"Christ, all this happened while I was out of here?" I said to Lanois.

He said, "What do you think?"

"I think we missed it."

I went into the kitchenette behind the courtyard and grabbed a beer out of the refrigerator and sank into a chair. One of Dan's assistants was sitting on the couch watching the tube. The ex-Klansman David Duke from Metairie in Jefferson Parish had been elected to the Louisiana State House of Representatives and he was being interviewed. He said that welfare wasn't working and that workfare would be better— make people on welfare work for the community instead of getting a free ride. He also wanted to put prisoners from state pens on work programs. Didn't want them getting a free ride, either. I hadn't seen Duke before; he looked like a movie star.

I gathered myself together and went back in to work with Dan. Jesus, I thought, this is only the first song. It should be easier than this. Lanois liked the tone of the song, asked what I didn't like about it. I told him that we couldn't turn it loose the way it was. We had to strip it down. With Lanois's help, I tried to make the song fly, but nothing was working. First off, Mason's part was clipped back, but then the kick and snare drum were out of place because they were playing to him and not to me. Once my original guitar was turned back up in the mix, the drums were out to lunch.

We lost two or three days just goofing around. Through it all, I started seeing that the song should have been more of an upbeat ballad. We tried breaking the song apart and adding melodic lines like a chorus, but it was too time consuming. Nothing was going to make any difference. Danny had a strong belief in the funk version. I didn't think we were communicating very well and it was beginning to break my bloody heart. At one point things really began to boil. He got so frustrated, he flashed into a rage, swung around, flinging a metallic dobro like it was some kind of toy and smashed it to the floor with furious actions. There was a momentary silence in the room. A young girl, who'd been cataloging tracks and taking notes, stopped grinning and left in tears. Poor doll. I felt terrible for her. Everything was beginning to collapse and we hadn't gotten started yet. We would have to let this song go. It was either too early or too late for "Political World." We'd have to put it away and listen to it later. It might sound better. That can happen.

Next song we tried was "Most of the Time." It didn't have a melody so I would just have to strum it 'til I found one. I never did come up with any definite melody, only generic chords, but Dan thought he heard something. Something that turned into a slow, melancholy song. On this, Danny was contributing as much as any musician. He added layers of parts and soon the song seemed to have some kind of attitude and purpose. Trouble was that the lyrics weren't putting me in there, where I wanted to be. It wasn't busting out the way it should. I could have easily given up five or six lines if I had phrased the verses differently. For what we were doing, though, Dan's treatment was fine. But it was just like the other song. I began to feel differently about it as we moved along. It seemed to have more to do about time itself than it did with me. I felt that the sound of a clock like Big Ben should be ticking right through the tune at various levels. A big-band treatment would have been okay, too. In my mind I was beginning to hear me singing the song with the Johnny Otis Orchestra. A lot of the lyrics needed to be shifted around and I began to feel blocked off. Danny put as much ambiance in this song as he could and he kept things from drifting, but this wasn't a song that I really felt like changing my grip on. You could change the lyrics, but the patterns were set. The tune was gaining weight by the minute and none of its clothes were fitting. It was all dammed up and stagnant.

We worked it to a standstill. Dan would have to be a shaman to make this work. The song, which seemed unfinished to begin with, had just become more unfinished as we rolled on. I wondered what I had gotten myself into. I thought I'd left all this recording aggravation in the past. I didn't need this. It's not like I despised the song, I just didn't have the will to work on it. The lyrics were so full of cloudy meaning and there was nothing in the song that was transforming itself, not even with all the ambiance.

After sitting around and talking for a while with Danny and Malcolm, I recorded the song "Dignity" with only Brian and Willie. This was the first song we did that delivered things and didn't just dream them. We listened to the playback and Dan got excited, said that he felt the song had plenty

of promise and arranged to cut it the next night with Rockin'
Dopsie and His Cajun Band. There was nothing the matter
with the song the way we had just cut it, with a minimum of instruments and the vocal up front, but I knew what Dan was
trying to do and I wanted to see him do it, so I didn't feel any
pressure or stress about recutting the song. I didn't think it
was unreasonable.

On the way back to the house I passed the local movie
theater on Prytania Street, where *The Mighty Quinn* was
showing. Years earlier I had written a song called "The Mighty
Quinn" which was a hit in England, and I wondered what the
movie was about. Eventually I'd sneak off and go there to see
it. It was a mystery, suspense, Jamaican thriller with Denzel
Washington as the mighty Xavier Quinn, a detective who solves
crimes. Funny, that's just the way I imagined him when I wrote
the song "The Mighty Quinn." Denzel Washington. He must
have been a fan of mine . . . years later he would play the
boxer Hurricane Carter, someone else I wrote a song about. I
wondered if Denzel could play Woody Guthrie. In my dimension of reality, he certainly could have.


At the house on Audubon Place the radio was always on in
the kitchen and always tuned to WWOZ, the great New Orleans station that plays mostly early rhythm and blues and
rural South gospel music. My favorite DJ, hands down, was
Brown Sugar, the female disc jockey. She was on in the midnight hours, played records by Wynonie Harris, Roy Brown,
Ivory Joe Hunter, Little Walter, Lightnin' Hopkins, Chuck
Willis, all the greats. She used to keep me company a lot
when everyone else was sleeping. Brown Sugar, whoever she

was, had a thick, slow, dreamy, oozing molasses voice—she sounded as big as a buffalo—she'd ramble on, take phone calls, give love advice and spin records. I wondered how old she could be. I wondered if she knew her voice had drawn me in, filled me with inner peace and serenity and would upend all my frustration. It was relaxing listening to her. I'd stare at the radio. Whatever she said, I could see every word as she said it. I could listen to her for hours. Wherever she was, I wished I could put all of myself in there.

WWOZ was the kind of station I used to listen to late at night growing up, and it brought me back to the trials of my youth and touched the spirit of it. Back then when something was wrong the radio could lay hands on you and you'd be all right. There was a country radio station, too, that came on early, before daylight, that played all the '50s songs, a lot of Western Swing stuff—clip clop rhythms, songs like, "Jingle, Jangle, Jingle," "Under the Double Eagle," "There's a New Moon over My Shoulder," Tex Ritter's "Deck of Cards," which I hadn't heard in about thirty years, Red Foley songs. I listened to that a lot. There'd been a station like that also broadcast into my hometown. In a weird sense, I felt like I was starting over, beginning to live my life again. There was a jazz station, too—played mostly current stuff—Stanley Clark, Bobby Hutcherson, Charles Earland, Patti Austin and David Benoit. New Orleans had the best radio stations in the world.

Elliot Roberts, who was booking my tour dates, had come to New Orleans for a visit. He showed me my upcoming tour schedule and I was disappointed. It was far different than what we had talked about. There were very few of the same towns that I'd played the previous year. These upcoming shows would be going to Europe. I told him that this wasn't what we talked about, that I needed to go back to the same towns that I played the previous year.

"You can't play the same towns every year, nobody's gonna get an erection over that. You gotta leave the towns alone. Leave 'em be for a while," he said.

I understood what Elliot was saying, but I didn't accept it. "I need to go back to the same places twice, even three times a year—it doesn't matter."

"You're held up in a certain way. You're mythological. Think about it like you think about Jesse James. There were a lot of bank robbers back then, a lot of jail breakers—a lot of holdup men, train robbers . . . but Jesse James is the only name people remember. He was mythological. You don't play the same towns every year, you don't rob the same banks."

"Boy, that sounds good," I said. The argument was pointless and it made no sense going into the depth of it.

I took Roberts to the studio with me where Lanois had already set up Rockin' Dopsie and His Cajun Band in the big parlor room. We started recording "Dignity" about nine o'clock. I knew what Lanois had in mind and thought that there might be something to it. The dichotomy of cutting this lyrically driven song with melodic changes, with a rockin' Cajun band, might be interesting . . . but the only way to find out, is to find out. Once we started trying to capture it, the song seemed to get caught in a stranglehold. All the chugging rhythms began imprisoning the lyrics. This style seemed to be oblivious to their existence. Both Dan and I became plainly perplexed. Every performance was stealing more energy. We recorded it a lot, varying the tempos and even the keys, but it was like being cast into sudden hell. The demo with just me and Willie and Brian had sounded effortless and it flowed smooth. Certainly, as Danny said, it didn't sound finished, but what recording ever does? Dopsie got almost as frustrated as me. It was a strange bull we were riding. He and his band never lost their composure, though. This song is not exactly a twelve-bar song and needed to project the perception of intimacy to be effective. It was becoming way too complicated and convoluted. An ambiance of texture and atmosphere is what the song called for and what Lanois is so good at. I couldn't figure out why we weren't getting it. You work hours on something and you get dizzy. After a while you lose your judgment.

At about three in the morning we had played ourselves out and just started playing any old stuff: "Jambalaya," "Cheatin' Heart," "There Stands the Glass"—country classics. Just fooling around, playing like we were on a party boat. Two of Dan's engineers had been changing shifts since the beginning, and it had been hot and sweaty all night. I was wearing a blue flannel shirt and it was soaked through. Sweat was pouring off my face. In the midst of all of this, I played another new song I had written, "Where Teardrops Fall." I showed it quickly to Dopsie and we recorded it. Took about five minutes and it wasn't rehearsed. In the finale of the song, Dopsie's saxophone player, John Hart, played a sobbing solo that nearly took my breath away. I leaned over and caught a glimpse of the musician's face. He'd been sitting there the whole night in the dark and I hadn't noticed him. The man was the spitting image of Blind Gary Davis, the singing reverend that I'd known and followed around years earlier. What was he doing here? Same guy, same cheeks and chin, fedora, dark glasses. Same build, same height, same long black coat—the works. It was eerie. Reverend Gary Davis, one of the wizards of modern music . . . like he'd been raised upright and was watching over things, keeping constant vigilance over what was happening. He peered across the room at me in an odd way, like he had the ability to see beyond the moment, like he'd thrown a rope line out to grip. All of a sudden I know that I'm in the right place doing the right thing at the right time and Lanois is the right cat. Felt like I had turned a corner and was seeing the sight of a god's face.

The next night, we began listening to all the different takes of "Dignity." Lanois had kept them all. There must have been more than twenty. Whatever promise Dan had seen in the song was beaten into a bloody mess. Where we had started from, we'd never gotten back to, a fishing expedition gone nowhere. In no take did we ever turn back the clock. We just kept winding it. Every take another ball of confusion. Takes that could almost make you question your own existence.

Then, from out of nowhere in the midst of it all, came "Where Teardrops Fall." It was just a three-minute ballad, but it made you stand straight up and stay right where you were. It's like someone had pulled the cord to stop the train. The song was beautiful and magical, upbeat, and it was complete. I was wondering if Danny was thinking the same thing, and he was. "I can't remember that at all," Danny said. Okay, we were going to forget about "Dignity" for a while. (We never did go back to it.) Lanois said that he liked the ballad, too, that it's got something, but—and it was a big "but"—he said we could do it better and I asked him how and he said that the timing was a little off and the song wavered. Maybe it did . . . three in the morning. We could get Mason and Daryl and whoever and lay down a better track. I said, sure, and went out the back door of the studio, through the courtyard down to Magazine Street to the ice cream parlor and stayed there a while, wanted to be by myself—unplugged the switchboard.

I thumbed through the local music paper and saw that Mick Jones, the quintessential guitarist from The Clash, was recovering from pneumonia. The report said that he nearly died. I wished that I had thought of him to play in my band. He'd have been perfect, but it was premature for me to think about that. Marianne Faithfull was recording a new record, too. She was the great grand dame and I used to know her. Hadn't seen her in a while. The paper said that she had a new attitude and feeling about life after going through rehab at Hazelden, a clinic up in Minnesota. I felt glad for her. Elton John was auctioning off all his furniture and costumes. In the pages was a photo of his pinball machine. It looked fantastic and I wished I was bidding on it.

I left the ice cream parlor, went back out on the sidewalk. A wet wind hit me in the face. Moonlight illuminated the glistening leaves and my footsteps disturbed a courtyard of cats. A dog snarled menacingly from behind a wrought-iron fence. A black sedan went by, a couple of winos in it—windows rolled down, Paula Abdul song blasting out of the speakers. I crossed the street as the car moved up the block, and walked back through Audubon Park towards the street I was staying on, off of St. Charles Avenue. Even with all the churches and temples and cemeteries, New Orleans doesn't have the psychic current of holy places. That's a cold, frozen fact. It takes you a while to figure that out. In a lot of places you have to change with the times. It's not necessary here. I got back to the house, went into the kitchen and sat there for a while, listened to Brown Sugar. She was playing "Dangerous Woman" by Little Junior Parker. Then I went upstairs and crawled under the sheets.

In the coming days some of my family would be visiting, and they wanted to go to the famous Antoine's for dinner. I didn't want to go but went anyway. We had dinner in the back room and I sat under a portrait of Princess Margaret in the same chair that supposedly Franklin Delano Roosevelt sat in. I only ordered the turtle soup. I didn't want to eat anything that would bog me down. Later, I would have to be back at Lanois's. I left the supper room early, walked out into a torrential thunderstorm, but I was glad I went. Glad I saw the place firsthand.

It had been raining off and on for the past three or four days, and now it was raining again. Danny had positioned everything just right to recut "Where Teardrops Fall." We were back in the same parlor room and with about four or five musicians. In no time we were off and running. We laid down what sounded musically to be a perfectly proper track, but I wasn't comfortable with it. It was hard to sing to— didn't seem to have the magic that the previous version had. I shrugged, couldn't get it, was having piss luck trying to cut this version. As a vocalist, it was like trying to scale the slippery trunk of a tree. I thought to myself, Why aren't we using the other one? The other track? What was the matter with it? Danny thought the other track wasn't right and of course, it wasn't—not in technical terms. It couldn't be fixed, but that was okay—there was no reason to interfere with it the way it was. It had a certain definite awe about it and eventually, Danny and I saw eye to eye, went back and listened to Dopsie's version and used it.

We cut "Series of Dreams," and although Lanois liked the song, he liked the bridge better, wanted the whole song to be like that. I knew what he meant, but it just couldn't be done. Though I thought about it for a second, thinking that I could probably start with the bridge as the main part and use the main part as the bridge. Hank Williams had done that once with the song "Lovesick Blues," but as much as I thought about it, the idea didn't amount to much and thinking about the song this way wasn't healthy. I felt like it was fine the way it was—didn't want to lose myself in thinking too much about changing it. Danny was struggling to help me make this song work and he had the confidence to try anything. He cared a lot. Sometimes I thought he cared too much. He would have done anything to make a song happen—empty the pans, wash dishes, sweep the floors. It didn't matter. All that mattered to him was getting that certain something and I understood that.

Lanois was a Yankee man, came from north of Toronto— snowshoe country, abstract thinking. Northerners think abstract. When it's cold, you don't fret because you know it's going to be warm again . . . and when it's warm, you don't worry about that either because you know it'll be cold eventually. It's not like in the hot places where the weather is always the same and you don't expect anything to change. Lanois's thinking was fine with me. I think abstract, too.

Lanois is technically minded and he's a musician, usually plays on every record he produces. He's got ideas about overdubbing and tape manipulation theories that he's developed with the English producer Brian Eno on how to make a record, and he's got strong convictions. But I'm pretty independent, too, and I don't like to be told to do something if I don't understand it. This was the problem we were going to have to work through. One thing about Lanois that I liked is that he didn't want to float on the surface. He didn't even want to swim. He wanted to jump in and go deep. He wanted to marry a mermaid. All that was fine with me. Off and on during the time we were cutting "Series of Dreams," he'd say to me something like, "We need songs like 'Masters of War,' 'Girl from the North Country,' or 'With God on Our Side.' " He began nagging at me, just about every other day, that we could sure use some songs like those. I nodded. I knew we could, but I felt like growling. I didn't have anything like those songs.

When we began working on "What Good Am I?" I had to hunt for a melody and after working on it for a suitable length of time Danny thought he heard something. I thought that I was on to something but hadn't quite found it yet. I was looking too hard. When it's right, you don't have to look for it. Maybe it was only a foot and a half away, I didn't know. But I had exhausted my energy and I thought I might as well just go with what Lanois liked, although it was too slow for my taste. Danny used layered rhythms to create a mood for this song. I liked the words, but the melody wasn't quite special enough—didn't have any emotional impact. Setting aside our personal differences, we worked on this song for a while and completed it.

I had heard there was a Tennessee Williams literary festival going on for the past week or two and I wanted to see what was left of it. So one night I went to Coliseum Street in the Garden District to one of the double gallery–style houses with a gabled roof, flanked by columns, in hopes to hear something about Tom, discover something about the wondrous truth of his plays. On paper they always seemed kind of stiff. You had to see them live onstage to get the full freak effect. I'd met Williams once in the early '60s, and he looked like the genius that he was. The society-sponsored lecture was ending as I got there. As I went in, most of the others were coming out, so I turned away and headed back to the recording studio, walking on Loyola Street past Lafayette Cemetery No. 2. Light rain was falling. Rats scurried across the telephone poles.

Later that night we began cutting "Ring Them Bells." There was one line in the song that I was trying to fix, but never did . . . the last line . . . "breaking down the distance between right and wrong." The line fit, but it didn't verify what I felt. Right *or* wrong, like it fits in the Wanda Jackson song, or right *from* wrong, like the Billy Tate song, that makes sense, but not right *and* wrong. The concept didn't exist in my subconscious mind. I'd always been confused about that kind of stuff, didn't see any moral ideal played out there. The concept of being morally right or morally wrong seems to be wired to the wrong frequency. Things that aren't in the script happen every day. If someone steals leather and then makes shoes for the poor, it might be a moral act, but it's not legally right, so it's wrong. That stuff troubled me, the legal and moral aspect of things. There are good deeds and bad deeds. A good person can do a bad thing and a bad person can do a good thing. But I never did get to fix the line. On this take it's outright, natural sound with little experimentation. I felt I could have done it unaccompanied. That aside, Lanois captured the essence of it on this, put the magic into its heartbeat and pulse. We cut this song exactly the way I found it . . . two or three takes with me on the piano, Dan on guitar and Malcolm Burn on keyboards. He definitely captured the moment. He might have even captured the whole era. He did the right thing—came up with an accurate, dynamic version. Anybody can hear it. The song sustains itself from beginning to end—Lanois brought out all its keen, harmonic sense. In this Dan was more than a sound man. He was like a doctor with scientific principles. I asked him once, "Danny. Are you a doctor?" "Yeah, but not of medicine," he smiled.

Lanois and his crew kept a bunch of vintage Harleys parked out back and in the courtyard of the studio. Mostly Panheads with Hydra-Glide front forks, chrome driving lamps, mostly solo seated, wide tires, tombstone taillights. I had to have one of these bikes. Mark Howard, one of Dan's engineers and motorcycle enthusiast found me one—a '66 Harley Police Special, out of Florida with a powder-coated frame, stainless steel spokes, black-powdered rim and hubs, everything original and it ran good. Once I got it, I began taking it out during breaks from the studio or early in the morning. I used to ride along Ferret Street all the way down to Canal, sometimes into East New Orleans over the Intercoastal waters or sometimes went over and parked it around Jackson Square, near St. Joseph's Cathedral. Once I took it into the Wildlife Gardens around Lake Borgne with its water views and benches, where Andrew Jackson and his ragtag army of pirates, Choctaws, free blacks, lawyers and merchants militia defeated Britain's finest, sent them back out to sea for good. Britain was supposed to have ten thousand troops and Jackson about four, but he overcame them anyway, so the history books say. Jackson said that he'd burn New Orleans to the ground before he'd surrender it. Jackson, Old Hickory, Master of Bloody Deeds—tall and rawboned, blue eyes and bushy gray hair, cantankerous, a backwoodsman, opposed the Bank of the United States. At least he didn't drop bombs killing civilians and innocent children for the glory of his nation's honor. He wouldn't be going to hell for that.

Once I rode the bike over to the Spanish Plaza and parked it at the foot of Canal Street. Nearby, a paddle wheeler was moored on the river, the chinka-chinka beat of a Cajun band on the boat sounded almost hysterical. Under the southernmost magnolia I started feeling something about a song called "Shooting Star," a song I hadn't written yet. I could vaguely hear it in my mind. The kind of song you hear when you're wide awake in your head and see and feel things, but all the rest of you is asleep. I didn't want to forget this. Before I left town, I wanted to write it and record it. I thought it might be something Lanois was looking for.

"Everything Is Broken" Lanois thought was a throwaway. I didn't think it was, but there was only one way to find out, only one way to cut it—one style and with plenty of tremolo. We recorded the song with the full band on the floor. Tony Hall on bass and Willie Green on drums. We cut it live in the big parlor room. Brian and I played the guitars. I was still playing the Tele. When you cut a song like this with a group of musicians, it's rare to get a day when all five or six feel good in the same kind of way at the same time. Dan played on this and contributed as much as anybody. I thought the song did just what it had to do, wouldn't have wanted to seriously change a thing about it. Danny didn't have to swamp it up too much, it was already swamped up pretty good when it came to him. Critics usually didn't like a song like this coming out of me because it didn't seem to be autobiographical. Maybe not, but the stuff I write does come from an autobiographical place.

Though Lanois showed little excitement over the track, he knew it wasn't a dog. I knew what he was looking for. He was looking for songs that defined me as a person, but what I do in the studio doesn't define me as a person. There's just too much small print in thousands of pages for anything like that to happen. He was helping me as a singer, though. As a singer, you could die without the right microphones and amps, and Lanois was doing his best to find the right combinations. I usually left the studio at night in a cold frame of mind. "Danny," I'd say sometimes. "Are we still friends?"

After being in New Orleans for about a month, I was up early and I rooted my wife out of bed. Daylight was two hours away. "What's wrong now?" she said. I hadn't thought that anything was wrong. Within minutes she had slipped out of her loose robe and was making coffee. By daybreak we were riding on the Harley, had crossed the Mississippi River into Bridge City and headed over towards Thibodaux on Route 90. No purpose in heading there, it was just a place to go. At Raceland, we got onto 308. I was feeling stuffy—needed to get out of town. Something wasn't clicking, like when the world is hidden from your eyes and you need to find it. If I wanted to keep awake for the rest of these sessions, I'd have to open a window and get a grip on something, and whatever it was I needed to be one hundred percent sure of it.

Crossing into Thibodaux, we rode near Bayou Lafourche. It was a clammy day, light rain off and on and the clouds were breaking up, heat lightning low on the horizon. The town has got a lot of streets with tree names, Oak Street, Magnolia Street, Willow Street, Sycamore Street. West 1st Street runs alongside the bayou. We walked on a boardwalk that ran out into the water above the eerie wetlands—small islands of grass in the distance and pontoon boats. It was quiet. If you looked you could spot a snake on a tree branch.

I moved the bike up close near an old water tower. We got off and walked around, walked along adjoining roads dwarfed by ancient cypress trees, some seven hundred years old. It felt far enough away from the city, the dirt roads surrounded by lush sugarcane fields, labyrinths of moss walls in crumbled heaps, marshlands and soft mud all around. On the bike again we cruised along Pecan Street, then over by St. Joseph's Church, which is modeled after one in Paris or Rome. Inside there's supposed to be the actual severed arm of an early Christian martyr. Nichols State University, the poor man's Harvard, is just up the street. On St. Patrick's Street we rode past the palatial grand homes and big plantation houses, deep porched and with many windows. There's an antebellum courthouse that stands next to clapboard halls. Ancient oak trees and decrepit shacks side by side. It felt good to be off by ourselves.

It was early afternoon and we'd been going for a while. Dust was blowing, my mouth was dry and my nose was clogged. Feeling hungry, we stopped into Chester's Cypress Inn on Route 20 near Morgan City, a fried chicken, fish and frog legs joint. I was beginning to get weary. The waitress came over to the table and said, "How about eating?" I looked at the menu, then I looked at my wife. The one thing about her that I always loved was that she was never one of those people who thinks that someone else is the answer to their happiness. Me or anybody else. She's always had her own built-in happiness. I valued her opinion and I trusted her. "You order," I said. Next thing I know, fried catfish, okra and Mississippi mud pie came to the table. The kitchen was next door in another building. Both the catfish and the pie were on cardboard plates, but I wasn't nearly as hungry as I thought I was—just ate the onion rings.

Later on, we rode south towards Houma. On the west side of the road there's cattle grazing and egrets, herons with slender legs standing in shallow bays—pelicans, houseboats, roadside fishing—oyster boats, small mud boats—steps that lead to small piers running out into the water. We kept rolling on, started crossing different kinds of bridges, some swinging, some lifting. On Stevensonville Road we crossed a canal bridge by a little country store and the road turned to gravel and began to wind treacherously through the swamps. The air smelled foul. Still water—humid air, rank and rotten. Kept riding south until we saw oil rigs and supply boats, then turned around and headed again towards Thibodaux. Thibodaux was neither here nor there and my mind started thinking opposites. Thinking about maybe going up to the Yukon country, someplace where we could really bundle up. By dusk we'd found a place to stay outside of Napoleonville. We pulled in for the night and I shut the bike down. It was a nice ride.

We stayed at a bed-and-breakfast cottage that was behind

a pillared plantation house with sculpted studded garden paths, a cream stucco bungalow that had a certain charm— stood like a miniature Greek temple. The room had a four poster comfortable bed and an antique table—the rest, camp style furnishings, and it came with a kitchenette equipped with utensils, but we didn't eat there. I laid down, listened to the crickets and wildlife out the window in the eerie blackness. I liked the night. Things grow at night. My imagination is available to me at night. All my preconceptions of things go away. Sometimes you could be looking for heaven in the wrong places. Sometimes it could be under your feet. Or in your bed.

Next day I woke up, felt like I had figured something out, why I wasn't feeling right about the recording sessions. Here's the thing—I wasn't looking to express myself in any kind of new way. All my ways were intact and had been for years. There wasn't much chance in changing now. I didn't need to climb the next mountain. If anything, what I wanted to do was to secure the place where I was at. I wasn't sure Lanois understood that. I guess I never made it plain, couldn't put it in so many words.

It had been raining off and on all night and now rain was sprinkling again. It was late morning when we left the motel. A nipping wind hit me in the face, but it was a beautiful day. The sky was dull gray. We climbed back on the blue Harley and rode down around Lake Verret, riding on high trails, cruising by twisted giant oaks, pecan trees—vines and cypress stumps down in the swamps. Got down almost as far as Amelia and then headed back—stopped at a gas station off Route 90 near Raceland. Across a vacant field stood an obscure roadside place, a gaunt shack called King Tut's Museum and it caught my eye. After filling the gas tank, we rode slowly across the cow path to the side of the shack. It was wood framed, an overhanging porch with support beams that had long ago rotted away—pickup truck full of vegetables parked out front and a junked out '50s Oldsmobile Golden Rocket up on blocks in the tall grass. A young girl was on the balcony beating the dust off a rug, dressed in pink gymnastic tights, had long black oiled ringlets and a bath towel around her shoulders. The dust hung like a red cloud in the air. We went up the short steps and I walked in. My wife stayed outside on a wooden swing bench.

The place sold trinkets, newspapers, sweets, handcraft items, baskets made of swamp cane that were woven in the area—elaborate patterns. There were figurines and sham jewels, some items in display cases, umbrellas, slippers, blue voodoo beads and votive candles. There were ironworks around the entryway, oak boughs—acorn motifs, a few bumper sticker signs. One said WORLD'S GREATEST GRANDPA. Another one said SILENCE. One said KEEP ON TRUCKIN'. The place was also a crawfish joint with a small counter on one side of the room. There were hog parts hanging from hooks on walls—hog jowls, hog ears, make you wanna squeal. It was run by an old-timer named Sun Pie, one of the most singular characters you'd ever want to meet. The man was short and wiry like a panther, dark face but with Slavic features, wore a narrow brimmed, flat topped straw hat. On his bones was the raw skin of the earth. The young girl up on the balcony was his wife. She looked like a schoolgirl. The place was a little too bright inside and the tables shined from polishing. Sun Pie was working on a high loft chair. It looked like it came out of a cathedral. It was disassembled in pieces, clamped up on the sides and glued. He was sandpapering an edge of a six-planed leg.

"You looking for a hot spot to fish?"

"No, just riding through."

"You could be doing worse," he says—pauses, "I used to do some of that," and he nodded in the direction of the blue cop bike. "Look around if you want to. Got some pretty nice stuff in here."

There were posters displayed, one of Bruce Lee, another of Chairman Mao. Behind the counter taped to the mirror was a wide, framed photograph showing the Great Wall of China. On the other brick wall was a jumbo sized American flag.

The radio was on from beyond a wall and the sound was coming through in static. The Beatles were singing, "Do You Want to Know a Secret." They were so easy to accept, so solid. I remembered when they first came out. They offered intimacy and companionship like no other group. Their songs would create an empire. It seemed like a long time ago. "Do You Want to Know a Secret." A perfect '50s sappy love ballad and nobody but them could do it. Somehow there was nothing wussy about it. The Beatles blasted away. Sun Pie put down his tools. Behind the man, there were double screen doors that swung open to the bayou. Sun Pie repaired boats in a trussed-up backyard, a yard full of crowbars, broken chains and moss covered logs. My wife walked in and Sun Pie looked towards the door, then back at me.

"You a praying man?" he said.

"Uh-huh."

"Good, gonna have to be when the Chinese take over."

He said it without looking at me. He had an odd way of

talking, made me feel like I wasn't in his place at all, like he had just strolled into my place. "You know, the Chinese were here at the beginning. They were the Indians. You know, the red man. The Comanche, the Sioux, the Arapaho, the Cheyenne—all them people—they were all Chinese. Came over here about the time when Christ was healing the sick. All the squaws and chiefs came from China—walked across from Asia, came down through Alaska and discovered this place. They became Indians a lot later."

I'd heard that story somewhere once, that the Bering Sea was actually a land mass at one time so that anybody could walk over it from Asia or Russia, so it's possible that what Sun Pie was saying was true.

"Chinese, huh?"

"Yeah, that's right. Trouble was that they split up into parties and tribes and started wearing feathers and forgot they were Chinese. They started wars with each other for no reason, one tribe against another. You could make enemies out of anybody. Even the best of friends. That's the nature of the downfall of the Indians. That's why when the white man came from Europe to conquer them they fell so easily. They were ripe like peaches and ready to fall."

I was curious about what Pie was saying and I sat down in one of the rickety chairs. "They're coming back, these Chinese, millions of them. It's been preordained, and they won't have to use force. They'll just walk in and take up where they left off."

Sun Pie carefully selected a chisel, began scraping on the back post of the chair. There were lions' heads on the leg rails and intricate swirling designs in the black wood. He was working close in. The Dale and Grace song "I'm Leaving It

Up to You" was playing on the radio. I thought I had seen a face like Sun Pie's before but couldn't remember just where. He had an unusual way of talking . . . slow but with slam bang action words. He put his tool down and smiled, got soft voiced and told me a little bit about himself. He wasn't distant or guarded. Said he'd been in jail once for cutting a man, that it got him into big trouble, but that the man had it coming. Said that I should turn in all my diamonds, emeralds and rubies and exchange everything for jade, because that will be the new currency when the Chinese get here with their fish and their meat. "People think I'm crazy, but I don't mind. The Chinese are solid—they don't use vulgar language. The Chinese nightingale will sing in the land. They don't have any ten commandments, either, don't need 'em. All the way from here to Peru, Chinese. You a prayin' man, huh? What do you pray for? You pray for the world?" I never thought about praying for the world. I said, "I pray that I can be a kinder person."

There was still a light drizzle outside, and you could hear it softly on the tin roof. New Orleans was beginning to pull on me and I was feeling the weight of the line. I looked through the window past the hanging baskets of ferns and white flowers, tried to see beyond the wisteria vines on the patio. Part of the sky was clear, but the light had a greenish glow at the edges.

"Sea of Love" came on the radio. It felt like I must have been cast off somewhere and it was time to go back and that if I had come out of New Orleans with any bitterness or hostility, it ought to be dead by now. "There used to be racetracks and stables around here," he said. "A hurricane came through about a hundred years ago, water twelve feet high.

Two thousand people gone—lost their lives. When the storm comes, you beg the Master, 'If you just keep me from getting killed, I'll do anything you say.' " He picked up a can of varnish from a old newspaper that was spread open on the floor. "Whom the Master wishes to kill, the Master kills." He dipped a small brush into the dripping can and began to paint strokes on one of the side rails of the chair. Then he stopped himself and laid the brush down across the top of the can. There were varnish splotches all over the newspaper, but you could still make out certain stuff, certain faces in the news. "That's a weapon," he said, pointing to the newspaper. "I just use it to protect my floor. It's a weapon in the hands of bad people. Miserable devils. They don't know beans." He picked up a long file with a wooden handle. "There's no equality down here. Some of us are special. Some of us aren't. Some down here are tougher and smarter than others, some are weaker and less wise. Can't help it. Can't help how you're born. Some down here make better doctors and some are better victims. Some down here are better thinkers. Some down here make better mechanics and better rulers. No one 'round here is a better carpenter than me, but I couldn't be a good lawyer. Can't read law. We're not even equal in our own races, some are at the top and some are at the bottom." He paused and picked up an oily rag. "I think all the good in the world might have already been done." Sun Pie talked in a language you couldn't misunderstand. "Bruce Lee came from a good family and he defeated them all, all the babies, all the greedy criminals, the ones with clawing hands, powerful men but worthless. They couldn't stand up to Bruce Lee. Their consciences, God help them, were vile and depraved." Sun Pie was one of the most unique characters, the kind of guy who would be the center of a procession in a parade, or maybe he'd be the nucleus of a mob.

My wife, who had been out on the patio reading her John le Carré book after wandering around in the store, had come back inside and was using an eyebrow pencil over by the window. We didn't have to communicate at all to know it was time for us to go. Sun Pie knew she was with me and he says, "What are you doing, man? You want to stay for supper or what?" A train whistle blew in the distance and brought me to my senses. There was something pleasurable about hearing it. I said I wasn't too positive we could do that. Sun Pie wore gold rimmed spectacles. Every once in a while sunlight would shoot off like sparks—like comets from a dark sky blasting off the rims.

"The Queen of Country Music was in here a while back, bought a brass ashtray."

"Who would that be?"

"Sweet Kitty Wells."

"Oh, yeah."

A subtle change comes over Sun Pie. He glanced over at the poster of Mao. "War is not a bad thing. It thins out the population. You got to let it all float up to the surface." In my mind's eye I saw blood being splattered and spilled. Whatever he was getting at, I didn't believe like that. "Does your conscience bother you? It doesn't matter, a man's conscience is useless, clear or guilty, a live man's is anyway." This conscience stuff would stick in my mind.

I was holding a cane and felt my hand tightening on it. I

made my way towards the door, looked out into the thick trees and then over at my pretty wife, who was looking back at me. I was thinking that if Sun Pie was an active man, I'd go to great lengths to get out of his way. "I'm ready," she said.

I started to buy one of the bumper stickers but Sun Pie gave it to me for free—the one that said WORLD'S GREATEST GRANDPA. That would come in handy in a few years, when I would need at least about a dozen of them. Sun Pie was inspiring, didn't play empty headed kid games. He was the right guy to run into at the right time, a guy who grooved on his own head.

"Got everything you need, then?" he asked.

"Yeah, but I need some more," I said.

He laughed, said he did, too. We walked across the boards of the porch and over to the blue Harley. The sun was shining and it was as hot as a branding iron. Then we climbed on the bike—I tooted the trumpet-style horn, put the pistons in the upper position and we headed towards the railroad tracks—stopped only once more, and that was at Jesuit Bend, but before nightfall we were back on St. Charles Avenue.

I'd gotten back to New Orleans with a clear head. I'd finish up what I started with Lanois, even write him a couple of songs I never would have written otherwise. One was "Man in the Long Black Coat" and the other was "Shooting Star." I'd only done that once before—did it for the producer Arthur Baker. Baker had helped me produce the album *Empire Burlesque* a few years earlier in New York City. All the songs were mixed and finalized except Baker kept suggesting that we should have an acoustic song at the end of the record, that it would bring everything to the right conclusion. I thought about it and I knew he was right, but I didn't have anything. The night the album was being completed, I told him I'd see what I could come up with, saw the importance of it. I was staying at the Plaza Hotel on 59th Street and had come back after midnight, went through the lobby and headed upstairs. As I stepped out of the elevator, a call girl was coming towards me in the hallway—pale yellow hair wearing a fox coat—high heeled shoes that could pierce your heart. She had blue circles around her eyes, black eyeliner, dark eyes. She looked like she had been beaten up and was afraid that she'd get beat up again. In her hand, crimson purple wine in a glass. "I'm just dying for a drink," she said as she passed me in the hall. She had a beautifulness, but not for this kind of world. Poor wretch, doomed to walk this hallway for a thousand years.

Later that night I sat at a window overlooking Central Park and wrote the song "Dark Eyes." I recorded it the next night with only an acoustic guitar and it was the right thing to do. It did complete the album.

New York City wasn't New Orleans, though. It wasn't the city of astrology. It didn't have any mysteries lurking in its vast recesses, mysteries built when and by whom no man could tell. New York was a city where you could be frozen to death in the midst of a busy street and nobody would notice. New Orleans wasn't like that.

My wife would be leaving soon. She had to go to Baltimore to be in a gospel play and we were sitting outside on the porch facing the veranda, sipping coffee, low thunder rolling in. She stuck her tongue in my ear. "That tickles," I said. My wife, who had the ability to see a grain of truth in just about anything, knew that the recording sessions hadn't been going easy and at times had become heated. "Don't go stoned crazy," she reminded me.

Later, I was going to go to the studio but changed my mind and fell asleep and woke up. Morning hadn't come, so I closed my eyes and went back to sleep again. I woke up. I'd slept the clock around and now it was night again. I went into the kitchen to make some coffee before leaving. The radio was on as usual. A singer was singing that life was monotonous, life is a drag. It was Eartha Kitt. I thought to myself, "That's the truth, Eartha. That's plenty good. I'm friends with ya. Go ahead and sing."

We recorded "What Was It You Wanted?" with the full band: Malcolm Burn on bass, Mason Ruffner on guitar, Willie Green on drums, Cyril Neville on percussion. I played guitar and harmonica. Lanois played guitar, too. There aren't any lyrics in the interludes, but there probably should have been. At the time it was more important to get the theme of the lyric across and to keep the rhythmic pulse going. I'd cut stranger songs. The way the microphones are placed makes the atmosphere seem to be texturally rich, jet lagged and loaded—Quaaludes, misty. It starts mixed and cooked in a pot like a gumbo, right from the downbeat, dreamy and ambiguous. We had to keep the song level and right-side up. Danny's sonic atmosphere makes it sound like it's coming out of some mysterious, silent land. The production gyrates and moves with all kinds of layered rhythms, and I don't think Barry White could have done it any better. In this song, all our interests coincided.

I started seeing that all these compressors, processors, vintage gear, preamps and the reverb echo effects that were being used added up to a certain romance of sound that Lanois had in his head. Everything was pretty much live the way you hear it. Dan didn't depend a lot on overdubbing, not that he wouldn't overdub an occasional instrument, he just didn't use it as a crutch. The song was like looking at words in a mirror and checking out the reverse images. It's like you set up a thick smokescreen and then put the real action ten miles away. In some takes "Disease of Conceit" was cut as a weeper blues with an insistent beat. B-flat gives it a dark edge. I am playing the piano but I'm playing blocked chords. Allen Toussaint might have played the same thing only better and it would have freed me up to play guitar, but that didn't happen. Arthur Rubinstein would have been the ultimate player. That would have been perfect. I could also hear the song being played as a march. It could have been recorded with a bugle band or a funeral band. That might have been even more perfect. We might have recorded four or five versions of this, every one going straight to the point and seeming to go down in an eternal second. None of these takes were ever swamped up at all.

We listened later to it on the big speakers with the bass jacked up and Danny said that we should leave it alone, that it's right the way it is. "Think so?" "Yeah, it's got something." That's the most you can ever get out of Lanois. He seldom showed any emotion or excitement over anything, unless he was whirling around and smashing guitars. That didn't happen often, though. The song came in ready form and not a thing was changed about it. The night we recorded it, there was a lightning storm outside—leaves slapping on the banana trees. Something was guiding the song. It was like Joan of Arc was out there. (Or Joan Armatrading.) Whoever it was, somebody was out there working like hell.

To get my brain into something else for a minute, I'd gone back to the local movie theater, this time to see *Homeboy* starring Mickey Rourke, who played a shy and awkward cowboy boxer named Johnny Walker. Christopher Walken was in it, too. Everybody in the movie was pretty good, but Mickey's acting was at the upper end. He could break your heart with a look. The movie traveled to the moon every time he came onto the screen. Nobody could hold a candle to him. He was just there, didn't have to say hello or good-bye. Just seeing him act gave me the inspiration to cut the last two songs for this album.

"Shooting Star" was one of the songs I wrote in New Orleans. I felt like I didn't write it so much as I inherited it. It would have been good to have a horn man or two on it, a throbbing hum that mingled into the music, but we had to cut it with what we had: Brian on guitar, Willie on drums, Tony on bass and Lanois on Omnichord, a plastic instrument that sounds like an autoharp—me playing guitar and harmonica. The song came to me complete, full in the eyes like I'd been traveling on the garden pathway of the sun and just found it. It was illuminated. I'd seen a shooting star from the backyard of our house, or maybe it was a meteorite.

In the big parlor room where we cut it there was no air conditioning so we had to keep going outside between takes. But that was the way I liked it anyway. I don't like air conditioning to start with. It's hard to cut songs in air conditioned rooms where all the good air is gone. In the courtyard, it was raining soup.

On "Shooting Star," I would have liked to have played combination string stuff with somebody else playing the rhythm chords, but we didn't get it that far. In this song, the microphones were pinned up in odd places. The band sounded full. It's not like we had an increased number of options in how to cut it. I was hoping that when it was finished it would at least sound cohesive, like the effect of three or four instruments coming off like a full orchestra. But that's hard to do with separate tracking. On one of the last takes, Dan had hyped the snare and captured the song in its essence. It was frigid and burning, yearning—lonely and apart. Many hundreds of miles of pain went into it.

New Orleans was heating up. The hundred percent humidity hadn't settled in but you could feel it coming. I'd gone over to the Lion's Den Club on Gravier Street to hear Irma Thomas, one of my favorite singers. She hadn't had a hit since the '60s, but she still was on the jukeboxes here with "Fever." Irma played at the Lion's Den Club frequently. I wanted to see her perform, maybe ask her about singing with me on "Shooting Star" and do something like the girl in Mickey and Sylvia. That would have been interesting.

Out in front of the club, a guy in a duck-bill cap was hosing down a car. Some people were sitting on porches and there were some revelers down the street. "She's not here tonight," the guy in the duck-bill cap said. The Stones, early in their career, had recorded Irma's version of "Time Is on My Side." Some newspaper writer once asked her, didn't that make her feel pretty good? Irma said that she didn't care, that she didn't write the song. Only those in the music business would understand that.

On the way back to the studio I was thinking that if I had

to do this again, I would have brought somebody to New Orleans with me, somebody that went back a ways—someone who I liked as a musician, who had ideas and could play them, who had come down the same musical path as me.

Lately I'd been thinking about Jim Dickinson and how it would have been good to have him here. Dickinson was in Memphis. He'd started out playing the same time as me, in about '57 or '58, listened to the same things and could play and sing pretty well. We were from opposite ends of the Mississippi River. Back then, rock and roll was hated and resented, and folk music even more so, and Dickinson stepped to the front in both. His influences were jug band and early rock-and-roll bebop, same as mine. He had played on the Stones' song "Wild Horses" and some other things, but he had recorded way before then, actually was the last artist to ever release a single on Sam Phillips's Sun Records with a song called "Cadillac Man." Jim had manic purpose. We had a lot of things in common and it would have been good to have him around. He had kids, too, that played music just like some of mine did. But I didn't bring anybody, didn't think to, didn't even bring any equipment. I guess I was skeptical to begin with. I wanted to see what Danny could do on his own. I was hoping he'd surprise me. And he did surprise me.

We recorded "Man in the Long Black Coat" and a peculiar change crept over the appearance of things. I had a feeling about it and so did he. The chord progression, the dominant chords and key changes give it the hypnotic effect right away—signal what the lyrics are about to do. The dread intro gives you the impression of a chronic rush. The production sounds deserted, like the intervals of the city have disappeared. It's cut out from the abyss of blackness—visions of a maddened brain, a feeling of unreality—the heavy price of gold upon someone's head. Nothing standing, even corruption is corrupt. Something menacing and terrible. The song came nearer and nearer—crowding itself into the smallest possible place. We didn't even rehearse the song, we began working it out with visual cues. Before the lyrics even came in, you knew that the fight was on. This is Lanois-land and couldn't have been coming from anywhere else. The lyrics try to tell you about someone whose body doesn't belong to him. Someone who loved life but cannot live, and it rankles his soul that others should be able to live. Any other instrument on the track would have destroyed the magnetism. After we had completed a few takes of the song, Danny looked over to me as if to say, This is it. It was.

I wasn't sure that we had recorded any historical tunes like what he had wanted, but I was thinking that we might have gotten close with these last two. "Man in the Long Black Coat" was the real facts. In some kind of weird way, I thought of it as my "I Walk the Line," a song I'd always considered to be up there at the top, one of the most mysterious and revolutionary of all time, a song that makes an attack on your most vulnerable spots, sharp words from a master.

I'd always thought that Sun Records and Sam Phillips himself had created the most crucial, uplifting and powerful records ever made. Next to Sam's records, all the rest sounded fruity. On Sun Records the artists were singing for their lives and sounded like they were coming from the most mysterious place on the planet. No justice for them. They were so strong, can send you up a wall. If you were walking away and looked back at them, you could be turned into stone. Johnny Cash's records were no exception, but they weren't what you expected. Johnny didn't have a piercing yell, but ten thousand years of culture fell from him. He could have been a cave dweller. He sounds like he's at the edge of the fire, or in the deep snow, or in a ghostly forest, the coolness of conscious obvious strength, full tilt and vibrant with danger. "I keep a close watch on this heart of mine." Indeed. I must have recited those lines to myself a million times. Johnny's voice was so big, it made the world grow small, unusually low pitched—dark and booming, and he had the right band to match him, the rippling rhythm and cadence of click-clack. Words that were the rule of law and backed by the power of God. When I first heard "I Walk the Line" so many years earlier, it sounded like a voice calling out, "What are you doing there, boy?" I was trying to keep my eyes wide opened, too.

I don't know how "Man in the Long Black Coat" could have been recorded without Lanois. Like Sam Phillips, he likes to push artists to the psychological edge, and he'd done that with me, but he didn't have to do any of that with this song.

Our time was drawing to a close. Danny and I were sitting in the courtyard, the same way we had when we first met. Wind whipped in the open doorway and another kicking storm was rumbling earthward. There was a hurricane a hundred miles away. The light had gone out of the day. In the trees, a solitary bird warbling. We did it as we damn well pleased and there was nothing more to say. When the record was all added up, I hoped it would meet head on with the realities of life. I was going to thank him, but sometimes you can do it without opening your mouth, you can live it. I'd come to town with a cacophony of ideas and spent all I had under the watching gods. There'd been a clashing of spirits at times, but nothing that had turned into a bitter or complicated struggle. In the end, there always has to be some compromise of personal interests and there was, but the record satisfied my purposes and his. I can't say if it's the record either of us wanted. Human dynamics plays too big a part, and getting what you want isn't always the most important thing in life anyway.

Although the record wouldn't put me back on the map in radio land, ironically I had two records on the charts, even one in the Top 10, *The Traveling Wilburys*. The other one was the *Dylan & the Dead* album. The record Danny and I had just done would get good reviews, but reviews don't sell records. Everyone who puts out a record gets at least one good review, but then there's always a new crop of records and a new set of reviews. Sometimes you make records and you can't give them away. The music business is strange. You curse it and you love it.

When we finished recording it felt like the studio could have gone up in a sheet of flame. It was so intense in there for the past couple of months or so. Lanois had created a haunting, not stumbling or halting album. He said he'd help me make a record and he didn't break his word. We went by circuitous ways but we got there. We were simpatico although I think I always heard the record as sounding more strident than he did. I know that he wanted to understand me more as we went along, but you can't do that, not unless you like to do puzzles. I think in the end, he gave up on that. A lot of the songs held up in a grand way and more than a few of them I've played plenty of times. I would have liked to been able to give him the kinds of songs that he wanted, like "Masters of War," "Hard Rain," "Gates of Eden," but those kinds of songs were written under different circumstances, and circumstances never repeat themselves. Not exactly. I couldn't get to those kinds of songs for him or anyone else. To do it, you've got to have power and dominion over the spirits. I had done it once, and once was enough. Someone would come along eventually who would have it again—someone who could see into things, the truth of things—not metaphorically, either—but really see, like seeing into metal and making it melt, see it for what it was and reveal it for what it was with hard words and vicious insight.

Danny asked me who I'd been listening to recently, and I told him Ice-T. He was surprised, but he shouldn't have been. A few years earlier, Kurtis Blow, a rapper from Brooklyn who had a hit out called "The Breaks," had asked me to be on one of his records and he familiarized me with that stuff, Ice-T, Public Enemy, N.W.A., Run-D.M.C. These guys definitely weren't standing around bullshitting. They were beating drums, tearing it up, hurling horses over cliffs. They were all poets and knew what was going on. Somebody different was bound to come along sooner or later who would know that world, been born and raised with it . . . be all of it and more. Someone with a chopped topped head and a power in the community. He'd be able to balance himself on one leg on a tightrope that stretched across the universe and you'd know him when he came—there'd be only one like him. The audience would go that way, and I couldn't blame them. The kind of music that Danny and I were making was archaic. I didn't tell him that, but that's how I honestly felt. With Ice-T and Public Enemy, who were laying the tracks, a new performer was bound to appear, and one unlike Presley. He wouldn't be swinging his hips and staring at the lassies. He'd be doing it with hard words and he'd be working eighteen hours a day.

Sun Pie had mentioned Elvis to me, said that Elvis was an Amazon woman, an enemy of democracy. At the time it sounded like crackpot talk, but at the same time I wasn't so sure.

Sometimes you say things in songs even if there's a small chance of them being true. And sometimes you say things that have nothing to do with the truth of what you want to say and sometimes you say things that everyone knows to be true. Then again, at the same time, you're thinking that the only truth on earth is that there is no truth on it. Whatever you are saying, you're saying in a ricky-tick way. There's never time to reflect. You stitched and pressed and packed and drove, is what you did.

Lanois would be moving on, too, to another pick up and move studio. Lanois was a walking concept. He slept music. He ate it. He lived it. A lot of what he did was pure genius. He steered this record with deft turns and jerks, but he did it. He stood in the bell tower, scanning the alleys and rooftops. My limited vision didn't permit me to see all around the thing. There were a lot of records out that were padded and schmaltzy odes to flunky-ism and neither one of us wanted to add to its ranks. When we began, that's about all we had in common. There's something magical about this record, though, and you might say that it was in the house or the parlor room or something, but there wasn't any magic in the house. It's what Lanois and me and Willie Green and Daryl and Brian Stoltz brought to the place that made it what it was. You live with what life deals you. We have to make things fit. The voice on the record was never going to be the voice of the martyred man of constant sorrow, and I think in the beginning, Danny had to come to terms with that, and when he gave that notion up, that's when things started to work. None of it was planned that way. Though I was incapable of taking a lot of his emotional trips seriously, we were kind of kindred spirits. In another millions of days, thousands of millions of days, what would it all mean? What does anything ever mean? I try to use my material in the most effective way. The songs were written to the glory of man and not to his defeat, but all of these songs added together doesn't even come close to my whole vision of life. Sometimes the things that you liked the best and that have meant the most to you are the things that meant nothing at all to you when you first heard or saw them. Some of these songs fit into that category. I suppose all these things are simple, matter of fact enough.

On the record, I had to make spur of the moment decisions which might not have had anything to do with the real situation. That was all right, though. It would have been good to vary the rhythms. There's all kinds of ways you can do that. Eight pulses to the measure—six—four. You could do things where in four bars you play four beats and emphasize the 1 and the 3 and obscure the 2. You can go on and on like that in endless ways, varying tempos and rhythms. It would have been good if someone was paying attention to that kind of stuff, the rhythm combinations within the song instead of the song. The song would take care of itself. That being said, I had wholehearted admiration for what Lanois did. A lot of it was unique and permanent. Danny and I would see each other again in ten years and we'd work together once more in a rootin' tootin' way. We'd make a record and start it all over, pick up where we left off.

# 5

# River of Ice

THE MOON was rising behind the Chrysler Building, it was late in the day, street lighting coming on, the low rumble of heavy cars inching along in the narrow streets below—sleet tapping against the office window. Lou Levy was starting and stopping his big tape machine—diamond ring gleaming off his pinky finger—cigar smoke hanging in the blue air. The place was like a room used for interrogation, a fixture like a fruit bowl hanging overhead and a couple of lamps, some brass ones on floor stands. Below my feet a patterned wood floor. It was a drab room and cluttered with trade magazines—*Cashbox*, *Billboard*, radio survey charts—an ancient filing cabinet in the corner. Besides Lou's old metal desk, there were a couple of wood chairs and I sat forward in one of them strumming songs off the guitar.

Recently I had called home. I did that at least a couple of times a month from one of the many public pay phones around town. The phone booths were like sanctuaries, step inside of them, shut the accordion type doors and you locked yourself into a private world free of dirt, the noise of the city blocked out. The phone booths were private, but the lines back home weren't. Back there every household had a party line. About eight or ten different houses all used the same line, only with different numbers. If you'd pick up the phone receiver, seldom would the line ever be clear. There were always other voices. Nobody ever said anything important over the phone and you didn't ramble on long. If you wanted to talk to people, you'd usually talk to them in the street, in vacant lots, fields or in cafes, never on the phone.

On the corner I put the dime in the slot and dialed the operator for long distance, called collect and the call went right through. I wanted everyone to know I was all right. My mother would usually give me the latest run of the mill stuff. My father had his own way of looking at things. To him life was hard work. He'd come from a generation of different values, heroes and music, and wasn't so sure that the truth would set anybody free. He was pragmatic and always had a word of cryptic advice. "Remember, Robert, in life anything can happen. Even if you don't have all the things you want, be grateful for the things you don't have that you don't want." My education was important to him. He would have wanted me to become a mechanical engineer. But in school, I had to struggle to get even decent grades. I was not a natural student. My mom, bless her, who had always stood up for me and was firmly on my side in just about anything and everything, was more concerned about "a lot of monkey business out there in the world," and would add, "Bobby, don't forget you have relatives in New Jersey." I'd already been to Jersey but not to visit relatives.

Lou snapped the big tape machine off after listening hard

to one of my original songs. "Woody Guthrie, eh? That's in-teresting. What made you want to write a song about him? I used to see him and his partner, Leadbelly—they used to play at the Garment Workers Hall over on Lexington Av-enue. You ever heard 'You Can't Scare Me, I'm Sticking to the Union'?" Sure I'd heard it.

"Whatever happened to him, anyway?"

"Oh, he's over in Jersey. He's in the hospital there."

Lou chomped away. "Nothing serious I hope. What other songs do you have? Let's put 'em all down."

I didn't have many songs, but I was making up some com-positions on the spot, rearranging verses to old blues ballads, adding an original line here or there, anything that came into my mind—slapping a title on it. I was doing my best, had to thoroughly feel I was earning my fee. Nothing would have convinced me that I was actually a songwriter and I wasn't, not in the conventional songwriter sense of the word. Defi-nitely not like the workhorses over in the Brill Building, the song chemistry factory that was only a few blocks away but might as well have been on the other side of the cosmos. Over there, they cranked out the home-run hits for radio playlists. Young songwriters like Gerry Goffin and Carole King, or Barry Mann and Cynthia Weil, or Pomus and Shuman, Leiber and Stoller—they were the songwriting masters of the Western world, wrote all the popular songs, all the songs with crafty melodies and simple lyrics that came off as works of power over the airwaves. One of my favorites was Neil Sedaka because he wrote and performed his own songs. I never crossed paths with any of those people because none of the popular songs were connected to folk music or the down-town scene.

What I was into was the traditional stuff with a capital *T* and it was as far away from the mondo teeno scene as you could get. Into Lou's tape recorder I could make things up on the spot all based on folk music structure, and it came natural. As far as serious songwriting went, the songs I could see myself writing if I was that talented would be the kinds of songs that I wanted to sing. Outside of Woody Guthrie, I didn't see a single living soul who did it. Sitting in Lou's office I rattled off lines and verses based on the stuff I knew— "Cumberland Gap," "Fire on the Mountain," "Shady Grove," "Hard, Ain't It Hard." I changed words around and added something of my own here and there. Nothing do or die, nothing really formulated, all major chord stuff, maybe a typical minor key thing, something like "Sixteen Tons." You could write twenty or more songs off that one melody by slightly altering it. I could slip in verses or lines from old spirituals or blues. That was okay; others did it all the time. There was little head work involved. What I usually did was start out with something, some kind of line written in stone and then turn it with another line—make it add up to something else than it originally did. It's not like I ever practiced it and it wasn't too thought consuming. Not that I would sing any of it onstage.

Lou had never heard any of this kind of thing before, so there was very little feedback from him. Once in a while he would stop the machine and have me start over on something. He'd say, "That's catchy," and then want me to do it again. When that happened, I usually did something different because I hadn't paid attention to whatever I just sung, so I couldn't repeat it like he just heard it. I had no idea what he was going to do with all this stuff. It was as anti–big mainstream as you could get. Leeds Music had published songs like "Boogie Woogie Bugle Boy," "C'est Si Bon," "Under Paris Skies," "All or Nothing at All," Henry Mancini songs like "Peter Gunn," "I'll Never Smile Again" and all the songs that were in *Bye Bye Birdie*, a big Broadway hit.

The one song that had hooked me up with Leeds Music, the one that convinced John Hammond to bring me over there in the first place, wasn't an outreaching song at all but more of an homage in lyric and melody to the man who'd pointed out the starting place for my identity and destiny— the great Woody Guthrie. I wrote the song with him in mind, and I used the melody from one of his old songs, having no idea that it would be the first of maybe a thousand songs that I would write. My life had never been the same since I'd first heard Woody on a record player in Minneapolis a few years earlier. When I first heard him it was like a million megaton bomb had dropped.

In the summer of '59 after leaving home early spring, I was in Minneapolis, having come down from Northern Minnesota—from the Mesabi Range, the iron mining country, steel capital of America. I'd grown up there in Hibbing but had been born in Duluth, about seventy-five miles away to the east on the edge of Lake Superior, the big lake that the Indians call Gitche Gumee. Though we lived in Hibbing, my father from time to time would load us into an old Buick Roadmaster and we'd ride to Duluth for the weekend. My father was from Duluth, born and raised there. That's where his friends still were. One of five brothers, he'd worked all his life even as a kid. When he was sixteen, he'd seen a car smash into a telephone pole and burst into flames. He jumped off his bicycle, reached in and pulled the driver out, smothering the driver's body with his own—risking his life to save someone he didn't even know. Eventually, he took accounting classes in night school and was working for Standard Oil of Indiana when I was born. Polio, which left him with a pronounced limp, had forced him out of Duluth—he lost his job and that's how we got to the Iron Range, where my mother's family was from. Near Duluth, I also had cousins across the suspension aerial bridge in Superior, Wisconsin, the notorious red-light, gambling town and I stayed with them sometimes.

What I recall mostly about Duluth are the slate gray skies and the mysterious foghorns, violent storms that always seemed to be coming straight at you and merciless howling winds off the big black mysterious lake with treacherous ten-foot waves. People said that having to go out onto the deep water was like a death sentence. Most of Duluth was on a slant. Nothing is level there. The town is built on the side of a steep hill, and you're always either hiking up or down.

One time my parents took me to see Harry Truman speak at a political rally in Duluth's Leif Erickson Park. Leif Erickson was a Viking who was supposed to have come to this part of country way before the Pilgrims had ever landed in Plymouth Rock. I must have been seven or eight at the time, but it's amazing how I can still feel it. I can remember the excitement of being there in the crowd. I was on top of one of my uncles' shoulders in my little white cowboy boots and cowboy hat. It was an exhilarating thing, being there—the cheers, the jubilation, the attentiveness to every word that Truman spoke . . . Truman was gray hatted, a slight figure, spoke in the same kind of nasal twang and tone like a country singer. I was mesmerized by his slow drawl and sense of seriousness and how people hung on every word he was saying. A few years later he would say that the White House was like a jail cell. Truman was down to earth. Once he even threatened a journalist who criticized his daughter's piano playing. He didn't do any of that in Duluth, though.

The upper Midwest was an extremely volatile, politically active area—with the Farmer Labor Party, Social Democrats, socialists, communists. They were hard crowds to please and not too much for Republicanism. John Kennedy, before he became president, when he was still a senator, had come up to Hibbing on the campaign trail but that was about six months after I left. My mother said that eighteen thousand people had turned out to see him at the Veterans Memorial Building and that people were hanging from the rafters and others were in the street, that Kennedy was a ray of light and had understood completely the area of the country he was in. He gave a heroic speech, my mom said, and brought people a lot of hope. The Iron Range was an area that very few nationally known politicians or any famous people ever made it through. (Woodrow Wilson had stopped there in the early part of the century and spoke from the back of a train. My mother had seen him, too, when she was ten years old.) If I had been a voting man, I would have voted for Kennedy just for coming there. I wished I could have seen him.

My mother's family was from a little town called Letonia, just over the railroad tracks, not far from Hibbing. When she grew up the town consisted of a general store, a gas station, some horse stables, and a schoolhouse. The world I grew up in was a little different, a little more modernized, but still mostly gravel roads, marshlands, hills of ice, steep skylines of trees on the outskirts of town, thick forests, pristine lakes large and small, iron mine pits, trains and one-lane highways. Winters, ten below with a twenty below wind-chill factor were common, thawing spring and hot, steamy summers—penetrating sun and balmy weather where temperatures rose over one hundred degrees. Summers were filled with mosquitoes that could bite through your boots—winters with blizzards that could freeze a man dead. There were glorious autumns as well.

Mostly what I did growing up was bide my time. I always knew there was a bigger world out there but the one I was in at the time was all right, too. With not much media to speak of, it was basically life as you saw it. The things I did growing up were the things I thought everybody did—march in parades, have bike races, play ice hockey. (Not everyone was expected to play football or basketball or even baseball, but you had to know how to skate and play ice hockey.) The other usual things, too, like swimming holes and fishing ponds, sledding and something called bumper riding, where you grab hold of a tail bumper on a car and ride through the snow, Fourth of July fireworks, tree houses—a witches' brew of pastimes. You could also easily hop an iron ore train by grabbing and then hanging on to one of the iron ladders on either side and ride out to any number of lakes where you could go out and jump in them. We did that a lot. As kids, we shot air guns, BB guns and the real thing—.22s—shot at tin cans, bottles or overfed rats in the town garbage dump. Also, we had rubbergun fights. Rubberguns were made from pine wood that were cut into *L*-shaped pieces. You'd grip the short end, which had a spring clothespin taped hard to the side. The rubber that we'd get from inner tubes back then was authentic, thick rubber that we'd cut into round strips, tie them in bows and stretch them from the hammer position, which was the top of the spring clothespin—stretch that all the way to the business end of the barrel. When you held the *L*-shaped gun in your grip (you could make them in varied sizes) and you squeezed it, the rubber would snap out with swift, violent force and you could hit a target to up to ten or fifteen feet away. You could hurt somebody. If you got hit with the rubber it stung like hell, burned and caused welts. These games would be played all day, one game after another. Usually you divided up sides in the beginning and hoped not to get popped in the eye. Some kids had three or four guns. If you got hit, you'd have to go to a certain spot under a tree and wait until the next game began. One year everything changed because the mines began using synthetic rubber on their tractors and trucks. Synthetic rubber wasn't as good or as accurate as real rubber. It just dropped off the end of your barrel with a plop or else flew about four feet and flopped to the ground. This just wasn't any good. I guess now, if you use real rubber, it would be like using dum-dum bullets.

Just about the same time that the synthetic rubber came into the picture, so did the big-screen drive-in movie. That was a family activity, though, because you had to have a car. There was other stuff going on. Dirt track stock car racing on cool summer nights, mostly '49 or '50 Fords, bashed in cars, coffin contraptions, humpbacked cages with roll bars and fire extinguishers—seats taken out, doors welded shut—bumpin' and rumblin', slammin' and swivelin' on a half mile track, summersaulting off the rails . . . tracks littered with junkyard cars. There were three-ring circuses that came to town a few times a year and full tilt carnivals complete with human oddities, showgirls and even geeks. I saw one of the last blackface minstrel shows at a county carnival. Nationally known country-western stars played at the Memorial Building, and once Buddy Rich and his big band came and played at the high school auditorium. The most thrilling event of the summer was when The King and His Court fast-pitch softball team came to town and challenged the best players in the county. If you liked baseball, this was the team to see. The King and His Court were four players: a pitcher, a catcher, a first baseman and a roving shortstop. The pitcher was awesome. Sometimes he pitched from second base, sometimes blindfolded, at times between his legs. Very few players ever got a hit off him, and The King and His Court never lost a game. Television was coming in, too, but not every home had one. Round picture tubes. Programs usually started broadcasting at about three o'clock in the afternoon with a test pattern that ran for a few hours and showed a few shows broadcast out of New York or Hollywood and then went off at around seven or eight. There wasn't much to watch . . . Milton Berle, Howdy Doody, the Cisco Kid, Lucy and her Cuban bandleader husband, Desi, the *Father Knows Best* family, where everybody's always dressed up even in their own house. It wasn't like in the big city, where there was a lot more happening on TV. We didn't get *American Bandstand* or anything like that. Of course, there were other things to do. Still, though, it was all small town stuff—very narrow, provincial, where everybody actually knows everyone.

Now at last I was in Minneapolis where I felt liberated and gone, never meaning to go back. I'd come into Minneapolis unnoticed, I rode in on a Greyhound bus—nobody was there to greet me and nobody knew me and I liked it that way. My mother had given me an address for a fraternity house on University Avenue. My cousin Chucky, whom I just slightly knew, had been the fraternity president. He was four years older than me and an all-around successful student in high school—captain of the football team, valedictorian, class president. It was no surprise that he'd become president of the fraternity. My mom said that she talked to my aunt about calling Chucky and letting me stay there—at least while the place was vacated during the summer and most of its members were gone. There were a couple of guys hanging around when I got there and one of them said that I could stay in one of the upstairs rooms, the one at the end of the hall. It was a nothing room with just a bunk bed and a table by a window without any curtains. I set my bags down and gazed out the window.

I suppose what I was looking for was what I read about in *On the Road*—looking for the great city, looking for the speed, the sound of it, looking for what Allen Ginsberg had called the "hydrogen jukebox world." Maybe I'd lived in it all my life, I didn't know, but nobody ever called it that. Lawrence Ferlinghetti, one of the other Beat poets, had called it "The kiss proof world of plastic toilet seats, Tampax and taxis." That was okay, too, but the Gregory Corso poem "Bomb" was more to the point and touched the spirit of the times better—a wasted world and totally mechanized—a lot of hustle and bustle—a lot of shelves to clean, boxes to stack. I wasn't going to pin my hopes on that. Creatively you couldn't do much with it. I had already landed in a parallel universe, anyway, with more archaic principles and values; one where actions and virtues were old style and judgmental things came falling out on their heads. A culture with outlaw women, super thugs, demon lovers and gospel truths . . . streets and valleys, rich peaty swamps, with landowners and oilmen, Stagger Lees, Pretty Pollys and John Henrys—an invisible world that towered overhead with walls of gleaming corridors. It was all there and it was clear—ideal and God-fearing—but you had to go find it. It didn't come served on a paper plate. Folk music was a reality of a more brilliant dimension. It exceeded all human understanding, and if it called out to you, you could disappear and be sucked into it. I felt right at home in this mythical realm made up not with individuals so much as archetypes, vividly drawn archetypes of humanity, metaphysical in shape, each rugged soul filled with natural knowing and inner wisdom. Each demanding a degree of respect. I could believe in the full spectrum of it and sing about it. It was so real, so more true to life than life itself. It was life magnified. Folk music was all I needed to exist. Trouble was, there wasn't enough of it. It was out of date, had no proper connection to the actualities, the trends of the time. It was a huge story but hard to come across. Once I'd slipped in beyond the fringes it was like my six-string guitar became a crystal magic wand and I could move things like never before. I had no other cares or interests besides folk music. I scheduled my life around it. I had little in common with anyone not like-minded.

I gazed out the second story window of the fraternity house overlooking University Avenue through the green elm trees and slow-moving traffic, low hanging clouds . . . the birds were singing. It was like a curtain was being lifted. It was early June and a fine spring day. There were just a few other guys in the house besides my cousin Chucky, and they hung around mostly in the mess hall, a kitchen in the basement that ran the length of the building. They had all recently graduated from the university and were working at odd jobs for the summer—were waiting to move on. Most days, they sat around playing cards and drinking beer in torn tee-shirts and cutoff jeans. Cocksmen. They paid me no mind. I saw that I could easily come and go and nobody would bother me here.

First thing I did was go trade in my electric guitar, which would have been useless to me, for a double-O Martin acoustic. The man at the store traded me even and I left carrying the guitar in its case. I would play this guitar for the next couple of years or so. The area around the university was known as Dinkytown, which was kind of like a little Village, untypical from the rest of conventional Minneapolis. It was mostly filled with Victorian houses that were being used as student apartments. School life wasn't in session, so these were mostly empty. I found the local record store in the heart of Dinkytown. What I was looking for were folk music records and the first one I saw was Odetta on the Tradition label. I went into the listening booth to hear it. Odetta was great. I had never heard of her until then. She was a deep singer, powerful strumming and a hammering-on style of playing. I learned almost every song off the record right then and there, even borrowing the hammering-on style.

With my newly learned repertoire, I then went further up the street and dropped into the Ten O'Clock Scholar, a Beat coffeehouse. I was looking for players with kindred pursuits. The first guy I met in Minneapolis like me was sitting around in there. It was John Koerner and he also had an acoustic guitar with him. Koerner was tall and thin with a look of perpetual amusement on his face. We hit it off right away. We already knew a few of the same songs like "Wabash Cannonball" and "Waiting for a Train." Koerner had just gotten out of the Marine Corps, was an aeronautical engineering student. He was from Rochester, New York, already married and had gotten into folk music a couple of years earlier than me, learned a lot of songs off of a guy named Harry Webber—mostly street ballads. But he played a lot of blues type stuff, too, traditional barroom kind of things. We sat around and I played my Odetta songs and a few by Leadbelly, whose record I had heard earlier than Odetta. John played "Casey Jones," "Golden Vanity"—he played a lot of ragtime style stuff, things like "Dallas Rag." When he spoke he was soft spoken, but when he sang he became a field holler shouter. Koerner was an exciting singer, and we began playing a lot together.

I learned a lot of songs off Koerner by singing harmony with him and he had folk records of performers I'd never heard at his apartment. I listened to them a lot, especially to The New Lost City Ramblers. I took to them immediately. Everything about them appealed to me—their style, their singing, their sound. I liked the way they looked, the way they dressed and I especially liked their name. Their songs ran the gamut in styles, everything from mountain ballads to fiddle tunes and railroad blues. All their songs vibrated with some dizzy, portentous truth. I'd stay with The Ramblers for days. At the time, I didn't know that they were replicating everything they did off of old 78 records, but what would it have mattered anyway? It wouldn't have mattered at all. For me, they had originality in spades, were men of mystery on all counts. I couldn't listen to them enough. Koerner had

some other key records, too, mostly on the Folkways label—
*Foc'sle Songs and Sea Shanties* was one that I could listen to
over and over again. This one featured Dave Van Ronk,
Roger Abrams, and some others. The record knocked me
out. It was full ensemble singing, hard driving harmonic
songs like "Haul Away Joe," "Hangin' Johnny," "Radcliffe
Highway." Sometimes Koerner and I sang some of those
songs as a duo. Another record he had was the Elektra folk
songs *Sampler* with a variety of artists. That's where I first
heard Dave Van Ronk and Peggy Seeger, even Alan Lomax
himself singing the cowboy song "Doney Gal," which I added
to my repertoire. Koerner had a few other records—some
blues compilations on the Arhoolie label where I first heard
Blind Lemon Jefferson, Blind Blake, Charlie Patton and
Tommy Johnson.

I listened a lot to a John Jacob Niles record, too. Niles was
nontraditional, but he sang traditional songs. A Mephistophe-
lean character out of Carolina, he hammered away at some
harplike instrument and sang in a bone chilling soprano
voice. Niles was eerie and illogical, terrifically intense and
gave you goosebumps. Definitely a switched-on character, almost like a sorcerer. Niles was otherworldly and his voice
raged with strange incantations. I listened to "Maid Freed
from the Gallows" and "Go Away from My Window" plenty of
times.

Koerner said that I had to meet a guy named Harry Webber and through him, I did. Webber was an English literary
professor, a tweed wearing, old fashioned intellectual. And
he did know plenty of songs, mostly roving ballads—stern
ballads, ones that meant cruel business. I learned one called
"Old Greybeard," about a young girl whose mother tells her

to go kiss a man who has been arranged for her to marry and the daughter tells the mother to go kiss him herself . . . that the old greybeard is now clean shaven. The song is sung in first, second and third person. I loved all these ballads right away. They were romantic as all hell and high above all the popular love songs I'd ever heard. You could exhaust all the combinations of your vocabulary without having to learn any vocabulary. Lyrically they worked on some kind of supernatural level and they made their own sense. You didn't have to make your own sense out of it. I used to sing another one, too, called "When a Man's in Love," where a boy in love feels no cold—he'll go through frosted snow to meet his girl, get her and take her to some silent place. I was beginning to feel like a character from within these songs, even beginning to think like one. "Roger Esquire," another song learned from Webber, was about money and beauty tickling the fancy and dazzling the eyes.

I could rattle off all these songs without comment as if all the wise and poetic words were mine and mine alone. The songs had beautiful melodies and were filled with everyday leading players like barbers and servants, mistresses and soldiers, sailors, farmhands and factory girls—their comings and goings—when they spoke in the songs they entered your life. But there was more to it than that . . . a lot more. Beneath it I was into the rural blues as well; it was a counterpart of myself. It was connected to early rock and roll and I liked it because it was older than Muddy and Wolf. Highway 61, the main thoroughfare of the country blues, begins about where I came from . . . Duluth to be exact. I always felt like I'd started on it, always had been on it and could go anywhere from it, even down into the deep Delta country. It was the same road, full of the same contradictions, the same one-horse towns, the same spiritual ancestors. The Mississippi River, the bloodstream of the blues, also starts up from my neck of the woods. I was never too far away from any of it. It was my place in the universe, always felt like it was in my blood.

Folklorist singers came through the Twin Cities also and you could learn songs from them, too—old-time performers like Joe Hickerson, Roger Abrams, Ellen Stekert or Rolf Kahn. Authentic folk records were as scarce as hens' teeth. You had to know people who had them. Koerner and some others had them, but the group was very small. Record stores didn't carry many of them, as there was very little demand. Performers like Koerner and myself would go anywhere to hear one by anybody we thought we hadn't heard. We once went over to St. Paul to somebody's house who supposedly had a 78 record of Blind Andy Jenkins singing "Death of Floyd Collins." The person wasn't at home and we never got to hear it. I did hear Tom Darby and Jimmy Tarleton, though, at the house of somebody's father who had owned an old copy of one of their records. I always thought that "A-wop-bop-a-loo-lop a-lop-bam-boo" had said it all until I heard Darby and Tarlton doing "Way Down in Florida on a Hog." Darby and Tarlton, too, were out of this world.

Koerner and I were playing and singing a lot together as a duo, but we each did our own thing separately. As for myself, I played morning, noon and night. That's all I did, usually fell asleep with the guitar in my hands. I went through the entire summer this way. In the fall, I was sitting at the lunch counter at Gray's drugstore. Gray's drugstore was in the heart of Dinkytown. I had moved into a room right above it. School was back in session and university life was picking up again. My cousin Chucky and his buddies had all moved away from the fraternity house, and the fraternity members, or would-be fraternity members, soon reappeared. They asked me who I was and what I was doing there. Nothing, I wasn't doing anything there . . . I was sleeping there. Of course I knew what was coming and quickly grabbed my bags and left. The room above Gray's drugstore cost thirty bucks a month. It was an okay place and I could easily afford it.

By this time, I was making three to five dollars every time I played at either one of the coffeehouses around or another place over in St. Paul called the Purple Onion pizza parlor. Above Gray's, the crash pad was no more than an empty storage room with a sink and a window looking into an alley. No closet or anything. Toilet down the hall. I put a mattress on the floor, bought a used dresser, plugged in a hot plate on top of that—used the outside window ledge as a refrigerator when it got cold. I was sitting at the counter at Gray's one day— winter had come early—wind howled across the Central Avenue Bridge outside and a carpet of snow was beginning to form on the ground. Flo Castner, who I'd known from one of the coffeehouses, the Bastille, had come in and sat down beside me. Flo was an actress in the drama academy, an aspiring thespian, odd looking but beautiful in a wacky way, had long red hair, was light skinned, dressed in black from head to foot. She had an uptown but folksy demeanor, was a mystic and transcendentalist—believed in the occult power of trees and things like that. She was also serious about reincarnation. We used to have strange conversations.

"In another life, I could have been you," she'd say.

"Yeah, but then I wouldn't have been the same person in that life."

"Yeah, that's right. Let's work on it."

On this particular day, we were just sitting around talking and she asked me if I'd ever heard of Woody Guthrie. I said sure, I'd heard him on the Stinson records with Sonny Terry and Cisco Houston. Then she asked me if I'd ever heard him all by himself on his own records. I couldn't remember having done that. Flo said that her brother Lyn had some of his records and she'd take me over there to hear them—that Woody Guthrie was somebody that I should definitely get hip to. Something about this sounded important and I became definitely interested. There wasn't much distance between the drugstore and her brother's house, maybe a half a mile or so. Her brother Lyn was an attorney for the city's social services—had thin, wispy hair, wore a bow tie and little James Joyce glasses. He had seen me and me him, a couple of times throughout the summer. I had heard him play a few folk songs, but he never said much and I never spoke to him. He had never invited me over to listen to anybody's records.

He was at home when Flo brought me by. He said it was okay to look through his record collection, pulled out a few record albums of old 78s and said I should listen to these. One was the *Spirituals to Swing Concert at Carnegie Hall*. This was a collection of 78s with Count Basie, Meade Lux Lewis, Joe Turner and Pete Johnson, Sister Rosetta Tharpe among many others. The other collection was the one that Flo had told me about—a Woody Guthrie set of about twelve double sided 78 records. I put one on the turntable and when the needle dropped, I was stunned—didn't know if I was stoned or straight. What I heard was Woody singing a whole lot of his own compositions all by himself . . . songs like "Ludlow Massacre," "1913 Massacre," "Jesus Christ," "Pretty Boy Floyd," "Hard Travelin'," "Jackhammer John," "Grand Coulee Dam," "Pastures of Plenty," "Talkin' Dust Bowl Blues," "This Land Is Your Land."

All these songs together, one after another made my head spin. It made me want to gasp. It was like the land parted. I had heard Guthrie before but mainly just a song here and there—mostly things that he sang with other artists. I hadn't actually heard him, not in this earth shattering kind of way. I couldn't believe it. Guthrie had such a grip on things. He was so poetic and tough and rhythmic. There was so much intensity, and his voice was like a stiletto. He was like none of the other singers I ever heard, and neither were his songs. His mannerisms, the way everything just rolled off his tongue, it all just about knocked me down. It was like the record player itself had just picked me up and flung me across the room. I was listening to his diction, too. He had a perfected style of singing that it seemed like no one else had ever thought about. He would throw in the sound of the last letter of a word whenever he felt like it and it would come like a punch. The songs themselves, his repertoire, were really beyond category. They had the infinite sweep of humanity in them. Not one mediocre song in the bunch. Woody Guthrie tore everything in his path to pieces. For me it was an epiphany, like some heavy anchor had just plunged into the waters of the harbor.

That day I listened all afternoon to Guthrie as if in a trance and I felt like I had discovered some essence of self-command, that I was in the internal pocket of the system feeling more like myself than ever before. A voice in my head said, "So this is the game." I could sing all these songs, every single one of them and they were all that I wanted to sing. It was like I had been in the dark and someone had turned on the main switch of a lightning conductor.

A great curiosity respecting the man had also seized me and I had to find out who Woody Guthrie was. It didn't take me long. Dave Whittaker, one of the Svengali-type Beats on the scene happened to have Woody's autobiography, *Bound for Glory*, and he lent it to me. I went through it from cover to cover like a hurricane, totally focused on every word, and the book sang out to me like the radio. Guthrie writes like the whirlwind and you get tripped out on the sound of the words alone. Pick up the book anywhere, turn to any page and he hits the ground running. Who is he? He's a hustling ex–sign painter from Oklahoma, an antimaterialist who grew up in the Depression and Dust Bowl days—migrated West, had a tragic childhood, a lot of fire in his life—figuratively and literally. He's a singing cowboy, but he's more than a singing cowboy. Woody's got a fierce poetic soul—the poet of hard crust sod and gumbo mud. Guthrie divides the world between those who work and those who don't and is interested in the liberation of the human race and wants to create a world worth living in. *Bound for Glory* is a hell of a book. It's huge. Almost too big.

His songs are something else, though, and even if you've never read the book, you'd know who he was through his songs. For me, his songs made everything else come to a screeching halt. I decided then and there to sing nothing but Guthrie songs. It's almost like I didn't have any choice. I liked my repertoire the way it was—stuff like "Cornbread, Meat and Molasses," "Betty and Dupree," "Pick a Bale of Cotton"—but I'd have to put it all on the back burner for a while,

didn't know if I'd ever get back to it. Through his compositions my view of the world was coming sharply into focus. I
said to myself I was going to be Guthrie's greatest disciple. It
seemed like a worthy thing. I even seemed to be related to him.
Even from a distance and having never seen the man, I could
perceive his face with a clearness. He looks not unlike my father in my father's early days. I knew little about Woody. I
wasn't even sure if he was alive anymore. The book makes it
seem like he was a character from the old past. Whittaker,
though, had got me up to date on him, that he was in ill health
somewhere in the East and I pondered that.

During the next few weeks I went back a few times to Lyn's
house to listen to those records. He was the only one who
seemed to have so many of them. One by one, I began singing
them all, felt connected to these songs on every level. They
were cosmic. One thing for sure, Woody Guthrie had never
seen nor heard of me, but it felt like he was saying, "I'll be
going away, but I'm leaving this job in your hands. I know I
can count on you."

Now that I crossed the divide, I was head over heels in singing
nothing but Guthrie songs—at house parties, in the coffeehouses, street singing, with Koerner, not with Koerner—if I
had a shower I would have sung them in there, too. There
were a lot of them and outside of the main ones, not easily to
be found. There were no reissues of his older records, there
were only the original ones, but I would move heaven and
earth to find them, even went to the Minneapolis public library to the Folkways section. (Public libraries were the one
place for some reason that had most of the Folkways records.)

I'd always be checking the repertoires of every out of town performer who came through to see what Guthrie songs they knew that I didn't, and I was beginning to feel the phenomenal scope of Woody's songs—the Sacco and Vanzetti ballads, Dust Bowl and children songs, Grand Coulee Dam songs, venereal disease songs, union and workingman ballads, even his rugged heartbreak love ballads. Each one seemed like a towering tall building with a variety of scenarios all appropriate for different situations. Woody made each word count. He painted with words. That along with his stylized type singing, the way he phrased, the dusty cowpoke deadpan but amazingly serious and melodic sense of delivery, was like a buzzsaw in my brain and I tried to emulate it any way I could. A lot of folks might have thought of Woody's songs as backdated, but not me. I felt they were totally in the moment, current and even forecasted things to come. I felt anything but like the young punk folksinger who had just begun out of nowhere six months previously. It felt more like I had instantly risen up from a noncommissioned volunteer to an honorable knight—stripes and gold stars.

Woody's songs were having that big an effect on me, an influence on every move I made, what I ate and how I dressed, who I wanted to know, who I didn't. In the late '50s and early '60s, teenage rebellion was beginning to make noise, but that scene hadn't appealed to me, not in a wholehearted way. It had no organized shape. The rebel-without-a-cause thing wasn't hands-on enough—even a lost cause, I thought, would be better than no cause. To the Beats, the devil was bourgeois conventionality, social artificiality and the man in the gray flannel suit.

Folk songs automatically went up against the grain of all

these things and Woody's songs even went against that. In comparison, everything else seemed one-dimensional. The folk and blues tunes had already given me my proper concept of culture, and now with Guthrie's songs my heart and mind had been sent into another cosmological place of that culture entirely. All the other cultures of the world were fine, but as far as I was concerned, mine, the one I was born into, did the work of them all and Guthrie's songs even went further.

The sun had swung my way. I felt like I'd crossed the threshold and there was nothing in sight. Singing Woody's songs, I could keep everything else at a safe distance. This fantasy was short-lived, however. Thinking that I was wearing the sharpest looking uniform and the shiniest boots around, all of a sudden I felt a jolt and was stopped short in my tracks. It felt like someone had taken a chunk out of me. Jon Pankake, a folk music purist enthusiast and sometime literary teacher and film wiseman, who'd been watching me for a while on the scene, made it his business to tell me that what I was doing hadn't escaped him. "What do you think you're doing? You're singing nothing but Guthrie songs," he said, jabbing his finger into my chest like he was talking to a poor fool. Pankake was authoritative and a hard guy to get past. It was known around that Pankake had a vast collection of the real folk records and could go on and on about them. He was part of the folk police, if not the chief commissioner, wasn't impressed with any of the new talent. To him nobody possessed any great mastery—no one could succeed in laying a hand on any of the traditional stuff with any authority. Of course he was right, but Pankake didn't play or sing. It's not like he put himself in any position to be judged.

He was a bit of a film critic, too. While other intellectual types might be discussing poetic differences between T. S. Eliot and e. e. cummings, Pankake would come up with arguments about why John Wayne was a better cowboy in *Rio Bravo* then he was in *Legend of the Lost*. He expounded on directors like Howard Hawks or John Ford, that they get Wayne when other directors don't. Maybe Pankake was right, maybe not. It wasn't that big a deal. Actually, as far as Wayne goes, I'd meet the Duke in the mid-'60s. He was the big male movie star at the time and was filming a war movie about Pearl Harbor, *In Harm's Way*, over in Hawaii. A girl I used to know in Minneapolis, Bonnie Beecher, had become an actress and was playing a supporting role. Me and my band, The Hawks, had stopped through there on our way to Australia and she invited me down to the set, a naval battleship. She introduced me to the Duke, who was in full military uniform, an army of people surrounding him. I watched him film a scene and then Bonnie brought me over to meet him. "I hear you're a folksinger," he said and I nodded. "Sing something," he said. I took out my guitar and sang "Buffalo Skinners" and he smiled, looked at Burgess Meredith who was sitting in a canvas chair, then he looked back at me and said, "I like that. Left that drover's bones to bleach, heh?" "Yup." He asked me if I knew "Blood on the Saddle." I did know "Blood on the Saddle," a little bit of it, anyway, but I knew "High Noon" better. I thought about singing it and maybe if I was standing there with Gary Cooper, I would have. But Wayne wasn't Gary Cooper. I don't know if he would have liked that song. The Duke was a massive figure. He looked like a heavy piece of hauled lumber, and it didn't seem like any man could stand shoulder to shoulder with him. Not anybody in the movies, anyway. I thought of asking him why some of his cowboy films were better than others, but it would have been crazy to do that. Or maybe it wouldn't have been . . . I don't know. In any case, I never would have dreamed that I'd be standing there on a battleship, somewhere in the Pacific singing for the great cowboy John Wayne, while back in Minneapolis face-to-face with Jon Pankake . . .

"You're trying hard, but you'll never turn into Woody Guthrie," Pankake says to me as if he's looking down from some high hill, like something has violated his instincts. It was no fun being around Pankake. He made me nervous. He breathed fire through his nose. "You better think of something else. You're doing it for nothing. Jack Elliott's already been where you are and gone. Ever heard of him?" No, I'd never heard of Jack Elliott. When Pankake said his name, it was the first time I'd heard it. "Never heard of him, no. What does he sound like?" John said that he'd play me his records and that I was in for a surprise.

Pankake lived in an apartment above McCosh's bookstore, a place that specialized in eclectic old books, ancient texts, philosophical political pamphlets from the 1800s on up. It was a neighborhood hangout for intellectuals and Beat types, on the main floor of an old Victorian house only a few blocks away. I went there with Pankake and saw it was true that he had all the incredible records, ones you never saw and wouldn't know where to get. For someone who didn't sing and play, it was amazing that he had so many. The record he took out and played for me first was *Jack Takes the Floor* on the Topic label out of London—an imported record, a very obscure one. There were probably only about ten of these discs in the whole U.S.A., or maybe Pankake had the only one in the country. I didn't know. If Pankake hadn't played it for me most likely I would have never heard it. The record started to spin and Jack's voice blasted into the room. "San Francisco Bay Blues," "Ol' Riley" and "Bed Bug Blues" go by in a flash. Damn, I'm thinking, this guy is really great. He sounds just like Woody Guthrie, only a leaner, meaner one, not singing the same Guthrie songs, though. I felt like I'd been cast into sudden hell.

Jack was some master of musical tricks. The record cover was mysterious, but not in an ominous way. It showed a character with certain careless ease, rakish looking, a handsome saddle tramp. He's dressed like a cowboy. His tone of voice is sharp, focused and piercing. He drawls and he's so confident it makes me sick. All that and he plays the guitar effortlessly in a fluid flat-picking perfected style. His voice leaps all over the room in a lazy way and he is explosive when he wants to be. You could hear that he had Woody Guthrie's style down pat and more. Another thing—he was a brilliant entertainer, something that most of the folk musicians didn't bother with. Most folk musicians waited for you to come to them. Jack went out and grabbed you. Elliott, who'd been born ten years before me, had actually traveled with Guthrie, learned his songs and style firsthand and had mastered it completely.

Pankake was right. Elliott was far beyond me. There were a few other Ramblin' Jack records that he had, too—one where he sings with Derroll Adams, a singer buddy of his from Portland who played banjo like Bascom Lamar Lunsford and sang in a dry and laconic witted style suiting Jack perfectly. Together they sounded like horses galloping.

They did "More Pretty Girls Than One," "Worried Man Blues" and "Death of John Henry." Jack alone was something else, though. On the cover of his record *Jack Takes the Floor,* you could almost see his eyes. They were saying something, but I knew not what. Pankake let me listen to the record repeated times. It was uplifting, but it was being thrown down at the same time. Pankake said something earlier, like Jack being the king of the folksingers, the city ones, anyway. Listening to him, you wouldn't doubt it. I don't know if Pankake was trying to enlighten me or put me down. It didn't matter. Elliott had indeed already gone beyond Guthrie, and I was still getting there. I had nothing near the compelling poise of self that I heard on the record.

I sheepishly left the apartment and went back out into the cold street, aimlessly walked around. I felt like I had nowhere to go, felt like one of the dead men walking through catacombs. It would be hard not to be influenced by the guy I just heard. I'd have to block it out of my mind, though, forget this thing, tell myself I hadn't heard him and he didn't exist. He was overseas in Europe, anyway, in a self-imposed exile. The U.S. hadn't been ready for him. Good. I was hoping he'd stay gone, and I kept hunting for Guthrie songs.

A few weeks later Pankake heard me playing again and was quick to point out that I didn't fool him, that I used to be imitating Guthrie and now I was imitating Elliott and did I think in some way that I was equivalent to him? Pankake said that maybe I should go back to playing rock and roll, that he knew I used to do that. I don't know how he knew—maybe he was a spy, too, but in any case, I wasn't trying to fool anybody. I was just doing what I could with what I had where I was. Pankake was right, though. You can't take only a few dance lessons and then think you are Fred Astaire.

Jon was one of the classic traditional folk snobs. They looked down on anything that smelled of commerciality and were vocal about it: groups like The Brothers Four, Chad Mitchell Trio, Journeymen, Highwaymen—the traditional folk snobs considered them all exploiters of a sacred thing. Okay, so that stuff didn't give me orgasms either. But they were no threat, so I didn't care about it one way or another. Most of the folk crowd trashed the commercial folk stuff. The popular perception of folk music were things like "Waltzing Matilda," "Little Brown Jug" and "The Banana Boat Song" and all that stuff had appealed to me a few years earlier so I didn't feel the need to put it down. To be fair, there were snobs on the other side, too—commercial folk snobs. These kind looked down on the traditional singers as being old-fashioned and wrapped in cobwebs. Bob Gibson, a clean-cut commercial folksinger from Chicago, had a big following and some records out. If he dropped in to see you perform he'd be in the front row. After the first or second song, if you weren't commercial enough, too raw or ragged around the edges, he might conspicuously stand up, make a fuss and walk out on you. There wasn't any middle ground and it seemed like everybody was a snob of one kind or another. I tried to keep everything in perspective.

Whatever I heard people say was irrelevant—both good or bad—didn't get caught up in it. I had no preconditioned audience anyway. What I had to do was keep straight ahead and I did that. The road ahead had always been encumbered with shadowy forms that had to be dealt with in one way or another. Now there was another one. I knew Jack was up there someplace and I hadn't missed what Pankake had said about him. It was true. Jack was the King of the Folksingers.

The "Queen of the Folksingers," that would have to be Joan Baez. Joan was born the same year as me and our futures would be linked, but at this time to even think about it would be preposterous. She had one record out on the Vanguard label called *Joan Baez* and I'd seen her on TV. She'd been on a folk music program broadcast nationwide on CBS out of New York. There were other performers on the show including Cisco Houston, Josh White, Lightnin' Hopkins. Joan sang some ballads on her own and then sat side by side with Lightnin' and sang a few things with him. I couldn't stop looking at her, didn't want to blink. She was wicked looking—shiny black hair that hung down over the curve of slender hips, drooping lashes, partly raised, no Raggedy Ann doll. The sight of her made me high. All that and then there was her voice. A voice that drove out bad spirits. It was like she'd come down from another planet.

She sold a lot of records and it was easy to understand why. The women singers in folk music were performers like Peggy Seeger, Jean Ritchie and Barbara Dane, and they didn't translate well to a modern crowd. Joan was nothing like any of them. There was no one like her. It would be a few years before Judy Collins or Joni Mitchell would come on the scene. I liked the older women singers—Aunt Molly Jackson and Jeanie Robinson—but they didn't have the piercing quality that Joan had. I'd been listening to a few of the female blues singers a lot, like Memphis Minnie and Ma Rainey, and Joan was in some kind of way more like them. There was nothing girlish about them and there was nothing girlish about Joan, either. Both Scot and Mex, she looked like a religious icon, like somebody you'd sacrifice yourself for and she sang in a voice straight to God . . . also was an exceptionally good instrumentalist.

The Vanguard record was no phony baloney. It was almost frightening—an impeccable repertoire of songs, all hard-core traditional. She seemed very mature, seductive, intense, magical. Nothing she did didn't work. That she was the same age as me almost made me feel useless. However illogical it might have seemed, something told me that she was my counterpart—that she was the one that my voice could find perfect harmony with. At the time there was nothing but distance and worlds and big divides between her and me. I was still stuck in the boondocks. Yet some strange feeling told me that we would inevitably meet up. I didn't know much about Joan Baez. I had no idea that she'd always been a true loner, kind of like me, but she'd been bounced around a lot and lived in places from Baghdad to San Jose. She had experienced a whole lot more of the world than I did. Even so, to think that she was probably more like me than me would have seemed a little excessive.

There was no clue from her records that she was interested in social change or any of that. I considered her lucky, lucky to get involved in the right kind of folk music early on, get up to her eyeballs in it—learn how to play and sing it in an expert way, beyond criticism, beyond category. There was no one in her class. She was far off and unattainable—Cleopatra living in an Italian palace. When she sang, she made your teeth drop. Like John Jacob Niles, she was mighty strange. I'd be scared to meet her. She might bury her fangs in the back of my neck. I didn't want to meet her, but I knew I would. I was going in the same direction even though I was way in back of her at the moment. She had the fire and I felt I had the same kind of fire. I could do the songs she did, for starters . . . "Mary Hamilton," "Silver Dagger," "John Riley," "Henry Martin." I could make them drop into place like she did, but in a different way. Not everyone can sing these songs convincingly. The singer has to make you believe what you are hearing and Joan did that. I believed that Joan's mother would kill somebody that she loved. I believed that. I believed that she'd come from that kind of family. You have to believe. Folk music, if nothing else, makes a believer out of you. I believed Dave Guard in The Kingston Trio, too. I believed that he would kill or already did kill poor Laura Foster. I believed that he'd kill someone else, too. I didn't think he was playing around.

As far as other singers around town, there were some but not many. There was Dave Ray, a high school kid who sang Leadbelly and Bo Diddley songs on a twelve-string guitar, probably the only twelve-string guitar in the entire Midwest—and then there was Tony Glover, a harp player who played with me and Koerner sometimes. He sang a few songs, but mostly played the harp—cupped it in his hands and played like Sonny Terry or Little Walter. I played the harp, too, but in a rack . . . probably the only harmonica rack at the time in the Midwest. Racks were impossible to find. I'd used a lopsided coat hanger for a while, but it only had sort of worked. The real harmonica rack that I found was in the basement of a music store on Hennipen Avenue, still in a box unopened from 1948. As far as harp playing went, I tended to keep it simple.

I couldn't play like Glover or anything, and didn't try to. I played mostly like Woody Guthrie and that was about it. Glover's playing was known and talked about around town, but nobody commented on mine. The only comment that I ever got was a few years later in John Lee Hooker's hotel room on Lower Broadway in New York City. Sonny Boy Williamson was there and he heard me playing, said, "Boy, you play too fast."

Eventually, it was time for me to get out of Minneapolis. Just like Hibbing, the Twin Cities had gotten a little too cramped, and there was only so much you could do. The world of folk music was too closed off and the town was beginning to feel like a mud puddle. New York City was the place I wanted to be and one snowy morning around daybreak after sleeping in the back room of the Purple Onion pizza parlor in St. Paul, the place where Koerner and I played . . . with only a few tattered rags in a suitcase and a guitar and harmonica rack, I stood on the edge of town and hitchhiked east to find Woody Guthrie. He was still the man. It was freezing and although I might have been slack in a lot of things, my mind was ordered and disciplined and I didn't feel the cold. Soon I was rolling through the snowy Wisconsin prairie fields, the looming shadows of Baez and Elliott were not far from my heels. The world I was heading into, although it would undergo a lot of changes, was really the world of Jack Elliott and Joan Baez. However true that might have been, I, too, had the axe in my hands and needed to tear out of there, head off to where life promised something more—felt that my own voice and guitar would be equal to the situation.


New York City, midwinter, 1961. Whatever I was doing was working out okay and I intended to stay with it, felt like I was closing in on something. I was playing on the regular bill at the Village Gaslight, the premier club on the carnivalesque MacDougal Street. When I began working there, the Gaslight was owned by John Mitchell, a renegade and raconteur, a Brooklynite. I only saw him a few times. He was ornery and combatant, had an exotic looking girl-friend who Jack Kerouac had based a novel on. Mitchell was already legendary. The Village was heavily Italian, and Mitchell hadn't taken even one step back from the local mafiosos. It was a known fact that he didn't make payoffs out of principle. The fire marshals, the police and the health inspectors were routinely invading the place. Mitchell, though, had lawyers and he took his battles to city hall and somehow the place stayed open. Mitchell carried a pistol and a knife. He also was a master carpenter. During my time there, some Mississippians bought the place sight unseen from a business opportunity ad in a magazine down South. Mitchell didn't tell anybody he was selling the club or that it would change ownership. He just sold the place and left the country.

The gothic folk club was located in the basement below the street, but it didn't seem like a basement because the floor had been lowered. About six or eight main performers alter-nated from darkness until dawn. The pay was sixty dollars weekly cash, at least that's what it was for me. Some performers might have been paid more. It was a huge step above the Greenwich Village basket-house scene.

Noel Stookey who later became part of Peter, Paul and Mary was the MC. Noel was an impressionist, a comedian and a singer and guitar player. He worked in a camera store during the day. At night he was dressed in a neat three-piece suit, was immaculately groomed, a little goatee, tall and lanky, Roman nose. Some people might have described him as aloof. Stookey looked like someone torn out of a page of some ancient magazine. He could imitate just about anything—clogged water pipes and toilets flushing, steamships and sawmills, traffic, violins and trombones. He could imitate singers imitating other singers. He was very funny. One of his more outrageous imitations was Dean Martin imitating Little Richard.

Hugh Romney, who later became the psychedelic clown Wavy Gravy, also performed down there. When he was Hugh Romney, he was the straightest looking cat you'd ever seen—always smartly dressed, usually in Brooks Brothers light gray suits. Romney was a monologist, gave long, intimate, unestablishmentarian raps, had squinty eyes, you could never tell if they were closed or opened. It was as if his sight was impaired. He'd walk onstage, squint into the blue spotlight and begin talking like he had just taken a long voyage and come back from a distant realm—like he had just gotten here from Constantinople or Cairo and he was going to enlighten you into some archaic mystery. It wasn't so much what he said, it was just in the way he said it. There were a few others around who did what he did, but Romney was the most known. Romney had been influenced by but was in no way on the same level as Lord Buckley.

Buckley was the hipster bebop preacher who defied all labels. No sulking Beat poet, he was a raging storyteller who did riffs on all kinds of things from supermarkets to bombs and the crucifixion. He did raps on characters like Gandhi and Julius Caesar. Buckley had even organized something called the Church of the Living Swing (a jazz church). With stretched out words, Buckley had a magical way of speaking. Everybody, including me, was influenced by him in one way or another. He died about a year before I got to town so I never got to see him; heard his records, though.

Some of the other musicians at the Gaslight were Hal Waters, an interpreter who sang folk songs in a refined way, John Wynn, who played gut-string guitar and sang folk songs in an operatic voice. Someone closer in temperament to me was Luke Faust, a five-string banjo player and singer who sang Appalachian ballads, another guy named Luke Askew, who later became an actor in Hollywood. Luke was from Georgia and he sang Muddy and Wolf and Jimmy Reed songs. He didn't play guitar but he had a guitar player. Luke was a white guy who sounded like Bobby Blue Bland.

Len Chandler played at the Gaslight, too. Len had originally come from Ohio and was a serious musician who had played oboe in the orchestra back home and could read and write and arrange symphonic music. He sang quasi-folk stuff with a commercial bent and was energetic, had that thing that people call charisma. Len performed like he was mowing down things. His personality overrode his repertoire. Len also wrote topical songs, front-page things.

Paul Clayton occasionally played sets down here, too. Paul got all his versions of songs by adapting transcriptions from old texts. He knew hundreds of songs and must have had a photographic memory. Clayton was unique—elegiac, very princely—part Yankee gentleman and part Southern rakish dandy. He dressed in black from head to foot and would quote Shakespeare. Clayton traveled regularly from Virginia to New York and back, and we got to be friends. His companions were out-of-towners and like him, a "caste apart"—had attitudes, but known only to themselves—a non-folky crowd. Authentic nonconformists—scufflers, but not the Kerouac types, not down and outers, not the kind that run the streets whose activities could be recognized. I liked Clayton and I liked his friends. Through Paul I met people here and there who said to me it was okay to stay at their apartments any time I needed it, and not to worry about it.

Clayton was good friends with Van Ronk, too. Dave Van Ronk, he was the one performer I burned to learn particulars from. He was great on records, but in person he was greater. Van Ronk was from Brooklyn, had seaman's papers, a wide walrus mustache, long brown straight hair which flew down covering half his face. He turned every folk song into a surreal melodrama, a theatrical piece—suspenseful, down to the last minute. Dave got to the bottom of things. It was like he had an endless supply of poison and I wanted some . . . couldn't do without it. Van Ronk seemed ancient, battle tested. Every night I felt like I was sitting at the feet of a timeworn monument. Dave sang folk songs, jazz standards, Dixieland stuff and blues ballads, not in any particular order and not a superfluous nuance in his entire repertoire. Songs that were delicate, expansive, personal, historical, or ethereal, you name it. He put everything into a hat and—presto—put a new thing out in the sun. I was greatly influenced by Dave. Later, when I would record my first album, half the cuts on it were renditions of songs that Van Ronk did. It's not like I planned that, it just happened. Unconsciously I trusted his stuff more than I did mine.

Van Ronk's voice was like rusted shrapnel and he could get a lot of subtle ramifications out of it—delicate, gentle, rough, explosive, sometimes all within the same song. He could conjure up anything—expressions of terror, expressions of despair. He also was an expert guitar player. All that, and he had a sardonic humorous side, too. I felt different towards Van Ronk than anyone else on the scene because it was him who brought me into the fold and I was happy to be playing alongside him night after night at the Gaslight. It was a real stage with a real audience and it was where the real action was. Van Ronk helped me in other ways, too. His apartment on Waverly Place had a couch I could crash on any time I wanted to. He also showed me around the regular haunts of Greenwich Village—the other clubs, mostly jazz clubs like Trudy Heller's, the Vanguard, the Village Gate and the Blue Note, and I got to see a lot of the jazz greats close up. As a performer Van Ronk did something else that I found intriguing.

One of his patented dramatic effects would be to stare intently at somebody in the crowd. He'd pin their eyes like he was singing just to them, whispering some secret, telling somebody something where their lives hung in the balance. He also never phrased the same thing the same way twice. Sometimes I'd hear him play the same song that he'd done in a previous set and it would hit me in a completely different way. He'd play something, and it was like I'd never heard it before, or not quite the way I remembered it. His pieces were perversely complex, although very simple. He had it all down and could hypnotize an audience or stun them, or he could make them scream and holler. Whatever he wanted. He was built like a lumberjack, drank hard, said little and had his territory staked out—full forward, all cylinders working. David was the grand dragon. If you were on MacDougal Street in the evening and out to see somebody play, he'd be the first and last vital choice of the night. He'd towered over the street like a mountain but would never break into the big time. It just wasn't where he pictured himself. He didn't want to give up too much. No puppet strings on him ever. He was big, sky high, and I looked up to him. He came from the land of giants.

Van Ronk's wife, Terri, definitely not a minor character, took care of Dave's bookings, especially out of town, and she began trying to help me out. She was just as outspoken and opinionated as Dave was, especially about politics—not so much the political issues but rather the highfalutin' theological ideas behind political systems. Nietzschean politics. Politics with a hanging heaviness. Intellectually it would be hard to keep up. If you tried, you'd find yourself in alien territory. Both were anti-imperialistic, antimaterialist. "What a ridiculous thing, an electric can opener," Terri once said as we walked past the shop window of a hardware store on 8th Street. "Who'd be stupid enough to buy that?"

Terri had managed to get Dave booked in places like Boston and Philly . . . even as far away as St. Louis at a folk club called Laughing Buddha. For me, those gigs were out of the question. You needed at least one record out even if it was on a small label to get work in any of those clubs. She did manage to come up with a few things in places like Elizabeth, New Jersey, and Hartford—once at a folk club in Pittsburgh, another in Montreal. Scattered things. Mostly I stayed around in New York City. I didn't really want to go out of town. If I wanted to be out of town, I wouldn't have come to New York City in the first place. I was fortunate to have the regular gig at the Gaslight and wasn't on any wild goose chase to go anywhere. I could breathe. I was free. Didn't feel constrained. Between sets I mostly hung out, drank shooters of Wild Turkey and iced Schlitz at the Kettle of Fish Tavern next door and played cards upstairs at the Gaslight. Things were working out fine. I was learning all I could and stayed keyed up. Once Terri offered to bring me over to meet Jac Holzman, who operated Elektra Records, one of the companies that released some of Dave's stuff. "I can get you an appointment. Do you want to sit down with him?" "I don't want to sit down with anybody, no." The idea didn't contain too much for me. Sometime later in the summer Terri managed to get me on a live radio folk extravaganza broadcast from Riverside Church up on Riverside Drive. Things were about to change for me again, to get new and strange.

Backstage the humidity was soaring. Performers came and went, waited to go on and milled around. As usual, the real show was backstage. I was talking to a dark-haired girl, Carla Rotolo, who I knew a little bit. Carla was Alan Lomax's personal assistant. Carla introduced me to her sister. Her sister's name was Susie but she spelled it Suze. Right from the start I couldn't take my eyes off her. She was the most erotic thing I'd ever seen. She was fair skinned and golden haired, full-blood Italian. The air was suddenly filled with banana leaves. We started talking and my head started to spin. Cupid's arrow had whistled by my ears before, but this time it hit me in the heart and the weight of it dragged me overboard. Suze was seventeen years old, from the East Coast. Had grown up in Queens, raised in a left-wing family. Her father had worked in a factory and had recently died. She was involved in the New York art scene, painted and made drawings for various publications, worked in graphic design and in Off-Broadway theatrical productions, also worked on civil rights committees—she could do a lot of things. Meeting her was like stepping into the tales of 1,001 Arabian nights. She had a smile that could light up a street full of people and was extremely lively, had a particular type of voluptuousness—a Rodin sculpture come to life. She reminded me of a libertine heroine. She was just my type.

For the next week or so I thought of her a lot—couldn't shut her out of my mind, was hoping I'd run into her. I felt like I was in love for the first time in my life, could feel her vibe thirty miles away—wanted her body next to mine. Now. Right now. Movies had always been a magical experience and the Times Square movie theaters, the ones like oriental temples were the best places to see them. Recently I'd seen *Quo Vadis* and *The Robe*, and now I went to sit through *Atlantis, Lost Continent* and *King of Kings*. I needed to shift my mind, get it off of Suze for a while. *King of Kings* starred Rip Torn, Rita Gam, and Jeffrey Hunter playing Christ. Even with all the heavy action on the screen, I couldn't tune into it. When the second feature, *Atlantis, Lost Continent* played, it was just as bad. All the death-ray crystals, giant fish submarines, earthquakes, volcanoes and tidal waves and whatnot. It might have been the most exciting movie of all time, who knows? I couldn't concentrate.

As fate would have it, I ran into Carla again and asked about her sister. Carla asked me if I'd like to see her. I said, "Yeah, you don't know how much," and she said, "Oh, she'd like to see you, too." Soon we met up and began to see each other more and more. Eventually we got to be pretty inseparable. Outside of my music, being with her seemed to be the main point in life. Maybe we were spiritual soul-mates.

Her mother Mary, though, who worked as a translator for medical journals, wasn't having it. Mary lived on the top floor of an apartment building on Sheridan Square and treated me like I had the clap. If she would have had her way, the cops would have locked me up. Suze's mom was a small feisty woman—volatile with black eyes like twin coals that could burn a hole through you, was very protective. Always make you feel like you did something wrong. She thought I had a nameless way of life and would never be able to support anybody, but I think it went much deeper than that. I think I just came in at a bad time.

"How much did that guitar cost?" she asked me once.

"Not much."

"I know, not much, but still something."

"Almost nothing," I said.

She glared at me, cigarette in her mouth. She was always trying to goad me into some kind of argument. My presence was so displeasing to her, but it's not like I'd caused any trouble in her life. It wasn't me who was responsible for the loss of Suze's father or anything. Once I said to her that I didn't think she was being fair. She stared squarely into my eyes like she was staring at some distant, visible object and said to me, "Do me a favor, don't think when I'm around." Suze would tell me later that she didn't mean it. She did mean it, though. She did everything in her power to keep us apart, but we went on seeing each other anyway.


This stifling scene was becoming problematic, signaling to me that I needed to get my own place, one with my own bed, stove and tables. It was about time. I guess it could have happened earlier, but I liked staying with others. It was less of a hassle, easier, with little responsibility—places where I could freely come and go, sometimes even with a key, rooms with plenty of hardback books on shelves and stacks of phonograph records. When I wasn't doing anything else, I'd thumb through the books and listen to records.

Not having a place of my own now was beginning to affect my supersensitive nature, so after being in town close to a year, I rented a third floor walk-up apartment at 161 West 4th Street at sixty dollars a month. It wasn't much, just two rooms above Bruno's spaghetti parlor, next door to the local record store and a furniture supply shop on the other side. The apartment had a tiny bedroom, more like a large closet, and a kitchenette, a living room with a fireplace and two windows that looked out over fire escapes and small courtyards. There was barely room enough for one person and the heat went off after dark and the place had to be heated by keeping both gas burners up full blast. It came empty. Quickly after moving in I built some furniture for the place. With some borrowed tools, I made a couple of tables, one which doubled as a desk. I also put together a cabinet and a bed frame. All the wood pieces had come from the store downstairs, and I fastened everything together with the accompanying hardware—galvanized nails, knockers and hinge plates, ⅜-inch square pieces of wrought iron, brass and copper, roundheaded wood screws. I didn't have to go far to get that stuff, it was all downstairs. I put it all together with hacksaws, cold chisels and screwdrivers—even made a couple of mirrors using an old technique I learned in a high school shop woodworking class using plates of glass, mercury and tin foil.

Besides playing music, I liked doing those kinds of things. I purchased a used TV, stuck it on top of one of the cabinets, bought a mattress and got a rug that I spread across the hardwood floor. I got a record player at Woolworth's and put it on one of the tables. The small room seemed immaculate to me and I felt that for the first time I had a place of my own.

Suze and I were spending more and more time together, and I began to broaden my horizons, see a lot of what her world was like, especially the Off-Broadway scene . . . a lot of LeRoi Jones's stuff, *Dutchman*, *The Baptism*. I also saw Gelber's junkie play, *The Connection*, the Living Theater's *The Brig*, and other remarkable plays. I went with her to where the artists and painters hung out, like Caffe Cino, Camino Gallery, Aegis Gallery. We went to see Comedia Del'Arte, a storefront on the Lower East Side that was built into a small theater with enormous puppets as big as people that jiggled and swung. I saw a couple of plays, one where a soldier, a prostitute, a judge and a lawyer were all the same puppet. The puppets, because of their size and the small, confining space, were odd, unsettling and confronting . . .

nothing like the funny wooden dummy, the tuxedoed Charlie McCarthy, the Edgar Bergen puppet who we all knew and loved so well.

A new world of art was opening up my mind. Sometimes early in the day we'd go uptown to the city museums, see giant oil-painted canvases by artists like Velázquez, Goya, Delacroix, Rubens, El Greco. Also twentieth-century stuff—Picasso, Braque, Kandinsky, Rouault, Bonnard. Suze's favorite current modernist artist was Red Grooms, and he became mine, too. I loved the way everything he did crushed itself into some fragile world, the rickety clusters of parts all packed together and then, standing back, you could see the complex whole of it all. Grooms's stuff spoke volumes to me. He was the artist I checked out most. Red's stuff was extravagant, his work cut like it was done by acid. All of his mediums—crayon, watercolor, gouache, sculpture or mixed media—collage tableaus—I liked the way he put the stuff together. It was bold, announced its presence in glaring details. There was a connection in Red's work to a lot of the folk songs I sang. It seemed to be on the same stage. What the folk songs were lyrically, Red's songs were visually—all the bums and cops, the lunatic bustle, the claustrophobic alleys—all the carnie vitality. Red was the Uncle Dave Macon of the art world. He incorporated every living thing into something and made it scream—everything side by side created equal—old tennis shoes, vending machines, alligators that crawled through sewers, dueling pistols, the Staten Island Ferry and Trinity Church, 42nd Street, profiles of skyscrapers. Brahman bulls, cowgirls, rodeo queens and Mickey Mouse heads, castle turrets and Mrs. O'Leary's cow, creeps and greasers and weirdos and grinning, bejeweled nude models, faces with melancholy looks, blurs of sorrow—everything

hilarious but not jokey. Familiar figures from history, too—
Lincoln, Hugo, Baudelaire, Rembrandt—all done with
graphic finesse, burned out as powerful as possible. I loved the
way Grooms used laughter as a diabolical weapon. Subcon-
sciously, I was wondering if it was possible to write songs like
that.

About that time I began to make some of my own drawings. I actually picked up the habit from Suze, who drew a
lot. What would I draw? Well, I guess I would start with
whatever was at hand. I sat at the table, took out a pencil
and paper and drew the typewriter, a crucifix, a rose, pen-
cils and knives and pins, empty cigarette boxes. I'd lose
track of time completely. An hour or two could go by and it
would seem like only a minute. Not that I thought that I was
any great drawer, but I did feel like I was putting an orderli-
ness to the chaos around—something like Red did, but he
did it on a much grander level. In a strange way I noticed
that it purified the experience of my eye and I would make
drawings of my own for years to come.

This was the same table that I'd sit at and compose songs.
Not quite yet, though. You have to take the lead from somewhere, and there were only a few performers around who
wrote songs and of them, my favorite was Len Chandler. But
I just thought that was his own personal thing and it wasn't
enough to inspire me to do it myself. As far as I was concerned, Woody Guthrie had written the greatest songs and
there was no way to top that. Eventually, though, while not
trying to reweave the world, I did compose a slightly ironic
song called "Let Me Die in My Footsteps." I based it on an
old Roy Acuff ballad. The song I wrote was inspired by the
fallout shelter craze that had blossomed out of the Cold

War. I suppose some considered it radical to come up with a song like that, but to me it wasn't radical at all. In Northern Minnesota fallout shelters didn't catch on, had no effect whatsoever on the Iron Range. As far as communists went, there wasn't any paranoia about them. People weren't scared of them, seemed to be a big to-do over nothing. Commies were symbolic of travelers from outer space. Mine owners were more to be feared, more of an enemy, anyway. Salesmen peddling fallout shelters had been turned away. Stores didn't sell them and nobody built them. Houses had thick-walled basements, anyway. Besides no one liked thinking that someone else might have one and you didn't. Or if you had one and someone else didn't, that might not be too good, either. It could turn neighbor against neighbor and friend against friend. You couldn't imagine having to confront some neighbor banging on your door saying something like, "Hey, look. It's a matter of life and death and our friendship ain't worth a bo diddley. Is that what you're trying to tell me?" How you could respond to a friend who was acting like a tyrant trying to force his way in, saying, "Listen I have young kids. My daughter's only three and my son is two. Before I let you close them out, I'll come to you with a gun. Now, quit the scam." There wasn't any honorable way out. Bomb shelters divided families and could create mutiny. Not that people weren't concerned about the mushroom cloud—they were. But salesmen hawking the bomb shelters were met with expressionless faces.

Besides that, the general opinion was, in case of nuclear attack all you really needed was a surplus Geiger counter. It might become your most prized possession, would tell you what's safe to eat and what's dangerous. Geiger counters were easy to get. In fact, I even had one in my New York apartment, so writing the song about the futility of fallout shelters was not that radical. It's not like I had to conform to any doctrine to do it. The song was personal and social at the same time, though. That was different. Even so, this song didn't break down any barriers for me or perform any miracle. Most everything I wanted to say I could usually find in an old folk song or in one of Woody's songs. When I began performing "Let Me Die in My Footsteps," I didn't even say I wrote it. I just slipped it in somewhere, said it was a Weavers song.

My perspective on all that was about to change. The air would soon shoot up in intensity and become more potent. My little shack in the universe was about to expand into some glorious cathedral, at least in songwriting terms. Suze had been working behind the scenes in a musical production at the Theatre de Lys on Christopher Street. It was a presentation of songs written by Bertolt Brecht, the antifascist Marxist German poet-playwright whose works were banned in Germany, and Kurt Weill, whose melodies were like a combination of both opera and jazz. Previously they had had a big hit with a ballad called "Mack the Knife" that Bobby Darin had made popular. You couldn't call this a play, it was more like a stream of songs by actors who sang. I went there to wait for Suze and was aroused straight away by the raw intensity of the songs . . . "Morning Anthem," "Wedding Song," "The World Is Mean," "Polly's Song," "Tango Ballad," "Ballad of the Easy Life." Songs with tough language. They were erratic, unrhythmical and herky-jerky—weird visions. The singers were thieves, scavengers or scallywags and they all roared and snarled. The entire world was narrowly confined between four streets. On the small stage, objects were barely discernable—lampposts, tables, stoops, windows, corners of buildings, moon shining through roofed-in courtyards—grim surroundings, creepy sensations. Every song seemed to come from some obscure tradition, seemed to have a pistol in its hip pocket, a club or a brickbat and they came at you in crutches, braces and wheelchairs. They were like folk songs in nature, but unlike folk songs, too, because they were sophisticated.

Within a few minutes I felt like I hadn't slept or tasted food for about thirty hours, I was so into it. The song that made the strongest impression was a show-stopping ballad, "A Ship the Black Freighter." Its real title was "Pirate Jenny," but I didn't hear that in the song so I didn't know what the real title was. It was sung by some vaguely masculine woman, dressed up like a scrubbing lady who performs petty tasks, goes about making up beds in a ratty waterfront hotel. What drew me into the song at first was the line about the ship the black freighter, that comes after every verse. That particular line took me back to the foghorns of ships that I'd heard in my youth and the grandiosity of the sounds had stuck in my mind. Seemed like they were right on top of us.

Duluth, even though it's two thousand miles from the nearest ocean, was an international seaport. Ships from South America, Asia and Europe came and went all the time, and the heavy rumble of the foghorns dragged you out of your senses by your neck. Even though you couldn't see the ships through the fog, you knew they were there by the heavy outbursts of thunder that blasted like Beethoven's Fifth— two low notes, the first one long and deep like a bassoon. Foghorns sounded like great announcements. The big boats came and went, iron monsters from the deep—ships to wipe out all spectacles. As a child, slight, introverted and asthma stricken, the sound was so loud, so enveloping, I could feel it in my whole body and it made me feel hollow. Something out there could swallow me up.

After I heard the song maybe a couple of times, I kind of forgot about the foghorns and got tuned in to the point of view of the maid, where she's coming from, and it's the driest, coldest place. Her attitude is so strong and burning. "The gentlemen" who she is making up beds for have no idea of the hostility inside of her and the ship, the black freighter, seems to be a symbol for some messianic thing. It's always getting closer and closer and maybe now it's even got its damn foot in the door. The scrubbing lady is powerful and she's masquerading as a nobody—she's counting heads. The song takes place in a hideous netherworld where soon, "every building . . . a flat one, the whole stinking place will be down to the ground." All except hers. Her building will be okay and she'll be safe and sound. Later in the song the gentlemen begin to wonder who lives there. They're in trouble, but they don't know it. They were always in trouble, but never knew it. People are swarming near the docks and the gentlemen are chained up and brought to her and she's asked if they should be killed now or later. It's up to her. The old scrubbing lady's eyes light up at the end of the song. The ship is shooting guns from its bow and the gentlemen are wiping the laughs off their faces. The ship is still turning around in the harbor. The old lady says, "Kill 'em right now, that'll learn 'em." What did the gentlemen do to deserve such a fate? The song doesn't say.

This is a wild song. Big medicine in the lyrics. Heavy action spread out. Each phrase comes at you from a ten-foot drop, scuttles across the road and then another one comes like a punch on the chin. And then there's always that ghost chorus about the black ship that steps in, fences it all off and locks it up tighter than a drum. It's a nasty song, sung by an evil fiend, and when she's done singing, there's not a word to say. It leaves you breathless. In the small theater when the performance reached its climactic end the entire audience was stunned, sat back and clutched their collective solar plexus. I knew why it did, too. The audience was the "gentlemen" in the song. It was their beds that she was making up. It was their post office that she was sorting mail in, and it was their school she was teaching in. This piece left you flat on your back and it demanded to be taken seriously. It lingered. Woody had never written a song like that. It wasn't a protest or topical song and there was no love for people in it.

Later, I found myself taking the song apart, trying to find out what made it tick, why it was so effective. I could see that everything in it was apparent and visible but you didn't notice it too much. Everything was fastened to the wall with a heavy bracket, but you couldn't see what the sum total of all the parts were, not unless you stood way back and waited 'til the end. It was like the Picasso painting *Guernica*. This heavy song was a new stimulant for my senses, indeed very much like a folk song but a folk song from a different gallon jug in a different backyard. I felt like I wanted to snatch up a bunch of keys and go see about that place, see what else was there. I took the song apart and unzipped it—it was the form, the free verse association, the structure and disregard for the known certainty of melodic patterns to make it seriously matter, give it its cutting edge. It also had the ideal chorus for the lyrics. I wanted to figure out how to manipulate and control this particular structure and form which I knew was the key that gave "Pirate Jenny" its resilience and outrageous power.

I'd think about this later in my dumpy apartment. I hadn't done anything yet, wasn't any kind of songwriter but I'd become rightly impressed by the physical and ideological possibilities within the confines of the lyric and melody. I could see that the type of songs I was leaning towards singing didn't exist and I began playing with the form, trying to grasp it—trying to make a song that transcended the information in it, the character and plot.

Totally influenced by "Pirate Jenny," though staying far away from its ideological heart, I began fooling around with things—took a story out of the *Police Gazette*, a tawdry incident about a hooker in Cleveland, a minister's daughter called Snow White, who killed one of her customers in a grotesque and ugly way. I started with that using the other song as a prototype and piled lines on, short bursts of lines . . . five or six freeform verses and used the first two lines of the "Frankie & Albert" ballad as the chorus. The lines that say, "Frankie was a good girl. Everybody knows. Paid a hundred dollars for Albert's new suit of clothes." I liked the idea of doing it, but the song didn't come off. I was missing something.

The alliance between Suze and me didn't turn out exactly to be a holiday in the woods. Eventually fate flagged it down and it came to a full stop. It had to end. She took one turn in the road and I took another. We just passed out of each others' lives, but before that, before the fire went out, we stayed together a lot at the West 4th Street apartment. During the summers there was more than enough stifling heat. The small place was like an oven full of suffocating air that you could just about chew and swallow. In the winter, there was no heat. It was biting cold and we kept each other warm snuggled under blankets.

Suze was there by my side when I began recording for Columbia Records. The events which led up to it were very unexpected, and I had never really fixed my gaze on any big recording company. I would have been the last one to believe it if you'd have told me I'd be recording for Columbia Records, one of the top labels in the country and one with big name mainstream artists like Johnny Mathis and Tony Bennett and Mitch Miller. What put me there amongst that crowd came about because of John Hammond. John had first seen and heard me at Carolyn Hester's apartment. Carolyn was a Texan guitar-playing singer who I knew and played with around town. She was going places and it didn't surprise me. Carolyn was eye catching, down-home and double barrel beautiful. That she had known and worked with Buddy Holly left no small impression on me and I liked being around her. Buddy was royalty, and I felt like she was my connection to it, to the rock-and-roll music that I'd played earlier, to that spirit.

Carolyn was married to Richard Fariña, a part-time novelist and adventurer who people said was with Castro in the Sierra Madre Mountains and had fought with the IRA. Whatever that was about, I thought he was the luckiest guy in the world to be married to Carolyn. We met over there at her apartment, me and guitarist Bruce Langhorne and stand-up bass player Bill Lee, whose four-year-old son would become the filmmaker Spike Lee. Eventually, Bruce and Bill would play on my records. They'd played with Odetta and could play everything from melodic jazz to rockin' blues. If you had them playing with you, that's pretty much all you would need to do just about anything.

Carolyn had asked me to play harmonica on some songs for her debut record on Columbia and to teach her a couple of other things that she had heard me do. I was happy to do that. Hammond had wanted to meet us and get everything in running order, to hear the songs Carolyn was thinking about recording. That's what the meeting was all about. That's where he first heard me. He heard my harp playing and guitar strumming, even heard me singing a few things in harmony with Carolyn, but I didn't notice him noticing me. I wouldn't have done that. I was just there for her and that was all. Before leaving he asked me if I recorded for anybody. He was the first authoritative figure who ever asked me that. He just kind of said it in passing. I shook my head, didn't hold my breath to hear him respond and he didn't and that was that.

Between that time and the next time I met him, it seemed like a tidal wave had happened, in my world anyway. I'd been playing at the most prominent folk club in America, the one called Gerde's Folk City, and was on the bill with a bluegrass band, The Greenbriar Boys, and had been given a rave review in the folk and jazz section of the *New York Times*. It was unusual because I was the second act on the bill and The Greenbriar Boys were hardly mentioned. I had played there once before and had gotten no review. This article appeared the night before Carolyn's recording session and the next day

Hammond saw the newspaper. The sessions went well and as everyone was packing up and leaving, Hammond asked me to come into the control booth and told me that he'd like me to record for Columbia Records. I said that, yeah, I would like to do that. It felt like my heart leaped up to the sky, to some intergalactic star. Inside I was in a state of unstable equilibrium, but you wouldn't have known it. I couldn't believe it. It seemed too good to be true.

My whole life was now about to be derailed. It seemed like eons ago since I'd been in Flo Castner's brother's apartment in southeast Minneapolis listening to the *Spirituals to Swing* album and the Woody Guthrie songs. Now, incredulously, I was sitting in the office of the man responsible for the *Spirituals to Swing* album and he was signing me to Columbia Records.

Hammond was a music man through and through. He spoke rapidly—short, cut phrases—and was edgy. He talked the same language as me, knew everything about the music he liked, all the artists he had recorded. He said what he meant and he meant what he said and could back it all up. Hammond was no bullshitter. Money didn't make much of an impression on him. Why would it? One of his forebears, Cornelius Vanderbilt, had stated somewhere, "Money? What do I care about money? H'ain't I got the power!" Hammond, who was a true American aristocrat, didn't give a damn about record trends or musical currents changing. He could do as he pleased with what he loved and had been doing it for a lifetime. He'd been giving opportunities to the humbled and the vulnerable for longer than anybody could remember. Now he was bringing me to the Columbia Records label—the center of the labyrinth. The folk labels had all turned me down. That was okay now. I was glad about it. I gazed around Mr. Hammond's office and saw a picture of a friend of mine, John Hammond Jr. John, or Jeep as we knew him on MacDougal Street, was about my age, a blues guitar player and singer. Later he'd become an acclaimed artist in his own right. When I met him he had just gotten back from college, and I think he had only been playing guitar for a short time. Sometimes we'd go over to his house, which was on MacDougal Street below Houston, where he'd grown up, and we listened to a lot of records out of an amazing record collection . . . mostly blues 78s and grassroots rock and roll. I never made the connection that he was the son of the legendary John Hammond until I saw the photograph and only then did I put it together. I don't think anybody knew who Jeep's father was. He never talked about it.

John Hammond put a contract down in front of me—the standard one they gave to any new artist. He said, "Do you know what this is?" I looked at the top page which said, *Columbia Records*, and said, "Where do I sign?" Hammond showed me where and I wrote my name down with a steady hand. I trusted him. Who wouldn't? There were maybe a thousand kings in the world and he was one of them. Before leaving that day, he'd given me a couple of records that were not yet available to the public that he thought might interest me. Columbia had bought the vaults of '30s and '40s secondary labels—Brunswick, Okeh, Vocalion, ARC—and would be releasing some of the stuff. One of the records that he gave me was The Delmore Brothers with Wayne Rainey, and the other record was called *King of the Delta Blues* by a singer named Robert Johnson. Wayne Rainey, I used to hear on the radio and he was one of my favorite harmonica players and singers, and I loved The Delmore Brothers, too. But I'd never heard of Robert Johnson, never heard the name, never seen it on any of the compilation blues records. Hammond said I should listen to it, that this guy could "whip anybody." He showed me the artwork, an unusual painting where the painter with the eye stares down from the ceiling into the room and sees this fiercely intense singer and guitar player, looks no more than medium height but with shoulders like an acrobat. What an electrifying cover. I stared at the illustration. Whoever the singer was in the picture, he already had me possessed. Hammond told me that he knew of him from way back, had tried to get him up to New York to perform at the famous Spirituals to Swing Concert but by that time he had discovered that Johnson was gone, had died mysteriously in Mississippi. He'd only recorded about twenty sides and Columbia Records owned all of them and was now about to reissue some.

John picked out a date on the calendar for me to come back and start recording, what studio to come to and all that, and I left high as a kite, took the subway back downtown and raced over to Van Ronk's apartment. Terri let me in. She'd been in the kitchen doing the domestic thing. The small kitchen was a mess—bread pudding on the stove—stale French bread with crusts on a cutting board—raisins and vanilla and eggs piled up. She was coating the bottom of a pan with margarine and waiting as the sugar was dissolving. "I got a record I want to play for Dave," I said as she let me in. Dave was reading the *Daily News*. In the pages, the American government was blasting away in Nevada, testing nuclear weapons. The Russians were testing nuclear weapons all over their country, too. James Meredith, a black student in Mississippi, was barred from getting into the classrooms at the state university. There were bad things in the news. Dave looked up, peering at me over a pair of horn-rimmed glasses. I had the thick acetate of the Robert Johnson record in my hands and I asked Van Ronk if he ever heard of him. Dave said, nope, he hadn't, and I put it on the record player so we could listen to it. From the first note the vibrations from the loudspeaker made my hair stand up. The stabbing sounds from the guitar could almost break a window. When Johnson started singing, he seemed like a guy who could have sprung from the head of Zeus in full armor. I immediately differentiated between him and anyone else I had ever heard. The songs weren't customary blues songs. They were perfected pieces—each song contained four or five verses, every couplet intertwined with the next but in no obvious way. They were so utterly fluid. At first they went by quick, too quick to even get. They jumped all over the place in range and subject matter, short punchy verses that resulted in some panoramic story—fires of mankind blasting off the surface of this spinning piece of plastic. "Kind Hearted Woman," "Traveling Riverside Blues," "Come On in My Kitchen."

Johnson's voice and guitar were ringing the room and I was mixed up in it. Didn't see how anybody couldn't be. But Dave wasn't. He kept pointing out that this song comes from another song and that one song was an exact replica of a different song. He didn't think Johnson was very original. I knew what he meant, but I thought just the opposite. I thought Johnson was as original as could be, didn't think him or his songs could be compared to anything. Dave later played some sides by Leroy Carr and Skip James and Henry Thomas, and said, "See what I mean?" I did see what he meant, but Woody had taken a lot of old Carter Family songs and put his own spin on them, too, so I didn't think much of whatever it meant. Dave thought Johnson was okay, that the guy was powerful but that it was all derivative. There was no point in arguing with Dave, not intellectually anyway. I had a primitive way of looking at things and I liked country fair politics. My favorite politician was Arizona Senator Barry Goldwater, who reminded me of Tom Mix, and there wasn't any way to explain that to anybody. I wasn't that comfortable with all the psycho polemic babble. It wasn't my particular feast of food. Even the current news made me nervous. I liked old news better. All the new news was bad. It was good that it didn't have to be in your face all day. Twenty-four-hour news coverage would have been a living hell.

I let Dave go back to his newspaper, said I'd see him later and put the acetate back in the white cardboard sleeve. It wasn't a printed cover. The only identification was written by hand on the disc itself and what it said was simply the name Robert Johnson and a listing of the songs. The record that didn't grab Dave very much had left me numb, like I'd been hit by a tranquilizer bullet. Later, at my West 4th Street apartment I put the record on again and listened to it all by myself. Didn't want to play it for anybody else.

Over the next few weeks I listened to it repeatedly, cut after cut, one song after another, sitting staring at the record player. Whenever I did, it felt like a ghost had come into the room, a fearsome apparition. The songs were layered with a startling economy of lines. Johnson masked the presence of more than twenty men. I fixated on every song and wondered how Johnson did it. Songwriting for him was some highly sophisticated business. The compositions seemed to come right out of his mouth and not his memory, and I started meditating on the construction of the verses, seeing how different they were from Woody's. Johnson's words made my nerves quiver like piano wires. They were so elemental in meaning and feeling and gave you so much of the inside picture. It's not that you could sort out every moment carefully, because you can't. There are too many missing terms and too much dual existence. Johnson bypasses tedious descriptions that other blues writers would have written whole songs about. There's no guarantee that any of his lines either happened, were said, or even imagined. When he sings about icicles hanging on a tree it gives me the chills, or about milk turning blue . . . it made me nauseous and I wondered how he did that. Also, all the songs had some weird personal resonance. Throwaway lines, like, "If today were Christmas Eve and tomorrow were Christmas Day," I could feel that in my bones—that particular yuletide time of the year. On the Iron Range it had been positively Dickensian. Just like the picture books: angels on Christmas trees, horse-drawn sleighs pushing through snowy streets, pine trees glistening with lights, wreaths strung over the downtown stores, Salvation Army band playing on the corner, choirs going from house to house caroling, fireplaces blazing, woolly scarves around your neck, church bells ringing. When December rolled around, everything slowed down, everything got silent and retrospective, snowy white, deep snow. I always thought Christmas was like that for everyone, everywhere. I couldn't imagine it not being like that forever. Johnson conjured that up in just a few swift strokes, like nothing else—not even the great "White Christmas." Everything for Johnson is legitimate prey. There's a fishing song called "Dead Shrimp Blues" unlike anything you could expect—a screwed-up fishing song with red-blooded lines that's way beyond metaphor. There's one about a Terraplane, a clunker of an automobile, probably the greatest car song. If you'd never seen a Terraplane and heard the song, you'd think it was streamlined and bullet shaped. Johnson's car song is way beyond metaphor, too.

I copied Johnson's words down on scraps of paper so I could more closely examine the lyrics and patterns, the construction of his old-style lines and the free association that he used, the sparkling allegories, big-ass truths wrapped in the hard shell of nonsensical abstraction—themes that flew through the air with the greatest of ease. I didn't have any of these dreams or thoughts but I was going to acquire them. I thought about Johnson a lot, wondered who his audience could have been. It's hard to imagine sharecroppers or plantation field hands at hop joints, relating to songs like these. You have to wonder if Johnson was playing for an audience that only he could see, one off in the future. "The stuff I got'll bust your brains out," he sings. Johnson is serious, like the scorched earth. There's nothing clownish about him or his lyrics. I wanted to be like that, too.

Eventually the record came out and it hit all the blues lovers like an explosion. A few researchers got transfixed on him and went looking for his past, whatever was left of it, and a few found it. Johnson recorded in the '30s, and in the

1960s there were still some folks around in the Delta who had known about him. Some even, who knew him. There'd been a fast moving story going around that he had sold his soul to the devil at a four-way crossroads at midnight and that's how he got to be so good. Well, I don't know about that. The ones who knew him told a different tale and that was that he had hung around some older blues players in rural parts of Mississippi, played harmonica, was rejected as a bothersome kid, that he went off and learned how to play guitar from a farmhand named Ike Zinnerman, a mysterious character not in any of the history books. Maybe because he didn't make records. He must have been an incredible teacher. Those who knew said that Ike showed Robert the rudiments of how to play like just about anybody and that Johnson did the rest on his own, that he mainly listened to records and got all of his approaches off those records. You can still hear them, the original records, the songs that were prototypes for all of Johnson's songs. This makes more sense. Johnson's even got a song called "Phonograph Blues" that's an homage to a record player with a rusty needle. John Hammond had told me that he thought Johnson had read Walt Whitman. Maybe he did, but it doesn't clear up anything. I just couldn't imagine how Johnson's mind could go in and out of so many places. He seems to know about everything, he even throws in Confucius-like sayings whenever it suits him. Neither forlorn or hopeless or shackled—nothing hinders him. As great as the greats were, he goes one step further. You can't imagine him singing, "Washington's a bourgeois town." He wouldn't have noticed or if he did, it would have been irrelevant.

More than thirty years later, I would see Johnson for myself in eight seconds' worth of 8-millimeter film shot in Ruleville, Mississippi, on a brightly lit afternoon street by some Germans in the late '30s. Some people questioned whether it was really him, but slowing the eight seconds down so it was more like eighty seconds, you can see that it really is Robert Johnson, has to be—couldn't be anyone else. He's playing with huge, spiderlike hands and they magically move over the strings of his guitar. There's a harp rack with a harmonica around his neck. He looks nothing like a man of stone, no high-strung temperament. He looks almost childlike, an angelic looking figure, innocent as can be. He's wearing a white linen jumper, coveralls and an unusual gilded cap like Little Lord Fauntleroy. He looks nothing like a man with the hellhound on his trail. He looks immune to human dread and you stare at the image in disbelief.

In a few years' time, I'd write and sing songs like "It's Alright Ma (I'm Only Bleeding)," "Mr. Tambourine Man," "Lonesome Death of Hattie Carroll," "Who Killed Davey Moore," "Only a Pawn in Their Game," "A Hard Rain's A-Gonna Fall" and some others like that. If I hadn't gone to the Theatre de Lys and heard the ballad "Pirate Jenny," it might not have dawned on me to write them, that songs like these could be written. In about 1964 and '65, I probably used about five or six of Robert Johnson's blues song forms, too, unconsciously, but more on the lyrical imagery side of things. If I hadn't heard the Robert Johnson record when I did, there probably would have been hundreds of lines of mine that would have been shut down—that I wouldn't have felt free enough or upraised enough to write. I wasn't the only one who learned a thing or two from Johnson's compositions. Johnny Winter, the flamboyant Texan guitar player born a couple of years after me, rewrote Johnson's song about the phonograph, turning it into a song about a television set. Johnny's tube is blown and his picture won't come in. Robert Johnson would have loved that. Johnny, by the way, recorded a song of mine, "Highway 61 Revisited," which itself was influenced by Johnson's writing. It's strange the way circles hook up with themselves. Robert Johnson's code of language was like nothing I'd heard before or since. To go with all of that, someplace along the line Suze had also introduced me to the poetry of French Symbolist poet Arthur Rimbaud. That was a big deal, too. I came across one of his letters called "Je est un autre," which translates into "I is someone else." When I read those words the bells went off. It made perfect sense. I wished someone would have mentioned that to me earlier. It went right along with Johnson's dark night of the soul and Woody's hopped-up union meeting sermons and the "Pirate Jenny" framework. Everything was in transition and I was standing in the gateway. Soon I'd step in heavy loaded, fully alive and revved up. Not quite yet, though.

Lou Levy had autonomy at Leeds Music Publishing company the same way John Hammond had autonomy at Columbia Records. Neither was a bureaucrat or egomaniac. Each came from an older world, a more ancient order, one with more piss 'n' vinegar. They knew where they belonged and they had guts to back up whatever their beliefs were. You didn't want to let them down. Whatever your dreams were, guys like these could make you realize them.

Lou shut off his tape machine and switched on some lamps. The songs I was recording for him were so unlike the big swinging ballads that he'd been used to. Night was coming on. Amber lights glowing from the windows across the street. The freezing sleet hit the side of the building like steel drums. Out the window it looked like diamonds slung onto black velvet. In the adjoining room I could hear the sound of Lou's secretary's racing feet going to shut tight one of the windows.

Lou's company would never publish any of my greatest songs. Al Grossman had seen to that. Grossman was the big-time manager around Greenwich Village. He had seen me around before but had paid me little mind. After my first record on Columbia had been released, there was a noticeable shift on his part to represent me. I welcomed the opportunity because Grossman had a stable of clients and was getting all of them work. When he began to represent me, the first thing he wanted to do was get me out of my Columbia Records contract. I thought that this was screwing around. Grossman informed me that I had been under twenty-one when I'd signed the contract, therefore I had been a minor, making the contract null and void . . . that I should go up to the Columbia offices and talk to John Hammond and tell him that my contract was illegal and that Grossman would be coming up to negotiate another one. Sure. I went up to see Mr. Hammond, but I had no intentions of doing that. Not if I had been offered a fortune would I have done it. Hammond had believed in me and had backed up his belief, had given me my first start on the world's stage, and no one, not even

Grossman, had anything to do with that. There was no way I'd go against him for Grossman, not in a million years. I knew that the contract would have to be straightened out, though, so I went to see him. The mere mention of Grossman's name just about gave him apoplexy. He didn't like him, said he was as dirty as they come and was sorry Grossman was representing me, though he said he would still be supportive. Hammond said that we should straighten this contract situation out right here and now before it becomes a pressing problem, and so we did that. A new young counsel for the record company came in and Hammond introduced me to him. An amendment to the old contract was drawn up and I signed it right then and there, now being twenty-one. The new counsel for the record company was the up-and-coming Clive Davis. Clive would take over Columbia Records full frontal in 1967.

Later when I told Grossman what I did, he just about went berserk. "What are you talking about?" he said. It wasn't what he expected. Grossman did get me out of my Leeds Music contract, though. I felt like that agreement didn't really matter and that Lou Levy hadn't really discovered me or could do anything with my songs anyway—at least not the ones I was doing then. I'd only been there as a favor to Hammond anyway. On this deal breaker, Grossman had given me $1,000, told me to go up and see Lou Levy, give the money to him and tell him that I wanted to buy my way out of the contract. I did that and Lou was only too happy to oblige. "Sure, son," he said. He was still smoking that damn cigar. "There's something unique about your songs, but I can't put my finger on it." I gave Lou the $1,000 and he gave me the contract back.

Grossman later put me with Witmark Music, an old line–style publishing company—the epitome of Tin Pan Alley, which published the standards "When Irish Eyes Are Smiling," "The Very Thought of You," "Jeepers Creepers," countless other big songs. My destiny wouldn't be made manifest up here at Leeds Music, but there was no way to know that in these moments while putting down my early songs into a tape recorder.

After Lou heard my Guthrie song, he asked me if I ever wrote any songs about baseball players. I told him I hadn't and he said that there were some players worth writing about. Lou was a baseball fanatic and could give you statistics on different players. One of the framed photos on the cabinet showed him standing shoulder to shoulder with Ford Frick, the commissioner of baseball. In another one he was at a charity function sitting at a table with Claire Ruth, the Babe's widow. He knew a lot about the game and asked me if I ever heard of Paul Waner. Lou said Paul was a hitter who could blast a ball back at a pitcher 150 miles an hour and break his face. He was that accurate. Opposing pitchers were scared to ever dare brush him back at the plate and that Ted Williams could do that, too . . . that a pitcher would rather throw the ball in the stands than take a chance on hitting either of them. Lou couldn't stand the home-run ball, thought it was the most boring aspect of the game . . . said that when a player hit one, he wanted his money back. He said all this while puffing away on a big stogie filling the room with formless clouds. I didn't follow baseball that much but I did know that Roger Maris who was with the Yankees was in the process of breaking

Babe Ruth's home-run record and that meant something. Maris was from Hibbing, Minnesota, of all places. Of course, I never heard of him there, nobody did. I was hearing a lot about him now, though, and so was the rest of the land. On some level I guess I took pride in being from the same town. There were other Minnesotans, too, that I felt akin to. Charles Lindbergh, the first aviator to fly nonstop across the Atlantic in the '20s. He was from Little Falls. F. Scott Fitzgerald, a descendant of Francis Scott Key, who wrote the words to "The Star-Spangled Banner" and who himself wrote *The Great Gatsby,* was from St. Paul. Fitzgerald was called "the prophet of the jazz age." Sinclair Lewis had won the Nobel Prize for Literature, the first American to do so. Lewis had written *Elmer Gantry* and was the master of absolute realism, had invented it. He was from Sauk Center, Minnesota. And then there was Eddie Cochran, one of the early rock-and-roll geniuses who was from Albert Lee, Minnesota. Native sons— adventurers, prophets, writers and musicians. They were all from the North Country. Each one followed their own vision, didn't care what the pictures showed. Each one of them would have understood what my inarticulate dreams were about. I felt like I was one of them or all of them put together.

The folk music scene had been like a paradise that I had to leave, like Adam had to leave the garden. It was just too perfect. In a few years' time a shit storm would be unleashed. Things would begin to burn. Bras, draft cards, American flags, bridges, too—everybody would be dreaming of getting it on. The national psyche would change and in a lot of ways it would resemble the Night of the Living Dead. The road out would be treacherous, and I didn't know where it would lead but I followed it anyway. It was a strange world ahead that would unfold, a thunderhead of a world with jagged lightning edges. Many got it wrong and never did get it right. I went straight into it. It was wide open. One thing for sure, not only was it not run by God, but it wasn't run by the devil either.